HIV AND DISABILITY

Updating the Social Security Listings

Committee on Social Security HIV Disability Criteria

Board on the Health of Select Populations

INSTITUTE OF MEDICINE
OF THE NATIONAL ACADEMIES

THE NATIONAL ACADEMIES PRESS
Washington, D.C.
www.nap.edu

THE NATIONAL ACADEMIES PRESS 500 Fifth Street, N.W. Washington, DC 20001

This study was supported by Contract No. SS00-09-30965 between the National Academy of Sciences and U.S. Social Security Administration. Any opinions, findings, conclusions, or recommendations expressed in this publication are those of the author(s) and do not necessarily reflect the view of the organizations or agencies that provided support for this project.

International Standard Book Number-13: 978-0-309-15701-8
International Standard Book Number-10: 0-309-15701-3

Additional copies of this report are available from The National Academies Press, 500 Fifth Street, N.W., Lockbox 285, Washington, DC 20055; (800) 624-6242 or (202) 334-3313 (in the Washington metropolitan area); Internet, http://www.nap.edu.

For more information about the Institute of Medicine, visit the IOM home page at: **www.iom.edu.**

Printed in the United States of America

Suggested citation: IOM (Institute of Medicine). 2010. *HIV and Disability: Updating the Social Security Listings.* Washington, DC: The National Academies Press.

"Knowing is not enough; we must apply.
Willing is not enough; we must do."
—Goethe

INSTITUTE OF MEDICINE
OF THE NATIONAL ACADEMIES

Advising the Nation. Improving Health.

THE NATIONAL ACADEMIES

Advisers to the Nation on Science, Engineering, and Medicine

The **National Academy of Sciences** is a private, nonprofit, self-perpetuating society of distinguished scholars engaged in scientific and engineering research, dedicated to the furtherance of science and technology and to their use for the general welfare. Upon the authority of the charter granted to it by the Congress in 1863, the Academy has a mandate that requires it to advise the federal government on scientific and technical matters. Dr. Ralph J. Cicerone is president of the National Academy of Sciences.

The **National Academy of Engineering** was established in 1964, under the charter of the National Academy of Sciences, as a parallel organization of outstanding engineers. It is autonomous in its administration and in the selection of its members, sharing with the National Academy of Sciences the responsibility for advising the federal government. The National Academy of Engineering also sponsors engineering programs aimed at meeting national needs, encourages education and research, and recognizes the superior achievements of engineers. Dr. Charles M. Vest is president of the National Academy of Engineering.

The **Institute of Medicine** was established in 1970 by the National Academy of Sciences to secure the services of eminent members of appropriate professions in the examination of policy matters pertaining to the health of the public. The Institute acts under the responsibility given to the National Academy of Sciences by its congressional charter to be an adviser to the federal government and, upon its own initiative, to identify issues of medical care, research, and education. Dr. Harvey V. Fineberg is president of the Institute of Medicine.

The **National Research Council** was organized by the National Academy of Sciences in 1916 to associate the broad community of science and technology with the Academy's purposes of furthering knowledge and advising the federal government. Functioning in accordance with general policies determined by the Academy, the Council has become the principal operating agency of both the National Academy of Sciences and the National Academy of Engineering in providing services to the government, the public, and the scientific and engineering communities. The Council is administered jointly by both Academies and the Institute of Medicine. Dr. Ralph J. Cicerone and Dr. Charles M. Vest are chair and vice chair, respectively, of the National Research Council.

www.national-academies.org

COMMITTEE ON SOCIAL SECURITY HIV DISABILITY CRITERIA

PAUL A. VOLBERDING (*Chair*), Professor and Vice Chair, Department of Medicine at the University of California–San Francisco, and Chief of the Medical Service, Veterans Affairs Medical Center, San Francisco

JOHN G. BARTLETT, Professor of Medicine, Division of Infectious Diseases at the Johns Hopkins University School of Medicine, Baltimore, Maryland

CARLOS DEL RIO, Professor and Chair, Hubert Department of Global Health at the Rollins School of Public Health and Professor of Medicine, Division of Infectious Diseases at the Emory University School of Medicine Atlanta, Georgia

PATRICIA M. FLYNN, Arthur Ashe Chair in Pediatric AIDS Research and Director of Clinical Research, Infectious Disease Department at St. Jude Children's Research Hospital, Memphis, Tennessee

LARRY M. GANT, Professor of Social Work, University of Michigan

IGOR GRANT, Distinguished Professor of Psychiatry and Director of HIV Neurobehavioral Research Programs, University of California–San Diego

H. CLIFFORD LANE, Clinical Director, National Institute of Allergy and Infectious Diseases at the National Institutes of Health, Rockville, Maryland

CELIA MAXWELL, Assistant Vice President for Health Sciences and Director of the Women's Health Institute, Howard University, Washington, DC

HEIDI M. NASS, Director of Treatment Education and Community Advocacy, University of Wisconsin Hospital HIV/AIDS Comprehensive Care Program, Madison

IRA SHOULSON, Louis C. Lasagna Professor of Experimental Therapeutics and Professor of Neurology, Pharmacology and Medicine, University of Rochester School of Medicine and Dentistry, New York

ANN BARTLEY WILLIAMS, Professor of Nursing and Associate Dean for Research, University of California–Los Angeles

Study Staff

SAMANTHA M. CHAO, Study Director
SUSAN R. McCUTCHEN, Senior Program Associate
ERIN E. WILHELM, Research Associate
JOI D. WASHINGTON, Senior Program Assistant
FREDERICK (RICK) ERDTMANN, Director, Board on the Health of Select Populations

Reviewers

This report has been reviewed in draft form by individuals chosen for their diverse perspectives and technical expertise, in accordance with procedures approved by the National Research Council's Report Review Committee. The purpose of this independent review is to provide candid and critical comments that will assist the institution in making its published report as sound as possible and to ensure that the report meets institutional standards for objectivity, evidence, and responsiveness to the study charge. The review comments and draft manuscript remain confidential to protect the integrity of the deliberative process. We wish to thank the following individuals for their review of this report:

SAM BOZZETTE, RAND Corporation
JANE BURGESS, VA Greater Los Angeles Medical Center
DWIGHT L. EVANS, University of Pennsylvania School of Medicine
KENNETH C. HERGENRATHER, The George Washington University
MARK ISHAUG, AIDS Foundation Chicago
MICHAEL S. SAAG, University of Alabama at Birmingham
ANDREW WIZNIA, Jacobi Medical Center
BARRY ZEVIN, San Francisco Department of Public Health

Although the reviewers listed above have provided many constructive comments and suggestions, they were not asked to endorse the conclusions or recommendations nor did they see the final draft of the report before its release. The review of this report was overseen by **HAROLD JAFFE,**

Centers for Disease Control and Prevention, and **KRISTINE M. GEBBIE,** School of Nursing Hunter College. Appointed by the National Research Council and Institute of Medicine, they were responsible for making certain that an independent examination of this report was carried out in accordance with institutional procedures and that all review comments were carefully considered. Responsibility for the final content of this report rests entirely with the authoring committee and the institution.

Preface

The Listing of Impairments (the Listings) of the Social Security Administration defines conditions for which disability can be accurately and efficiently determined with high specificity, granting a disability allowance only for those truly disabled. The Listings specify in detail the requirements for such an allowance based on the material submitted by the claimant and supported by medical records. In this system, those applying for disability benefits not allowed after the initial evaluation still can be deemed disabled, but only after a longer process of functional assessment and potentially appeal and examination. Therefore, it is critical that the Listings accurately reflect current understanding of the disease in question, specifically because this understanding affects the individual's prognosis and expected level of function in the workplace.

HIV infection as a disabling condition has evolved in fundamental ways since the listings for HIV infection were last updated in 1993. Then, HIV infection and its end-stage disease, AIDS, were rapidly fatal and essentially untreatable. AIDS was defined primarily by the diagnosis of one or more otherwise unusual opportunistic infections or cancers—ones that arose because of severe HIV-induced immune deficiency. The HIV Infection Listings, appropriately at the time, were largely based on a history of diagnosis of these opportunistic diseases. Antiretroviral therapy in 1993 was of very modest potency, with only slight improvement in the immune system damaged by HIV infection.

New drugs and the concept of drug combinations evolved dramatically after 1996. HIV infection is now considered a chronic condition which, in optimal settings, allows high levels of functioning and prolonged survival. Combinations of antiretroviral drugs suppress HIV replication, enabling a recovery of immune function as reflected in circulating CD4+ T-lymphocytes to normal or near-normal levels in most persons. Success in treatment, however, is far from universal. Many HIV-infected persons harbor virus already resistant to one or more antiretroviral drugs, limiting CD4 recovery. Others are diagnosed at very advanced disease stages or at an older age, both predictors of poor response to treatment. Many others find the lifelong requirement for consistently excellent medication adherence to be impossible or are suffering from the side effects of current or previous antiretroviral therapy. Today, although many of the opportunistic diseases once common are now uncommon, they are still seen. Many patients respond well to treatment, but others, even in the era of potent HIV medications, fail to achieve control of HIV replication or are diagnosed in extremely late disease stages and have rapid progression or disabling complications. For all these reasons, the HIV Infection Listings are in urgent need of reconsideration and revision.

The Social Security Administration commissioned the Institute of Medicine to examine the current listings for HIV infection and to suggest how they might be updated, considering the substantial changes in the disease since the introduction of potent combinations of antiretroviral drugs beginning in 1996. A committee of experts in HIV management and outcomes was created to address this charge and drafted a series of recommendations presented in this report. The committee had public hearings, reviewed the relevant literature, and commissioned data analyses from several of the largest ongoing cohort studies of HIV-infected persons. The committee also obtained input from the Centers for Disease Control and Prevention and other credible sources of information regarding HIV infection and disability. The committee used this information along with the expertise of its members in formulating recommendations for HIV-infected children and adults. Because HIV-infected children vary from adults in some specific conditions, their needs were the topic of a separate chapter.

Categories of Recommended HIV Disability Allowances in This Report

Low CD4 Count

Although disability allowances in the 1993 Listings were based primarily on a diagnosis of an AIDS-related opportunistic infection or malignancy, the committee believes a more important indicator of disability today is a low CD4 cell count, specifically at or below 50 cells/mm^3, because this is a direct marker of HIV disease stage and a predictor of short-term mortality risk as well as of attenuated antiretroviral therapy response. Many of the most serious opportunistic diseases that form the 1993 Listings occur in individuals with low CD4 cell counts and thus would be captured by new Listings as recommended. The committee recommends that this allowance should be reviewed periodically—3 years would be most practical—to assess the magnitude and stability of the individual's response to antiretroviral treatment.

Imminently Fatal Conditions

By contrast, the committee found several HIV-induced diseases that remain so serious that they warrant a permanent disability allowance. These diseases are severely disabling, have a high short-term mortality risk, and respond minimally to conventional treatment.

HIV-Associated Conditions Without Listings Elsewhere in Other Body Systems

Disability allowance was also recommended for another group of conditions associated with HIV infection or side effects of treatment if the affected person also had functional limitations using standards already used under the existing listings. These conditions limit the affected person's ability to function in the workplace. Because recovery from these may be possible with antiretroviral therapy, the committee recommended that disability should, as with low CD4 counts, be considered a disability for 3 years and be reviewed regularly.

HIV-Associated Diseases With Existing Listings Elsewhere

Many HIV-infected persons experience a higher rate or earlier onset of diseases already included in the Listings in other body systems. For example, cardiovascular disease and chronic kidney disease are increasing problems in the HIV-infected population, but the current Listings for those organ systems adequately define a pathway to disability allowance. The committee believes, in these cases, that the cross-reference to those listings is the most efficient approach.

Finally, the committee addressed means to improve the utility of the HIV Infection Listings. The committee recommended an ongoing review of the forms employed to best capture the information needed for allowance determination, and rewriting all introductory material for those most directly involved in the determination process. The committee believes wider access to deidentified disability data would enable research aimed at continuously improving the process. Finally, the committee recommended broadening the array of health care professionals who are allowed input into the determination process, reflecting the many professionals involved in contemporary medical care.

The committee thanks all those individuals and groups who provided input for this report and especially the staff of the Institute of Medicine, whose expertise and dedication to this analysis were a model of professionalism.

Paul Volberding, *Chair*
Committee on Social Security
HIV Disability Criteria

Acknowledgments

The committee and staff would like to thank those who presented statements and presentations at the public workshops held on December 7, 2009, in Washington, DC, and on February 11, 2010, in Irvine, CA:

Bebe Anderson, Lambda Legal
Brent Braveman, University of Illinois
Liza Conyers, University of Pittsburgh
Judith Currier, University of California–Los Angeles
Robert Heaton, University of California–San Diego
Kevin Malone, Client of Whitman-Walker Clinic
J. Scott Pritchard, Oregon Disability Determination Services and Medical Consultants Ad Hoc Committee of the National Association of Disability Examiners
Michael Saag, University of Alabama and HIV Medical Association
Susan Smith, National Association of Disability Examiners

We would also like to acknowledge and thank those individuals and groups who provided the committee and staff with data to inform the committee's discussions:

Brian Agan, Uniformed Services University of the Health Sciences
Keri Althoff, Johns Hopkins University
John Brooks, Centers for Disease Control and Prevention
Lynn E. Eberly, University of Minnesota
The EuroSIDA Study Group
Stephen J. Gange, Johns Hopkins University
Kelly Gebo, Johns Hopkins University
Michael Horberg, Kaiser Permanente

Lisa P. Jacobson, Johns Hopkins University
Amy Justice, Yale University
Mari Kitahata, University of Washington
Rosemary McKaig, National Institutes of Health
Amanda Mocroft, University College London
Richard Moore, Johns Hopkins University
Michael Saag, University of Alabama and HIV Medical Association
Luke Shouse, Centers for Disease Control and Prevention
Janet P. Tate, Yale University

The committee would also like to thank the following Disability Determination Services offices and their staff for meeting with committee members and explaining the disability process:

Detroit, MI
Hartford, CT
La Jolla, CA
Madison, WI
Nashville, TN
New York, NY
Oakland, CA
Timonium, MD
Washington, DC
Worcester, MA

In addition, we would to acknowledge and thank those individuals who provided the committee with their insights during the report process: Tony Burns, Client of Whitman-Walker Clinic; Richard Elion, Whitman-Walker Clinic; Erin Loubier, Whitman-Walker Clinic; and George Mathas, Client of Whitman-Walker Clinic.

We would like to extend a special thanks to Howard Goldman, who served as an unpaid consultant to the committee. Dr. Goldman offered his support and guidance to the committee throughout the process.

In addition, many Institute of Medicine staff members helped throughout the study process. The study staff would like to thank LaVita Coates-Fogle, Andrea Cohen, Linda Kilroy, Pamela McCray-Ramsey, Michael McGeary, William McLeod, and Jon Sanders for giving their time and support to further the committee's efforts during the study process.

Finally, we would like to thank and recognize the support from the U.S. Social Security Administration for sponsoring this study. In particular, we would like to thank Barry Eigen, Sheila Everett, Monte Hetland, Johanna Klema, Cathy Lively, Joanna Marashlian, Mike O'Connor, Kevin Parmer, Paul Scott, Art Spencer, Janet Truhe, and Cheryl Williams.

Contents

Summary

The human immunodeficiency virus (HIV) attacks the immune system, resulting in a progressive immunodeficiency that predisposes the infected person to opportunistic infections and cancers. This immunodeficiency is eventually fatal in nearly all cases in the absence of potent antiretroviral treatment. The advanced stage of HIV-induced immunodeficiency is termed acquired immunodeficiency syndrome or AIDS.

Before the availability of potent therapy in 1996, AIDS resulted in death in less than 2 years in most cases, usually as a direct result of one or more opportunistic infections or cancers. Advances in HIV research have led to the widespread availability of potent combination antiretroviral therapy, which has dramatically changed the course of HIV infection, making it a chronic, manageable disease in many people. These advances have important implications for treatment and outcomes as well as policies addressing the disease.

The U.S. Social Security Administration (SSA) responded early to the HIV/AIDS epidemic by providing disability benefits beginning in 1983 to people diagnosed with AIDS. In 1993 it adopted disability criteria for HIV (i.e., the HIV Infection Listings) as an administrative tool to more rapidly adjudicate claims. These criteria were loosely based on the Centers for Disease Control and Prevention's (CDC's) definition of AIDS. Despite the remarkable advances in HIV/AIDS management resulting from the availability of potent antiretroviral therapy in 1996, the HIV Infection Listings have not been substantially revised. In 2009, SSA asked the Institute of Medicine to establish the Committee on Social Security HIV Disability

Criteria to recommend improvements to the HIV Infection Listings (see Box S-1 for the statement of work).

Throughout its discussions, the committee acknowledged that listings cannot be viewed in a vacuum. The committee recognized that HIV/AIDS outcomes are improved by adhering to potent antiretroviral regimens. Adherence requires timely diagnosis of HIV infection, linkage and retention in HIV care, as well as continuous access and adherence to these drugs and to expert medical care. Recognition of this connection is critical because Social Security benefits have a great impact on access to care and treatment for people living with HIV/AIDS. Qualifying for Social Security disability benefits in many states is seen as an entrée to other public programs, such as Medicare and Medicaid and housing programs. The *2010 Patient Protection and Affordable Care Act* will undoubtedly affect these social programs and others, but it is too early to determine how the Social Security disability program will be affected. While the issues of adherence and access to care are critical in the discussion of Social Security disability benefits, in-depth discussion about the means by which people receive treatment and medications are outside the committee's scope.

SOCIAL SECURITY DISABILITY EVALUATION PROCESS

SSA pays disability benefits through two programs: Social Security Disability Insurance (SSDI) and Supplemental Security Income (SSI). To qualify, individuals must meet SSA's definition of disability, which differs for adults and children,[1] defined as follows:

- Adults: "an inability to engage in any substantial gainful activity[2] by reason of any medically determinable physical or mental

[1] Social Security considers children to be those under the age of 18.

[2] The term substantial gainful activity (SGA) is used to describe a level of work activity and earnings. Work is "substantial" if it involves doing significant physical or mental activities or a combination of both. For work activity to be substantial, it does not need to be performed on a full-time basis. Work activity performed on a part-time basis may also be substantial gainful activity. "Gainful" work activity is work performed for pay or profit; work of a nature generally performed for pay or profit; or work intended for profit, whether or not a profit is realized. The amount of monthly earnings considered as SGA depends on the nature of the person's disability. The Social Security Act specifies a higher SGA amount for statutorily blind persons. If a person's impairment is anything other than blindness, earnings averaging over $1,000 a month (for the year 2010) generally demonstrate SGA. For a statutorily blind person, earnings averaging over $1,640 a month (for the year 2010) generally demonstrate SGA for SSDI.

BOX S-1
Statement of Work

An ad hoc committee of medical experts will conduct a study to assist the Social Security Administration (SSA) on HIV disability issues. The committee will review the current medical criteria for disability resulting from HIV infection in SSA's Listing of Impairments ("the Listings") and identify areas in which the HIV Infection Listings should be revised and updated based on current medical knowledge and practice. Specifically, the committee will (1) conduct a comprehensive review of the relevant research literature and current professional practice guidelines; (2) assess the current HIV Infection Listings in light of current research knowledge and evidence-based medical practice; and (3) produce a short report with specific recommendations for revision of the HIV Infection Listings based on evidence (to the extent possible) and professional judgment (where evidence is lacking).

impairment(s)[3] which can be expected to result in death or which has lasted or can be expected to last for a continuous period of not less than 12 months."

- Children: a child is "considered disabled if he has a medically determinable physical or mental impairment which results in marked and severe functional limitations, and which can be expected to result in death or which has lasted or can be expected to last for a continuous period of not less than 12 months."

For adults applying for SSDI or SSI, SSA uses a five-step sequential evaluation process to determine whether a claimant is disabled (see Figure S-1). The process is modified for children applying for SSI benefits.

At Step 1, SSA determines whether the claimant is engaging in substantial gainful activity. If not, the claim progresses to Step 2 to determine whether the claimant has a severe impairment that significantly limits the claimant's ability to perform basic work activities (e.g., standing and sitting). If the claimant is found to have a severe impairment then SSA determines whether it satisfies the medical condition found in the Listing of Impairments, also referred to as the Listings. Adult claims not allowed

[3] A medically determinable impairment (MDI) is an impairment that results from anatomical, physiological, or psychological abnormalities which can be shown by medically acceptable clinical and laboratory diagnostic techniques. The MDI must be established by medical evidence consisting of signs, symptoms, and laboratory findings, not only by a person's statement of symptoms.

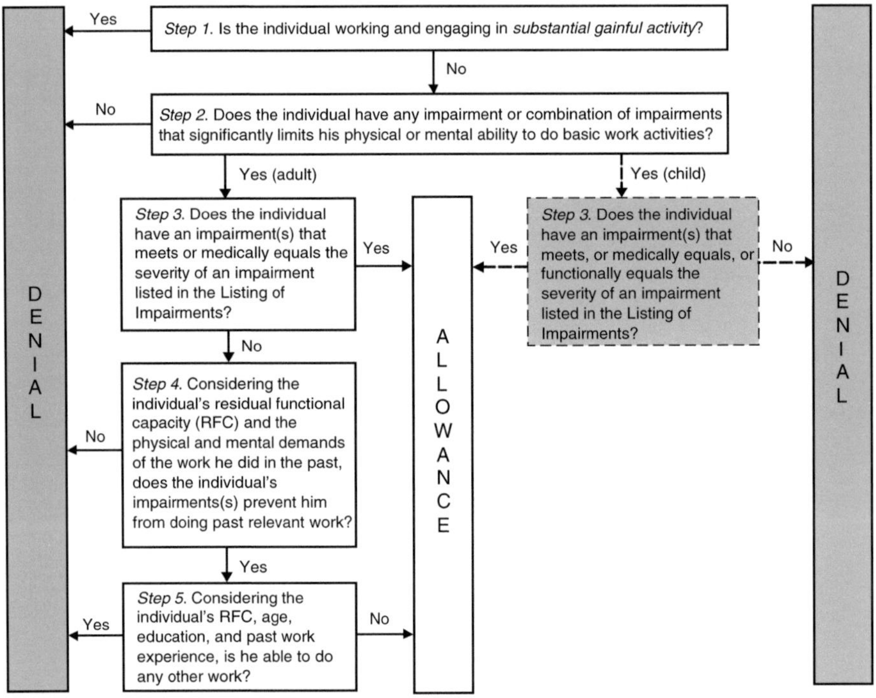

FIGURE S-1 Social Security Administration five-step sequential evaluation process.

at the Listings level proceed to Step 4 and, if necessary, Step 5, which considers a claimant's ability to perform past work and to do other work in the national economy, respectively. This is assessed through a time- and resource-intensive process based on all relevant medical and other evidence in the case record.

For children under age 18 applying for SSI benefits, Steps 1 and 2 are the same. At Step 3, the considerations are whether a child's impairment meets or medically equals a listing; if the claim does not meet or medically equal a listing, it may be found to *functionally equal* a listing. To make this determination, SSA assesses the interactive and cumulative effects of all of the child's impairments in terms of six domains of functioning: (1) acquiring and using information; (2) attending and completing tasks; (3) interacting and relating with others; (4) moving about and manipulating objects; (5) caring for yourself; and (6) health and physical well-being.

The Listing of Impairments

To save time and resources, and to ease the administrative burden of determining the functional capacity of each claimant, SSA adopted a list of serious medical conditions (the Listings), which are applied at Step 3 of the sequential evaluation process. The Listings consist of Part A (primarily for adults) and Part B (applies to children in cases where specific considerations are needed) and are organized into 14 body systems for adults and 15 for children (e.g., musculoskeletal, respiratory, neurological). The listing for each body system begins with a narrative introductory text that defines key concepts and terms used in that body system. Each body system and listing is identified by a number. For example, the immune system disorders body system for Part A is Listing 14.00, and HIV infection is Listing 14.08. The Part A HIV Infection Listing consists of 11 sublistings, from 14.08A to 14.08K, and the Part B HIV Infection Listing consists of 12 sublistings, from 114.08A to 114.08L.

In determining whether an individual is disabled, SSA decides whether the claimant's impairment *meets* or *medically equals* a listing, as explained below:

- Meets: If the evidence in a case establishes the presence of all the criteria required by one of the listings, then the claimant's impairment meets that specific listing; and
- Equals: If an individual is not found to meet the exact requirements of a specific listing, he can still be found disabled if the impairment is at least equal in severity and duration to the criteria of any listed impairment, as established by the relevant evidence in the claimant's case record.

REVISING THE HIV INFECTION LISTING

SSA's Listing of Impairments needs to be highly valid and reliable to efficiently and effectively recognize disabled claimants. The committee developed the following principles on which a new Listing ought to be based:

- Reflect current medical practice;
- Determine severity fairly;
- Use objective evidence, to the extent possible;
- Incorporate work-related functioning, to the extent possible;
- Be simple and easy to implement; and
- Use flexible language to account for changes in the disease and its treatment over time.

The committee considered incorporating measures of work-related functioning to complement declines in organ or physical functioning because many patients with HIV/AIDS show a decline in functional abilities after diagnosis and as their diseases progress. Additionally, comorbid conditions often lead to a more disabling condition than would be predicted from the sum of their individual effects. The committee concludes that measures of functional capacity are critical in assessing whether patients living with HIV/AIDS can participate meaningfully in social and employment activities. However, upon reviewing the literature, the committee found no single test to measure the overall functional capacity or functional limitation of an individual with HIV. Functional limitations in adults are primarily assessed in three domains (i.e., physical, mental, neurocognitive), but are difficult to define or measure in a cost-effective and reproducible manner.

Without strong, valid, and easy-to-conduct functional measures, the committee sought to identify current equivalents to the earlier CDC definition of AIDS in the context of disability. Upon evaluating the medical literature, the committee identified four categories under which claimants should be considered disabled: those with CD4 $\leq$ 50 cells/mm^3; those with imminently fatal or severely disabling HIV-associated conditions; those with HIV-associated conditions without listings elsewhere in the Listing of Impairments; and those with HIV-associated conditions with listings elsewhere in the Listing of Impairments.

Low CD4 Count

The committee tried to identify a laboratory marker that could be used to make decisions about functional impairment and disability, but no direct associations were found. In the absence of such associations, the committee considered measures predictive of disease progression, morbidity, and mortality as surrogate markers of disability.

The CD4+ T-cell (also known as CD4 cells or T-cells) count is a common standard laboratory marker of disease stage for HIV/AIDS patients. The 1993 CDC AIDS definition was expanded to include a CD4 count below 200 cells/mm^3 as indicative of an AIDS diagnosis. Varying CD4 levels indicate different levels of disease severity. A CD4 $\leq$ 50 cells/mm^3 has been associated with poorer response to antiretroviral therapy, increased short-term all-cause mortality, and increased incidence of HIV-associated illnesses. Additionally, the majority of early mortalities from those with opportunistic infections occur at CD4 $\leq$ 50 cells/mm^3. Although CD4 count is a continuous variable, CD4 $\leq$ 50 cells/mm^3, as compared to other values, is most indicative of severe advanced immunodeficiency. It is comparable to the previous CDC AIDS definition based on opportunistic infections and cancers in its ability to indicate impairment. Although other clinical markers exist, such as HIV plasma viral load, none predict disease stage as well as CD4 count. The HIV viral load is clinically useful in monitoring the response to antiretroviral therapy and is a good predictor of the rate of CD4 decline, but it is not a direct measure of disease stage.

Although widely accepted measures of HIV functional impairments are limited, a strong relationship exists between advanced immune impairment and clinical outcomes, including mortality. The committee concludes that a threshold can be drawn at CD4 ≤ 50 cells/mm^3 as an indicator of disability. Because CD4 count can change in response to antiretroviral therapy, claimants allowed disability under such a listing should be periodically reevaluated. The committee believes 3 years would allow for a sustained response and is the maximum practical period for SSA reassessment.

RECOMMENDATION 1. SSA should use CD4 count as an indicator of disability. Specifically, CD4 ≤ 50 cells/mm^3 is an indicator that a claimant's HIV infection is disabling. This allowance should be reevaluated periodically by SSA.

Imminently Fatal or Severely Disabling HIV-Associated Conditions

A number of imminently fatal or severely disabling HIV-associated conditions exist, even in the era of potent antiretroviral therapy. These rare but very aggressive diseases will likely lead to death or severe disability within a year and patients are unlikely to improve. Although much less common than early in the epidemic, these generally untreatable conditions resemble the AIDS-defining infections or cancers that were considered appropriate for disability allowance in the current listing. The committee therefore concludes that claimants with these conditions need to be considered separately from other HIV infection claimants and that these conditions should be specifically included in the HIV Infection Listings as permanent disabilities.

RECOMMENDATION 2. SSA should make disability determination allowances permanent for imminently fatal and/or severely disabling HIV-associated conditions. These conditions may be appropriate as compassionate allowances. These include the following:

- **HIV-associated dementia;**
- **Multicentric Castleman's disease;**
- **Kaposi's sarcoma involving the pulmonary parenchyma;**
- **Primary central nervous system lymphomas;**
- **Primary effusion lymphoma; and**
- **Progressive multifocal leukoencephalopathy.**

Other Severe HIV-Associated Conditions

A new set of nonimminently fatal medical conditions associated with HIV infection has emerged in recent years. Among these are conditions also seen in the general population, including cardiovascular disease and osteoporosis. In the United States, these and other HIV-associated conditions have become leading causes of morbidity and mortality for persons living with HIV infection. They can be the result of the disease itself, adverse effects of HIV treatments, comorbid diseases, or from the treatment of those conditions. Additionally, longer recognized conditions such as distal sensory polyneuropathy also continue to be disabling.

The committee believes that the presence of an opportunistic infection or a manifestation of HIV alone is no longer sufficient to declare a person unable to work. However, the combination of clinical severity and limited functional capacity would allow for an appropriate determination of disability to be made. The severity of such conditions can be assessed by coupling objective tests of medical impairment with an evaluation of functioning. Although few measures of functioning exist for people living with HIV/AIDS, three measures of functioning are currently used in other areas of the Listing of Impairments, including 14.08K of the HIV Infection Listing: ability to perform activities of daily living; maintenance of social functioning; and completion of tasks in a timely manner due to deficiencies in concentration, persistence, or pace. This sublisting is the second most frequently used sublisting, leading the committee to conclude that disability examiners are comfortable with using these measures. In the absence of a single, widely used measure of functioning for people living with HIV/AIDS, the committee believes these three measures should be retained in revisions to improve the effectiveness of the Listing.

RECOMMENDATION 3. SSA should continue to include measures of functional capacity in the HIV Infection Listings and update these measures with research advances.

Although opportunistic infections now occur at a lower rate, they can still be associated with early mortality. The committee believes the majority of HIV-infected people with severe opportunistic infections would be captured by a CD4 $\leq$ 50 cells/mm^3 listing; disability assessment could also be triggered by poor functional status.

Some HIV-associated conditions are not addressed in other sections of the Listing of Impairments, while others are. The committee considered the two groups separately because if a current listing does not exist for conditions that can be truly disabling, a path to receive disability benefits will need to be identified. Having a condition with a current listing elsewhere also provides a path to being deemed disabled in Step 3.

HIV-Associated Conditions Without Listings Elsewhere

The committee suggests that a Listing be developed that identifies potentially severe HIV-associated conditions currently without listings elsewhere in the Listing of Impairments (i.e., outside of Listings 14.08 and 114.08). An assessment of functioning should be completed in disability claims that present with (1) HIV-associated conditions, (2) adverse effects of treatment for HIV or comorbid conditions, or (3) other significant, documented symptoms (e.g., fatigue, malaise, pain). To account for the unpredictable nature of HIV and its treatment, allowances made under these parameters should be considered a disability for 3 years following the last documentation of the manifestation, adverse effects, or symptoms. This time period reflects the fact that HIV is now generally a manageable chronic disease and that the immunologic and functional status of many HIV claimants is likely to improve once they are engaged in care and receiving therapy. It should be noted that the benefits of therapy may decrease as comorbidities continue to develop, therefore requiring regular reevaluation.

RECOMMENDATION 4. Comorbidities induced by HIV infection or adverse effects of treatment should be considered disabling if they markedly limit functioning in one or more of the following areas: ability to perform activities of daily living; maintenance of social functioning; or completion of tasks in a timely manner due to deficiencies in concentration, persistence, or pace. This includes, but is not limited to, the following conditions:

- **Diarrhea;**
- **Distal sensory polyneuropathy;**
- **HIV-associated neurocognitive disorders;**
- **HIV-associated wasting syndrome;**
- **Kaposi's sarcoma;**
- **Lipoatrophy or lipohypertrophy; and**
- **Osteoporosis.**

Symptoms such as fatigue, malaise, and pain should also be considered if found to limit functioning. Periodically, SSA should reevaluate claims made using these comorbidities, consistent with the reevaluation of other disability allowances.

HIV-Associated Conditions With Listings Elsewhere

The committee identified a number of HIV-associated conditions with high morbidity and mortality currently represented in other sections of the Listing of Impairments. The prevalence of these diseases is growing among HIV-infected populations and will likely increase as these populations live longer. HIV infection typically results in an increased risk of developing comorbid conditions and an accelerated rate of progression to a severe or fatal outcome. However, the literature suggests the disability caused by comorbid conditions is not usually clinically distinct and therefore is captured by other disability listings.

Upon assessment of the criteria currently in the Listing of Impairments for these other conditions, the committee determined that these were appropriate for assessing disability for people also infected with HIV. Because the condition is not unique, the committee concluded that current, existing listings are adequate for determining disability resulting from these conditions in HIV-infected people. Comorbid conditions should be cross-referenced to other listings and follow the disability criteria of those listings.

RECOMMENDATION 5. SSA should cross-reference the following HIV-associated conditions to existing listings:

- **Cardiovascular disease (Listings 4.00 and 104.00);**
- **Chronic kidney disease, including HIV-associated nephropathy (Listings 6.00 and 106.00);**
- **Diabetes (Listings 9.08 and 109.08);**
- **Hepatitis (Listings 5.05 and 105.05); and**
- **Malignancies (Listings 13.00 and 113.00), not otherwise specified in the report.**

Recommendation 5 differs from Recommendation 4 in two ways. First, the duration of these allowances should follow the durations identified by the other sublistings. However, if it is found in the literature that HIV coinfection causes changes to the disease not effectively captured in other disability listings, SSA may want to consider adding the disease to the HIV Infection Listings. Second, the conditions discussed in this recommendation are not linked to functional criteria to allow for the conditions to be easily cross-referenced.

Concepts Specific to Children

When children receiving disability benefits reach age 18, they need to reapply to sustain their benefits. This can result in HIV-infected children switching from Part B (114.08) to Part A (14.08) to qualify as disabled. To allow for a smooth transition, the committee recommends that the listing specific to children follow as closely as possible to the Listing in Part A of the SSA Listing of Impairments.

RECOMMENDATION 6. SSA should ensure that the HIV Infection Listings in Parts A and B of the SSA Listing of Impairments are constructed similarly. However, conditions specific to children not found in adults should also be listed in Part B, including age-appropriate CD4 and developmental criteria, neurological manifestations of HIV infection, and HIV-related growth disturbance.

Because of the differences in CD4 count and percentage and prognosis between children and adults, Recommendation 1 needs to be modified for children, but still easily abstracted from the medical record. Count, percentage, or both may be available in medical records, but recent studies indicate that CD4 percentage adds little to the prognostic value of CD4 count. Based on approximate equivalency for the various age groups for HIV disease progression and death, the committee suggests the age-specific CD4 count and percentage criteria for children shown in Table S-1.

The conditions listed in Recommendation 2 are also rare in children but have been reported. Accordingly, a similar listing should be included in the pediatric HIV Infection Listing. Modifications should include the replacement of HIV-associated dementia with the current listing for neurological manifestations of HIV infection (currently 114.08G). Even in the era of combination antiretroviral therapy, neurological manifestations still present serious challenges for children. Therefore, neurological manifestations in children and adolescents should be maintained under Part B. In addition, growth development is an important indicator of their health and is seen as one of the most sensitive indicators of disease progression. Growth disturbance or failure to grow has been associated with rapid progression from asymptomatic HIV infection to AIDS in children thus leading to shorter survival. As a result, the committee concluded that the current listing for growth disturbance (currently 114.08H) should be retained in Part B.

In Part B, the measures of functioning used in Recommendation 4 should reflect measures relevant to children—developmental and emotional disorders of newborn and younger infants (currently paragraphs A–E of 112.12) and organic mental disorders (currently paragraphs B1–B2 of 112.02).

Although the conditions contained in Recommendation 5 are not common in children, they do occur and may become more evident as perinatally infected children continue to age. Additionally, there are current pediatric listings for these conditions that would be applicable. Therefore, the com-

TABLE S-1 Proposed Disabling CD4 Count Ranges for Children

Age Range	Suggested CD4 Count	Suggested CD4 Percentage
< 1 year	≤ 500 cells/mm^3	< 15 percent
1–5 years	≤ 200 cells/mm^3	< 15 percent
> 5 years	≤ 50 cells/mm^3	N/A

NOTE: N/A = not applicable.

mittee concludes that Recommendation 5 should also be applied to the Part B HIV Infection Listings.

MAXIMIZING THE UTILITY OF THE LISTINGS

The success of the HIV Infection Listings relies in part on how it is used, including general guidance for how to implement the Listings, how to reflect future changes in clinical practice, and how to more effectively obtain medical evidence.

Guidance for how to interpret and implement the Listings is in the introductory text, which precedes each section of the Listing of Impairments. The intended audience is broad and includes claimants and their families, the general public, disability examiners, medical consultants, and adjudicators. According to some disability examiners and medical consultants, the introductory text helps guide interpretation of the Listings, but at the same time it is confusing, disjointed, and difficult to read. In an effort to improve the usability of the introductory text, the committee believes that it should be reorganized and simplified.

RECOMMENDATION 7. SSA should rewrite the introductory text for Parts A and B of the SSA Listing of Impairments by:

- **a. Simplifying and reorganizing the text to address the appropriate audiences; and**
- **b. Consolidating all HIV references into one section.**

It will be important to reflect changes in the management and care of HIV infection in future revisions. Areas of particular concern for future assessments include long-term adverse events of treatment; newly emerging clinical manifestations of HIV infection; and consequences of nonadherence and resistance to HIV therapies. SSA should monitor these issues and others and consider adding them to the HIV Infection Listings as appropriate.

Data can be very informative in making the listings as effective as possible. SSA collects detailed data on each claim submitted and to an extent uses the data to inform its processes. Evaluations of these data can be important in identifying trends and patterns to help revise and inform the relevancy of the Listings. In addition, these data currently are not available for public use. However, making deidentified data publicly accessible for relevant analysis could result in improving the timeliness and applicability of the HIV Infection Listings.

RECOMMENDATION 8. SSA should use its database to maximize the utility of the HIV Infection Listings by:

- **a. Collecting and analyzing data to evaluate their effectiveness; and**

b. Making data more widely accessible for outside analysis to better inform their currency and efficiency.

The initial information SSA uses to adjudicate a claim is generally acquired through the medical record, SSA disability application forms, and supplemental documents submitted by other health professionals. The committee expects that these forms will be updated to reflect Listing revisions and include measures of impairment, disability, and functioning. The forms should also be responsive to the decision-making needs of disability examiners and medical consultants.

Finally, the information that SSA uses to make its decisions often comes from an "acceptable medical source."[4] While "other sources"[5] may have more meaningful and informative interactions with a claimant, their opinions may not receive equal weight to an "acceptable medical source." The current hierarchy of health professionals delineated in the determination process may not be appropriate, especially when discussing functional ability. The committee concludes that SSA ought to consider including a wide array of licensed health professionals as acceptable medical sources (e.g., nurses, dentists, allied health professionals) for determining the functional effects of impairments.

CONCLUSION

An opportunity exists to improve the effectiveness of the HIV Infection Listings. The current Listings represent a time prior to the availability of effective antiretroviral therapy when HIV/AIDS was defined largely by having an opportunistic infection or malignancy resulting in a fatal outcome in a short period of time. Widespread availability of combination antiretroviral therapies has dramatically changed the course of HIV/AIDS. For many individuals it is now a chronic, manageable disease that is no longer characterized solely by opportunistic infections and malignancies. More importantly, HIV infection no longer equates with being permanently disabled. Instead, disability in HIV-infected claimants can now be more precisely identified by clinical markers and specific sets of medical conditions. By revising the HIV Infection Listings to better reflect current clinical practice, SSA will be able to more accurately identify those who need Social Security disability benefits.

---

[4] "Acceptable medical sources" are defined by SSA to include licensed physicians, psychologists, optometrists, qualified speech-language pathologists, and psychological consultants.

[5] "Other sources" are defined by SSA to include other medical sources such as naturopaths, chiropractors, and audiologists; educational personnel; public and private social welfare agency personnel; and nonmedical sources such as spouses, parents, and clergy.

1

Introduction

The human immunodeficiency virus (HIV) is a retrovirus that attacks the immune system, resulting in a progressive disruption of immune function. The most serious consequence of HIV infection is acquired immunodeficiency syndrome (AIDS). In the early days of the epidemic, HIV infection led to almost certain death. Additionally, the high incidence of mother-to-child transmission of HIV resulted in many infants acquiring HIV infection from their mothers during pregnancy or delivery, or postpartum through breastfeeding. Advances in therapy—particularly combination antiretroviral therapies—have dramatically changed the course of HIV infection to a chronic, manageable disease. These life-extending treatments require lifelong daily medications that may have significant side effects. More recently, patients with HIV infection have been noted to have an increased incidence of a number of serious chronic conditions typically associated with aging. The combination of having a complex disease that requires an equally complex treatment regimen can be disabling, potentially leaving individuals unable to function and conduct daily activities.

Many people living with HIV/AIDS, especially those diagnosed at a late stage, are unable to work and need some level of public assistance. Early in the epidemic, the U.S. Social Security Administration (SSA) expanded its disability benefits program beginning in 1983 to help support people living with AIDS. It adopted disability criteria for HIV, loosely organized around the 1987 AIDS-defining illnesses identified by the Centers for Disease Control and Prevention, and in 1993 developed the HIV Infection Listings.

Although the course of HIV/AIDS and complications associated with treatment have changed dramatically since the beginning of the epidemic,

SSA's HIV disability criteria (i.e., the HIV Infection Listings) have not been substantially updated to reflect these changes. In 2009, SSA asked the Institute of Medicine (IOM) to recommend revisions to the Listings, for which the IOM established the Committee on Social Security HIV Disability Criteria.

The severity of HIV infection and its disabling nature are why SSA originally added HIV to its disability listings. It is the history and progression of medical management that necessitates revision of how SSA considers HIV as an emerging disability, how the Listings reflect the current state of clinical practice, and how they address the specific needs of people living with HIV/AIDS.

SOCIAL SECURITY DISABILITY

SSA pays disability benefits through two programs: Social Security Disability Insurance (SSDI) and Supplemental Security Income (SSI).

In 2008, more than 12 million people received Social Security disability benefits, and SSA expected to process more than 3.3 million new disability applications claims in fiscal year 2010 (see Table 1-1) (SSA, 2010a).

THE DISABILITY EVALUATION DECISION PROCESS

Definition of Disability

To be eligible for disability benefits under SSDI, a person must be insured for benefits, be younger than full retirement age, have filed an application for benefits, and have a Social Security-defined disability. SSA defines disability as "an inability to engage in any substantial gainful activity[1] by reason of any medically determinable physical or mental impairment(s)[2] which can be expected to result in death or which has lasted or can be

[1] The term substantial gainful activity (SGA) is used to describe a level of work activity and earnings. Work is "substantial" if it involves doing significant physical or mental activities or a combination of both. For work activity to be substantial, it does not need to be performed on a full-time basis. Work activity performed on a part-time basis may also be substantial gainful activity. "Gainful" work activity is work performed for pay or profit; work of a nature generally performed for pay or profit; or work intended for profit, whether or not a profit is realized. The amount of monthly earnings considered as SGA depends on the nature of the person's disability. The Social Security Act specifies a higher SGA amount for statutorily blind persons. If a person's impairment is anything other than blindness, earnings averaging over $1,000 a month (for the year 2010) generally demonstrate SGA. For a statutorily blind person, earnings averaging over $1,640 a month (for the year 2010) generally demonstrate SGA for SSDI.

[2] A medically determinable impairment (MDI) is an impairment that results from anatomical, physiological, or psychological abnormalities which can be shown by medically acceptable clinical and laboratory diagnostic techniques. The MDI must be established by medical evi-

TABLE 1-1 Number of 2007 Initial Allowances and Benefit Amounts

	Number of Allowances		Average Monthly Benefit
	HIV	All SSA Disability	
Adults			
SSDI only	1,429[a]	361,496[b]	$1,064[c]
SSI only	2,769[a]	165,860[c]	$596[c]
SSDI and SSI	3,524[a]	272,446[c]	$714[c]
Children			
SSI only	56[a]	157,550[c]	$555[d]
Total	7,778	957,352	

NOTE: SSDI = Social Security Disability Insurance; SSI = Supplemental Security Insurance.
SOURCES: [a]Unpublished data set provided by SSA; [b]SSA, 2008a; [c]SSA, 2008b; [d]SSA, 2007.

expected to last for a continuous period of not less than 12 months." In addition, individuals under the age of 18 are considered disabled if they have a medically determinable physical or mental impairment, which results in marked and severe functional limitations, and which can be expected to result in death or which has lasted or can be expected to last for a continuous period of not less than 12 months.

Five-Step Sequential Evaluation Process

For adults applying for SSDI or SSI benefits, SSA uses a five-step sequential evaluation process to determine whether a claimant is disabled (see Figure 1-1).[3] This process is different for children under age 18.

At Step 1, SSA determines whether the claimant is engaging in substantial gainful activity. If not, the claim progresses to Step 2 to determine whether the claimant has a severe impairment that significantly limits the claimant's ability to perform basic work activities (e.g., standing and sitting). If the claimant is found to have a severe impairment, then SSA determines whether it satisfies the medical condition criteria found in the Listing of Impairments, also referred to as the Listings. This serves as an

dence consisting of signs, symptoms, and laboratory findings, not only by a person's statement of symptoms.

[3]SSA has three additional ways to expedite decisions: (1) flagging TERI (TERminal Illness) cases for expedited processing; (2) using a predictive model to identify QDD (Quick Disability Determination) cases that are highly likely to be allowed and processing them within 20 days; and (3) using CAL (Compassionate ALlowances) to approve cases with certain diagnoses—either terminal (e.g., gallbladder cancer) or permanently disabling (e.g., mixed dementia).

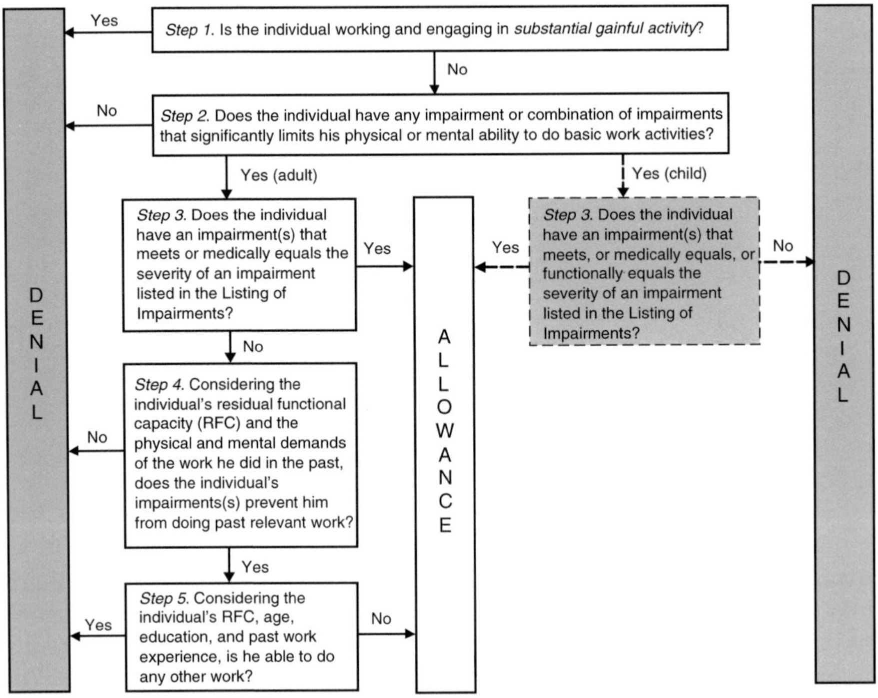

FIGURE 1-1 Social Security Administration five-step sequential evaluation process.

administrative expedient to quickly identify allowances for both SSDI and SSI. In determining whether a claimant is disabled, SSA decides whether the claimant's impairment *meets* or *medically equals* a listing. Those terms are defined as follows:

- Meets: If the evidence in a case establishes the presence of all the criteria required by one of the listings, then the claimant's impairment meets that specific listing; and
- Equals: If a claimant's impairment is not found to meet the exact requirements of a specific listing, he can still be found disabled if the impairment is at least equal in severity and duration to the criteria of any listed impairment, as established by the relevant evidence in the claimant's case record.

Claims may also be cross-referenced to other listings, a procedure that allows claims to be decided based on the specific requirements of an existing listing. It is important to note that a claimant whose impairment does not meet or medically equal a listing is *not* denied benefits at this step.

Adult claims not allowed at Step 3 (the Listings level) proceed to Step 4 and, if necessary, Step 5, which considers a claimant's ability to perform past work and to do other work in the national economy, respectively. To do this, SSA assesses the claimant's residual functional capacity (RFC) through a time- and resource-intensive process, based on all relevant medical and other evidence in the case record. At Step 4, SSA uses the RFC to help determine the claimant's capacity to do past relevant work (defined as jobs held during the previous 15 years). If SSA determines the claimant is unable to perform past relevant work, the claim progresses to Step 5.

At Step 5, SSA evaluates the claimant's capacity to adjust to any other kind of work. To make this final determination, SSA considers the claimant's age, education, work experience, and the RFC. Generally, the greater the age, the lower the educational attainment, and/or the lower the skill level of previous jobs held by the claimant, the more likely SSA will be to allow the claim. If the claimant is found capable of performing other work, he is not considered disabled. If he cannot perform other work, he is considered disabled based on medical–vocational factors.

For children under age 18 applying for SSI benefits, Steps 1 and 2 are the same. At Step 3, the considerations are whether a child's impairment meets or medically equals a listing. A child's impairment that does not meet or medically equal the requirements of a specific listing may be found to *functionally equal* a listing. To make this determination, SSA assesses the interactive and cumulative effects of all of the child's impairments in terms of six domains of functioning: (1) acquiring and using information; (2) attending and completing tasks; (3) interacting and relating with others; (4) moving about and manipulating objects; (5) caring for yourself; and (6) health and physical well-being. Domains are broad areas of functioning intended to capture all of what a child can or cannot do in activities at home, at school, and in the community, compared to other children of the same age who do not have impairments. For a child's impairment to functionally equal the Listings, it must result in "marked" limitations[4] in two domains of functioning or an "extreme" limitation in one domain.[5] Step 3 is the final step in the process for children under age 18 applying for

[4] A "marked" limitation is found when a child's impairment(s) interferes seriously with his ability to independently initiate, sustain, or complete activities. A "marked" limitation also means a limitation that is "more than moderate" but "less than extreme." It is the equivalent of the functioning one would expect to find on standardized testing with scores that are at least 2, but less than 3, standard deviations below the mean.

[5] An "extreme" limitation is found when a child's impairment(s) interferes very seriously with his ability to independently initiate, sustain, or complete activities. An "extreme" limitation also means a limitation that is "more than marked," and is the rating given to the worst limitation. It is the equivalent of the functioning one would expect to find on standardized testing with scores that are at least 3 deviations below the mean.

SSI benefits. Steps 4 and 5 do not apply to children's claims because these steps focus on a claimant's ability to work.

THE LISTING OF IMPAIRMENTS

History and Purpose

When the SSDI program began in 1956, SSA was faced with quickly processing a large number of claims. To ease the administrative burden of determining the functional capacity of each claimant, SSA adopted a list of serious medical conditions (the Listings) and incorporated it as Step 3 of the sequential evaluation process. Most adult claims not allowed based on the Listings require the lengthy RFC assessment to determine whether a claimant can perform past relevant work. Thus, the Listings are an administrative expedient that allows SSA to process many cases more efficiently, saving time and resources. The percentage of initial allowances made at Step 3 based on the Listings has declined steadily, from more than 90 percent in the early years of the program to 70 percent in the 1980s to 49 percent in 2009 (SSA, 2010b).

In creating or revising the Listings, one of SSA's concerns is that the criteria describe impairments that are severe enough to prevent a claimant from doing any gainful activity, regardless of his age, education, and work experience. By setting the severity standard of the Listings at a higher level (inability to engage in any gainful activity)—referred to as "listing-level severity"—than its disability standard (inability to engage in any *substantial* gainful activity), SSA is able to identify a significant number of allowances and to have confidence that these cases would be allowed if they were subject to a more comprehensive disability assessment at Steps 4 and 5. Further, SSA wants the criteria in the Listings to be clear and easy to apply so that adjudicators can allow claims quickly under the Listings.

Structure

The Listings consist of Part A (primarily for adults) and Part B (applies to children in cases where specific considerations are needed) and are organized into 14 and 15 body systems, respectively (e.g., musculoskeletal, respiratory, neurological; see Appendix A for the full Listings). Listings for each body system begin with a narrative introductory text that defines key concepts and terms used in that body system. Each body system and listing is identified by a number; for example, the immune system disorders body system for Part A is 14.00 and Part B is 114.00. The Part A HIV Infection Listing consists of 11 sublistings (14.08A to 14.08K) and the Part B HIV Infection Listing consists of 12 sublistings (114.08A to 114.08L).

DECISION PROCESS

Initial Decisions

Most Social Security disability claims are initially processed through a network of local SSA field offices and state agencies, usually called Disability Determination Services (DDSs). DDSs, which are fully funded by the federal government, are responsible for developing and evaluating medical evidence and making the initial disability determination.

SSA field office staff are responsible for verifying nonmedical eligibility requirements. If the nonmedical eligibility requirements are met, the field office then sends the case to the DDS for evaluation of disability. The DDS first attempts to obtain medical records from the claimant's medical sources. If that evidence is unavailable or insufficient to make a determination, the DDS will arrange for a consultative examination to obtain the additional information needed. This information is preferred to be from the claimant's treating source, but the DDS may also obtain it from an independent source.

Based on all the medical and other information, the DDS staff make the initial disability determination. Determinations are most often made by an adjudicative team composed of a medical consultant (e.g., a licensed physician) and a disability examiner. Reasonable efforts must be made to ensure that an appropriate specialist evaluates cases involving mental disorders or those involving children.

Appeals Process

After the initial decision, applicants have the opportunity to appeal the determination, following an administrative process that is the same for adult and child claims. There are four levels of appeal: reconsideration, administrative hearing by an administrative law judge (ALJ), review by the appeals council, and federal court review. If the claimant disagrees with the initial disability decision, he may request a reconsideration. A different adjudicative team in the DDS then reviews the initial decision.

If the claimant disagrees with the reconsideration decision, he may ask for a hearing before an ALJ. A claimant may appear before the ALJ in person with an attorney or other representative. The ALJ may ask for testimony from a "medical expert," although usually the decision is usually based on the claimant's RFC rather than the Listings. The ALJ may reverse the denial (thus allowing the claim), affirm the denial, or remand the case to the DDS for further development.

If the claimant disagrees with the hearing decision, he may ask for a review by the SSA's appeals council. If the claimant disagrees with the appeals council's decision, the claimant may file a civil lawsuit in a federal court.

MEDICAL EVIDENCE

The DDS is responsible for developing a claimant's medical history for at least the previous 12 months in most claims. This includes statements or reports from the claimant or his treating source, and information about the impact of an impairment and its related symptoms on a claimant's ability to work. Every reasonable effort is made to obtain medical reports from the claimant's treating source or other medical sources. The DDS evaluates every medical opinion received regardless of source, but does not have to give every opinion equal weight. The treating source is given "controlling weight" if the opinion is well supported by medically acceptable clinical and laboratory diagnostic techniques and is not inconsistent with other substantial evidence in the case record.

If the treating source's report contains a conflict or ambiguity that must be resolved, lacks necessary information, or does not appear to be based on medically acceptable clinical and laboratory diagnostic techniques, the DDS may recontact the treating source for additional evidence or clarification. If the treating source will not or cannot provide the information needed to decide the case, the DDS can order and pay for a consultative examination.

"Acceptable medical sources" are sources who can provide evidence to establish a medically determinable impairment (see Box 1-1). The term

BOX 1-1
Acceptable Medical Sources

- *Licensed physicians* (medical or osteopathic doctors)
- *Licensed or certified psychologists* (included are school psychologists or other licensed or certified individuals with other titles who perform the same function as a school psychologist in a school setting, for purposes of establishing mental retardation, learning disabilities, and borderline intellectual functioning only)
- *Licensed optometrists*, for purposes of establishing visual disorders (except in the U.S. Virgin Islands, licensed optometrists, for the measurement of visual acuity and visual fields only)
- *Licensed podiatrists*, for purposes of establishing impairments of the foot, or foot and ankle only, depending on whether the state in which the podiatrist practices permits the practice of podiatry on the foot only, or the foot and ankle
- *Qualified speech-language pathologists*, for purposes of establishing speech or language impairments only ("qualified" means that the speech-language pathologist must be licensed by the state professional licensing agency, or be fully certified by the state education agency in the state in which he practices, or hold a Certificate of Clinical Competence from the American Speech-Language-Hearing Association)

"other medical sources" describes sources that may provide evidence to show the severity of a claimant's impairment and how it affects his ability to work. Other sources include medical sources not listed in Box 1-1 (e.g., nurse practitioners, physicians assistants, naturopaths, chiropractors, audiologists, and therapists), educational personnel (e.g., school teachers, counselors, daycare center workers), and public and private social welfare agency personnel. Nonmedical sources such as spouses, parents and other caregivers, siblings, other relatives, friends, neighbors, and clergy may also be consulted.

If the treating source's opinion is not given controlling weight, DDS personnel consider a number of factors in weighing evidence, whether from the treating source or others. For example, SSA may consider the existence of an examining relationship (i.e., evidence from a source who has examined the claimant has more weight than a source who has not), length of the treatment relationship, supportability, and other factors that support or contradict the opinion, when weighing evidence.

REVISING AND UPDATING THE LISTINGS

The Listings were first published as regulations in 1968. The first significant revision to the Listings regulations occurred in 1977, when SSA published a new set of listings criteria that would apply to children under age 18. In 1979, SSA comprehensively updated and revised all the adult listings. In 1984, Congress directed SSA to revise its mental disorders listing criteria, which it published in 1985. Later the same year, SSA updated listings for most of the other body systems. The 1985 regulations added expiration dates to all body systems. The law does not require SSA to periodically update the criteria in the Listings, but as SSA noted at the time, it would periodically review and update the Listings based on medical advancements in disability evaluation and treatment and program experience.

The 1985 updates were the last comprehensive revision to the Listings. Since then, SSA has focused on updates that are more targeted—addressing single body systems, or even individual listings. During the mid-1990s, SSA suspended listings revisions in anticipation of a fundamental redesign of the disability decision-making process; however, an internal reassessment of its disability initiatives led SSA to resume its efforts to update all body systems on a continuous basis.

Over time, SSA has added steps to the revision process to expand input from outside of the agency. Rather than beginning the revision process by issuing new draft rules in a Notice of Proposed Rulemaking (NPRM) in the *Federal Register*, SSA may begin by issuing an Advance Notice of Proposed Rulemaking (ANPRM), which announces its intention to update a specific body system and asks for suggestions from the public. SSA may also hold one or more outreach meetings, at which researchers, clinicians, patients, and patient representatives discuss specific impairments, focusing on how existing listings could be revised or on adding new listings. After these additional steps, SSA drafts proposed rules and publishes an NPRM for public comment before being issued Final Rules. It is important to note that revisions to listings apply only to new claimants, and are not applied retroactively to those previously allowed.

Since the development of the HIV Infection Listings in 1993, three ANPRMs have been published (2003, 2006, and 2008). SSA received comments ranging from specific edits (e.g., expand HIV encephalopathy to include AIDS dementia complex) to broader suggestions about the types of evidence collected and the expertise of disability examiners. Commenters also suggested that SSA recognize advances in care such as new manifestations and identification of clinical markers in the HIV Infection Listings. The committee reviewed all the public comments submitted in response to these notices and considered them over the course of its deliberations.

THE HIV INFECTION LISTINGS[6]

In 2009, 7,816 allowances were made based on meeting or medically equaling the HIV Infection Listings (14.08 and 114.08). The total number of claims involving the HIV Infection Listings has decreased steadily from approximately 30,000 claims in 1999 to approximately 25,000 in 2009, in part due to the changing management of HIV. The total allowance rate for all adult HIV infection claims fell from 39 percent in 1999 to 30 percent in 2009. For child claims involving HIV infection, the allowance rate declined from 26 percent in 1999 to 12 percent in 2009.

For 14.08, the number of allowances per sublisting has stayed somewhat steady from 1999 to 2009 (Figure 1-2), with a few exceptions. Allowances made under sublisting 14.08C (protozoan or helminthic infections) decreased in 2008, while 14.08B (fungal infections) increased dramatically. These changes can be attributed largely to a reclassification of *Pneumocystis* pneumonia from a protozoan to a fungal infection. Also, the number of allowances for malignant neoplasms increased from 1999 to 2009. These patterns are likely to change over time in response to the evolving management of the disease. Patterns in Step 3 allowances for Part B (114.08) could not be determined because the total number of claims was low, limiting their significance (Figure 1-3). The three most and least used 14.08 sublistings in 2009 are listed in Table 1-2.

For adults, allowances can be made on the basis of meeting the List-

[6] All data from this section are derived from an unpublished data set provided by SSA. Data were current as of December 31, 2009.

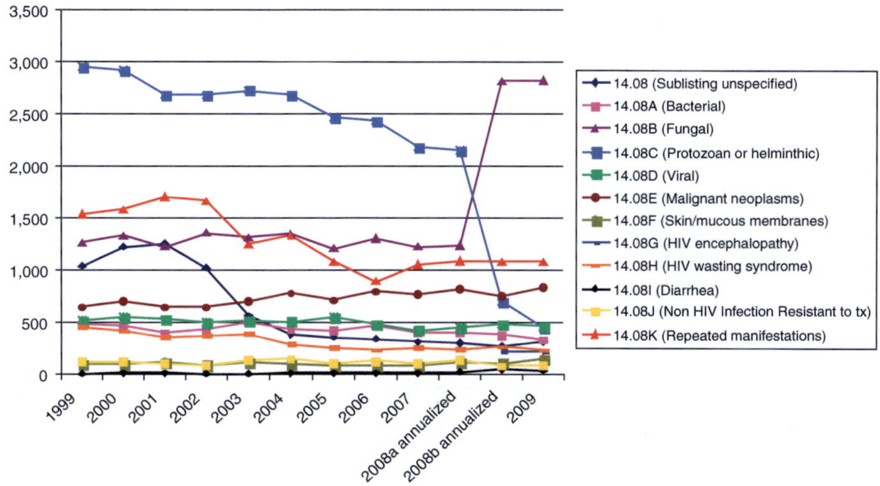

FIGURE 1-2 Allowances by sublisting, 14.08, 1999–2009.
NOTE: 2008 data were annualized to account for changes made to Listing 14.08 that took effect on June 16, 2008.
SOURCE: Unpublished data set provided by SSA.

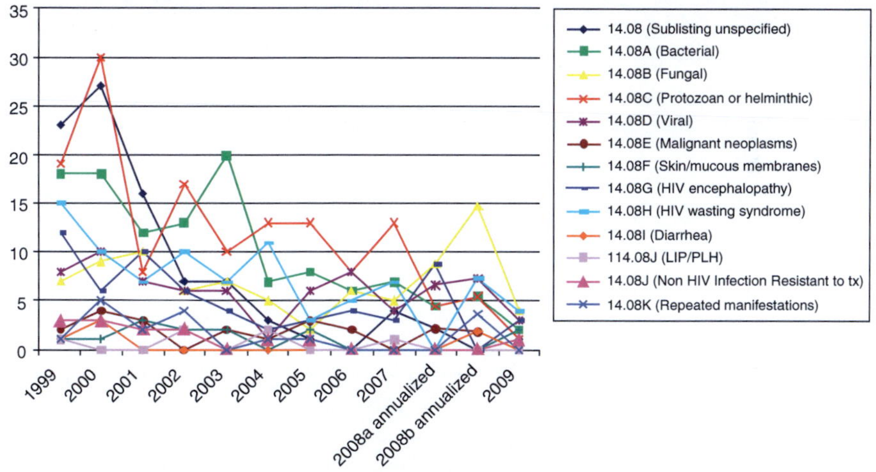

FIGURE 1-3 Allowances by sublisting, 114.08, 1999–2009.
NOTE: 2008 data were annualized to account for changes made to Listing 114.08 that took effect on June 16, 2008. LIP/PLH = Lymphoid interstitial pneumonitis/pulmonary lymphoid hyperplasia complex.
SOURCE: Unpublished data set provided by SSA.

TABLE 1-2 Most and Least Used Sublistings of 14.08

Most Used Sublistings	Description	Number of Allowances
14.08B	Fungal infections	2,820
14.08K	Repeated manifestations	1,079
14.08E	Malignant neoplasms	839
Least Used Sublistings		
14.08F	Conditions of the skin or mucous membranes	154
14.08J	Resistant to treatment or require hospitalization or recurrent intravenous treatment	92
14.08I	Diarrhea	50

NOTE: 114.08 ranged from no allowances in 114.08E, I, J, and L to four allowances in 114.08B and H.
SOURCE: Unpublished data set provided by SSA.

ings (Step 3), equaling the Listings (Step 3), or medical–vocational factors (Step 5). Between 1999 and 2009, approximately 35 percent of all adult HIV claims were allowed (22 percent met the Listing, 7 percent medically equaled the Listing, and 6 percent were medical–vocational decisions). Of those adults denied disability status, 40 percent occurred at Step 5 (ability to perform other work) and 28 percent occurred at Step 4 (ability to perform past work). Over the same time period, an average of 22 percent of claims for children were allowed (14 percent met the Listing, 4 percent medically equaled the Listing, and 4 percent functionally equaled the Listing).

FUNCTIONAL ASSESSMENT OF THE PATIENT WITH HIV/AIDS

HIV/AIDS requires consideration of multiple domains, including medical and psychosocial factors. Work-related functional assessments to more precisely characterize the degree of impairment experienced by the patients living with HIV/AIDS are difficult to conduct, but are necessary as people are living longer with HIV/AIDS and its associated complications (see Appendix D). Many patients with HIV/AIDS show a decline in functional abilities after diagnosis and as their disease progresses (Braveman et al., 2006).

Categories of Functional Assessment

There are three primary domains of functional assessments: physical, mental, and neurocognitive. Measuring limitations in each of these domains helps to create an overall assessment of the functional capacity of an individual. Domain descriptions are as follows:

- *Physical domain:* Physical functioning is the ability to independently perform an activity, the lack of which can be a measure of physical disability, associated with medical conditions and treatment side effects, mental health, and/or lifestyle factors (Oursler et al., 2006). The physical domain generally includes objective criteria based on clinical assessments and biological markers. Measuring individuals' ability to perform activities of daily living and instrumental activities of daily living are another way to measure functional capacity.
- *Mental domain:* Mood and substance abuse disorders are common comorbidities among HIV-infected populations that can lead to functional impairment and potential disability. Significant mental disorders such as depression and anxiety are seen in 25 to 50 percent of individuals living with HIV infection (Pence et al., 2006). Alcoholism is a particularly challenging disease for the HIV/AIDS population, and can lead to increased immune suppression (Fama et al., 2007).
- *Neurocognitive domain:* Neurocognitive impairments play a significant role in the function of HIV-infected individuals, even among antiretroviral-treated individuals (Ellis et al., 2009; Grant, 2008; Heaton et al., 2010). HIV causes neurocognitive disorder either as a primary, direct effect of HIV infection or as a consequence of an opportunistic infection (Ellis et al., 2009). Learning and retrieving new information is one of the most challenging issues facing HIV-infected individuals exhibiting neurocognitive limitation. Other problems include difficulty in maintaining attention, disturbances in executive function, and delayed word retrieval (Grant, 2008).

Tools to Measure Functional Capacity

An objective, clear, and specific test to assess how individuals with HIV/AIDS are affected by all three domains does not currently exist. However, measurement tools exist that separately assess activities of daily living in the physical domain, depression scores in the mental domain, and neurocognitive impairments. There are also assessments to qualitatively measure the patient experience through narrative. These assessments spanning multiple domains of functioning are considered valid and predictive in the literature.

Assessment of an individual's ability to engage in activities of daily living and instrumental activities of daily living is usually determined based on the extent to which he can independently initiate and maintain participation in an ongoing manner. Physical assessments may be as simple as testing an individual's ability to lift objects and sit or stand for periods of time, or can be as complicated as testing the ability to independently manage a medication regimen or shop for groceries. Employment-related assessments may also be administered, such as asking the individual to take apart an object and reassemble it.

For example, the Occupational Performance History Interview (OPHI-II) is designed to provide information about a patient's ability to perform and participate in activities of daily living (Levin et al., 2007). The instrument includes three scales of self-measurement (see Box 1-2) and a qualitative measure for the interviewer to record the patient's life history (often described as "narrative") and any patterns the patient may exhibit (described as the "narrative slope").

Persons with HIV can also develop or have a preexisting mental health impairment. A wide range of impairments exists in people infected with HIV, including major depression, anxiety, bipolar disorder, HIV-associated mania, schizophrenia, apathy, and delirium. Structured psychiatric evaluations that lead to diagnoses and care regimens include the interchangeably used *Diagnostic and Statistical Manual of the American Psychiatric Association* (DSM-IV-TR) and the *International Classification of Disorders* (ICD-10). Standardized, validated, and widely used diagnostic protocols include self-report scales such as the Beck, Hamilton, or Zung Depression inventories. Clinician-administered protocols include the Composite International Diagnostic Interview and the Profile of Mood States, which are more comprehensive assessments of multiple emotional domains.

Specific tests are available to measure the impact of the neurocognitive challenges associated with HIV infection. These include the California Verbal Learning Test (verbal memory), Benton Visual Retention Test (visual memory), Finger Tapping Test (psychomotor skills), Halstead Category Test (concept learning), and the Wisconsin Card Sorting Test (executive func-

BOX 1-2
Three Scales of Self-Measurement

- *Occupational Identity:* Perceptions of self; an opportunity for participation in culturally recognized and named roles
- *Occupational Competence:* Perceptions of ability to engage in and sustain a pattern of productive and satisfying occupational behavior
- *Occupational Setting:* Environment

tion). These well-studied measurement tools are accepted for their ability to accurately capture patients' abilities in the specified areas. These tests are also well received because they are not cost prohibitive (Grant, 2008).

Additional functional assessments may include an individual's general abilities, as indicated by intelligence or memory tests. These tests may be useful to assess an individual's capacity in the multiple domains because the final outcome of functional impairment may not be the result of impairments from a single domain.

Importance of Functional Assessment

Individuals infected with HIV continue to experience multiple effects from their condition. It is important to measure limitations of work-related function by assessing the ability of patients living with HIV/AIDS to effectively participate in social and employment activities in meaningful ways. Currently, a test or evaluation does not exist to measure the overall work-related functional capacity or functional limitation of an individual with HIV. However, tools are available to measure the effects of conditions that impair functioning in adults, including physical functioning, mental disorders, and neurocognitive deficits. Assessing an individual's functional capacity based on these multiple domains is increasingly important, as co-morbid conditions often lead to a more disabling condition than would be predicted from the sum of their individual effects (Antinori et al., 2007). Evaluating the six domains of functioning in children as identified by SSA is also critical to determine the level of impairment for children, especially in the initial stages of development. The committee concludes that measures of functional capacity ought to continue to be important in the HIV Infection Listings.

IOM COMMITTEE

Methods

To address its statement of task of providing guidance to the SSA about how to increase the utility of the HIV Infection Listings, the committee assessed the evidence about HIV and clinical markers of functioning, disability, and return to work. This included a review of the literature and collection of data from SSA, the Centers for Disease Control and Prevention, and various cohorts, including EuroSIDA, the Multicenter AIDS Cohort Study, the North American AIDS Cohort Collaboration on Research and Design, the U.S. Military HIV Natural History Study, and the Veterans Aging Cohort Study. Over the course of the 12-month study, the committee met in person three times, engaged the public through two public workshops, and received statements from various stakeholder organizations. Committee members also conducted site visits at nine DDSs across the country.

Considerations for Developing a Listing

SSA's Listing of Impairments needs to be both highly valid and reliable to efficiently and effectively recognize disabled claimants. Striking a balance between sensitivity and specificity is difficult in any clinical diagnostic test, and also holds true for the Listings. SSA would prefer that the Listings have the greatest positive predictive value at the risk of identifying fewer individuals who actually meet the definition of disability (i.e., "false negatives"). The committee's recommendations and conclusions are offered in an effort to support the construction of such a listing.

The committee developed the following principles on which new HIV Infection Listings ought to be based:

- Reflect current medical practice;
- Determine severity fairly;
- Be based on objective evidence, to the extent possible;
- Incorporate work-related functioning, to the extent possible;
- Be simple and easy to implement; and
- Use flexible language to account for changes in the disease and its treatment over time.

These principles were important in guiding the committee's work and were formed to be consistent with the committee's understanding of SSA's internal processes.

Scope of the Report

The committee's statement of work can be found in Box 1-3. Throughout its discussions, the committee acknowledged that the Listings cannot be viewed in a vacuum. Of particular importance are the issues of medication adherence and access to care. The committee recognized that improved HIV/AIDS outcomes are made possible by adhering to potent antiretroviral regimens, which require continuous access to medical care. Recognition of this connection is critical because Social Security benefits have a great impact on access to care for people living with HIV/AIDS. Qualifying for Social Security disability benefits in many states is seen as an entrée to other public programs, such as Medicare, Medicaid, and housing programs. The 2010 *Patient Protection and Affordable Care Act* undoubtedly will affect these social programs and others, such as those funded by the *Ryan White*

BOX 1-3
Statement of Work

An ad hoc committee of medical experts will conduct a study to assist the Social Security Administration (SSA) on HIV disability issues. The committee will review the current medical criteria for disability resulting from HIV infection in SSA's Listing of Impairments ("the Listings") and identify areas in which the HIV Infection Listings should be revised and updated based on current medical knowledge and practice. Specifically, the committee will (1) conduct a comprehensive review of the relevant research literature and current professional practice guidelines; (2) assess the current HIV Infection Listings in light of current research knowledge and evidence-based medical practice; and (3) produce a short report with specific recommendations for revision of the HIV Infection Listings based on evidence (to the extent possible) and professional judgment (where evidence is lacking).

Care Act, that provide many HIV-infected people with access to care and medication. However, it is too early to determine how the new law will specifically impact the Social Security disability program. Although the issues of adherence and access to care are critical in the discussion of Social Security disability benefits, in-depth discussion about the means by which people receive treatment and medications was deemed outside the committee's scope.

REPORT STRUCTURE

This report consists of eight chapters, of which this introduction is the first. Chapter 2 reviews current concepts in HIV. Chapters 3 through 6 introduce and explain the committee's recommendations with respect to the Part A HIV Infection Listing (14.08). Recommendations regarding Part B (114.08) are discussed in Chapter 7. Chapter 8 provides a discussion of other actions SSA could take to enhance implementation of the HIV Infection Listings, as well as how the introductory text should be revised.

SSA asked the committee to address a list of specific questions. Appendix B provides an index of the committee's responses to each question throughout the report.

REFERENCES

Antinori, A., G. Arendt, J. Becker, B. Brew, D. Byrd, M. Cherner, D. Clifford, P. Cinque, L. Epstein, K. Goodkin, M. Gisslen, I. Grant, R. Heaton, J. Joseph, K. Marder, C. Marra, J. McArthur, M. Nunn, R. Price, L. Pulliam, K. Robertson, N. Sacktor, V. Valcour, and V. Wojna. 2007. Updated research nosology for HIV-associated neurocognitive disorders. *Neurology* 69(18):1789–1799.

Braveman, B., G. Kielhofner, G. Albrecht, and C. Helfrich. 2006. Occupational identity, occupational competence and occupational settings (environment): Influences on return to work in men living with HIV/AIDS. *Work* 27(3):267–276.

Ellis, R. J., P. Calero, and M. D. Stockin. 2009. HIV infection and the central nervous system: A primer. *Neuropsychology Review* 19(2):144–151.

Fama, R., J. C. Eisen, M. J. Rosenbloom, S. A. Sassoon, C. A. Kemper, S. Deresinski, A. Pfefferbaum, and E. V. Sullivan. 2007. Upper and lower limb motor impairments in alcoholism, HIV infection, and their comorbidity. *Alcoholism: Clinical & Experimental Research* 31(6):1038–1044.

Grant, I. 2008. Neurocognitive disturbances in HIV. *International Review of Psychiatry* 20(1):15.

Heaton, R., D. Clifford, D. Franklin Jr., S. Woods, C. Ake, F. Vaida, R. Ellis, S. Letendre, T. Marcotte, J. Atkinson, M. Rivera-Mindt, O. Vigil, M. Taylor, A. Collier, C. Marra, B. Gelman, J. McArthur, S. Morgello, D. Simpson, J. McCutchan, I. Abramson, A. Gamst, C. Fennema-Notestine, T. Jernigan, J. Wong, and I. Grant for The CHARTER Study Group. 2010 (in press). HIV-associated neurocognitive disorders persist in the era of potent antiretroviral therapy. *Neurology.*

Levin, M., G. Kielhofner, B. Braveman, and L. Fogg. 2007. Narrative slope as a predictor of work and other occupational participation. *Scandinavian Journal of Occupational Therapy* 14(4):258–264.

Oursler, K. K., J. L. Goulet, D. A. Leaf, A. Akingicil, L. I. Katzel, A. Justice, and S. Crystal. 2006. Association of comorbidity with physical disability in older HIV-infected adults. *AIDS Patient Care and STDs* 20(11):782–791.

Pence, B. W., W. C. Miller, K. Whetten, J. J. Eron, and B. N. Gaynes. 2006. Prevalence of DSM-IV–defined mood, anxiety, and substance use disorders in an HIV clinic in the Southeastern United States. *Journal of Acquired Immune Deficiency Syndromes* 42(3):298–306.

SSA (Social Security Administration). 2007. *SSI annual statistical report.* Washington, DC: SSA.

SSA. 2008a. *Annual statistical report on the Social Security Disability Insurance Program.* Washington, DC: SSA.

SSA. 2008b. *SSI annual statistical report.* Washington, DC: SSA.

SSA. 2010a. *Social Security news release: Social Security helps states with mounting disability claims.* http://www.ssa.gov/pressoffice/pr/est-pr.htm (accessed April 15, 2010).

SSA. 2010b. *A historical look at initial adult disability determinations that meet or equal a medical listing(s).* Paper presented at IOM Committee of Medical Experts to Assist Social Security on Disability Issues, Washington, DC, April 21.

2

Current Concepts in HIV/AIDS

EVOLUTION OF THE EPIDEMIC

The first cases of AIDS were reported in the United States in 1981 (CDC, 2001). At that time the average life expectancy for a person diagnosed with AIDS was 6 months (Satriano et al., 2005). Subsequent advances in treatment, particularly the use of combination antiretroviral therapy, have transformed HIV/AIDS into a chronic, manageable condition. A 35-year-old person diagnosed with HIV infection has an estimated life expectancy of 32 years, depending on nadir CD4 (Hogg et al., 2008). In the setting of these successes, however, patients with HIV infection still face many challenges.

As treated patients live longer, illnesses typically associated with an aging population, such as cardiovascular disease, osteoporosis, and diabetes, are being seen at increased frequency. Some of these conditions may be related to treatment, and others may be related to the chronic inflammatory state associated with HIV infection. Furthermore, self-management and adherence to the sometimes complex treatment regimens required by HIV/AIDS represent an ongoing and lifelong challenge for many patients. Finally, the remarkable advances in combination antiretroviral therapy are of little value to those who are unable to access state-of-the-art care, including treatments for conditions associated with HIV infection.

In 2008, the Centers for Disease Control and Prevention (CDC) estimated that more than 56,000 incident HIV cases occurred in the United States in 2006 (the most recent year data are available) (Hall et al., 2008). As mortality rates have declined due to improvements in treatment, the cumulative number of people living with HIV/AIDS has steadily increased. In 2006, the CDC estimated approximately 1.1 million people were living with HIV/AIDS in the United States (CDC, 2008). Over the past decade, the prevalence of HIV/AIDS in the United States has risen disproportionately among some racial and ethnic groups. Slightly more than 50 percent of HIV-positive individuals in the United States are African Americans, and 18 percent are Hispanic/Latino (CDC, 2007). In addition, adolescents and young adults account for an increasing proportion of all new cases of HIV infection. While 29 percent of people living with HIV/AIDS in the United States are between the ages of 13 and 29, this age group accounts for 34 percent of all new cases of HIV (Hall et al., 2008).

Pathogenesis of HIV

HIV damages the immune system by (1) depleting a critical element of the body's immune system, the CD4+ T-cell pool (CD4 cells), and (2) causing a state of generalized activation and inflammation of the immune system. As a consequence of these two changes, patients with HIV infection are at an increased risk of other infectious diseases and virus-associated cancers as well as an array of noninfectious diseases. The diagnoses and clinical conditions associated with HIV infection are listed in Table C-1 (see Appendix C). In addition to the secondary complications of HIV infection, the virus is capable of directly infecting the nervous system, leading to neurocognitive dysfunction (Grant, 2008).

Comorbidities of HIV

Although the list of opportunistic infections and neoplasms associated with HIV infection is well characterized and has been relatively stable since the beginning of the epidemic, a new set of serious complications of HIV infection has emerged in recent years (Table C-1). These conditions have replaced opportunistic infections as the leading cause of death in patients with HIV infection (Buchacz et al., 2010). It is believed that the ongoing immune activation and inflammation characteristic of HIV infection in patients with or without treatment and manifest by elevated levels of interleukin-6 and D-dimer is responsible, at least in part, for these problems. It has been suggested that HIV infection leads to an accelerated senescence of multiple organ systems, or premature aging. Complicating this picture is the fact that many of these same problems are seen as side effects of some medications used to treat HIV infection.

The presence of comorbidities such as major depressive disorder, other mental disorders, or substance abuse may affect neurocognition in HIV-positive individuals. Cognitive limitations may impair many patients and range from marginal to severe (Valcour et al., 2004; Vance and Struzick, 2007). Cognitive dysfunction can have a major impact on a patient's ability to maintain activities of daily living, remain employed, or engage in other regular activities such as driving.

Common comorbidities among HIV-infected populations with and without neurocognitive disorder include psychiatric and behavioral disorders, which can lead to functional impairment and potential disability. Within psychiatric disorders, major depression, delirium, and anxiety are seen in 25 to 50 percent of individuals living with HIV infection (Pence et al., 2006). Studies have suggested the risky behaviors associated with bipolar disorder or schizophrenia may lead to higher prevalence rates of HIV infection among affected populations. These disorders are somewhat less common than major depression, but if untreated may lead to impairment and disability (Vlassova et al., 2009). Behavioral disorders include untreated drug dependence, which can lead to impairment and disability. Injection drug use can lead to immune suppression and increased HIV transmission (Fama et al., 2009; Vlassova et al., 2009). Cocaine, amphetamine, and alcohol abuse can also lead to increased immune suppression (Fama et al., 2009), decreased adherence, and poor virologic outcomes (Vlassova et al., 2009). Psychological reactions to negative life experiences can lead to posttraumatic stress disorder, seen in 13 to 20 percent of individuals living with HIV infection. Posttraumatic stress disorder cooccurs with major depression and substance use disorders in 25 to 50 percent of individuals living with HIV infection and is associated with lower CD4 counts and incompletely suppressed viral load (Vranceanu et al., 2008).

HIV and Aging

A growing number of older adults are affected by HIV/AIDS, including those who have aged with the disease due to advances in treatment as well as individuals who have been infected later in life. In 2007, the largest number of new infections occurred among those ages 40 to 44. Furthermore, according to CDC estimates for 2007, 28 percent of HIV-infected adults were over age 45. New aspects of chronic HIV infection will likely become apparent as the HIV/AIDS population ages.

Older age is associated with more rapid progression of HIV infection. Research has linked age as an independent prognostic factor for patients with HIV (Egger et al., 2002). Patients older than age 50 who began combination antiretroviral therapy showed higher clinical progression of disease, including higher rates of mortality, compared to younger patients beginning treatment (Kirk and Goetz, 2009). Furthermore, untreated older adults progress to AIDS and death much faster than younger individuals. In addition, older adults may experience longer-term effects from the virus, treatment, and comorbidities compared to younger people. Researchers and treating clinicians may need to consider differentiating between those recently infected at an older age and those who were infected at a younger age and have grown older with the disease due to improvements in therapy (Stoff et al., 2004). Older adults may be diagnosed later in disease progression, as many age-related illnesses can mimic HIV-associated symptoms (Kirk and Goetz, 2009).

MANAGEMENT OF HIV/AIDS

In the beginning of the epidemic, researchers and clinicians struggled to understand the nature of the immune defect and the identity of the causative agent. With the discovery of HIV as the causative agent of AIDS, work proceeded rapidly to identify and develop inhibitors of critical steps in the viral life cycle (see Figure 2-1). In 1987, monotherapy with the nucleoside analogue zidovudine (ZDV, also known as azidothymidine [AZT]) became the first licensed treatment for patients with AIDS. Although this treatment saved lives, its effects were relatively short lived because the virus was able to develop resistance to the single agent. The licensure of ZDV was rapidly followed by the development of a series of additional nucleoside analogues, followed by the introduction of nonnucleoside reverse transcriptase inhibitors, protease inhibitors, fusion inhibitors, entry inhibitors, and integrase inhibitors.

Used in combination, these drugs lead to substantial suppression of HIV replication for extended periods of time. Despite this success, these drugs are not able to eradicate the virus and patients currently must remain on therapy for the remainder of their lives. Even brief lapses in therapy can lead to increases in viral replication and subsequent immune system and other end organ damage.

The overall goal of combination antiretroviral therapy (also known as highly active antiretroviral therapy or HAART) is to limit the ability of the virus to replicate and thus limit its ability to damage the host. Following the widespread use of combination antiretroviral therapy in the United States in the mid-1990s, the mortality rate due to AIDS declined steeply (see Figure 2-2). Continued success in the future will depend to a large extent on the ability to engage HIV-infected persons in care early in the course of their infection and to support them in adhering to treatment regimens. Successful treatment regimens begin with early diagnosis of HIV infection. Research has shown that patients have better outcomes when they begin combination antiretroviral therapy regimens before their CD4 counts decline to fewer than 350 cells/mm^3, compared to patients who begin treatment at a more advanced stage of disease (Egger et al., 2002). A broader discussion of CD4 count and prognosis is included in Chapter 3.

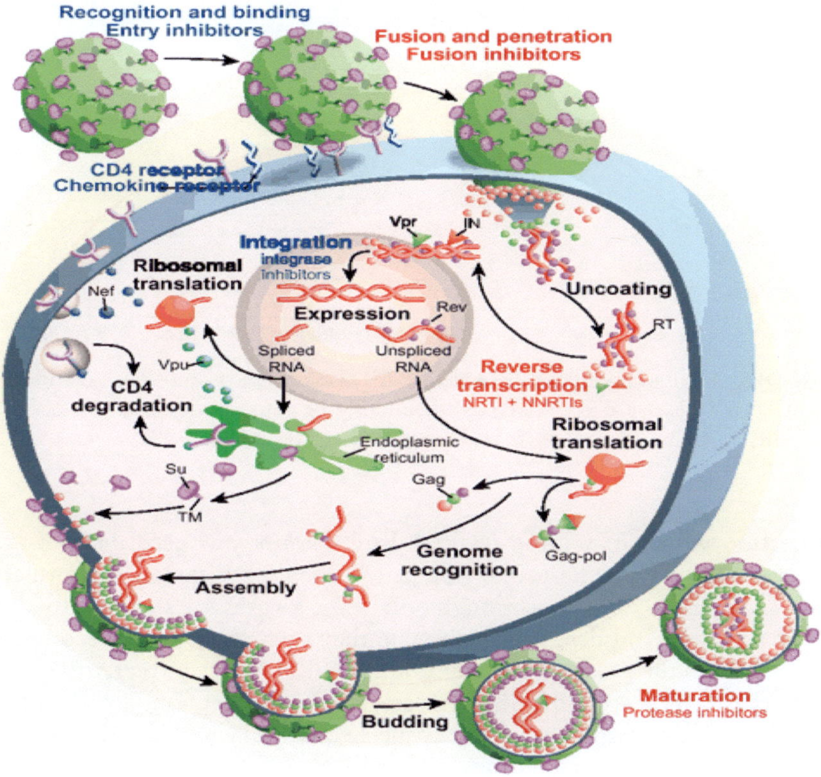

FIGURE 2-1 Replication cycle of HIV with stages to initiate treatment.
NOTE: NNRTI = nonnucleoside reverse transcriptase inhibitor; NRTI = nucleoside reverse transcriptase inhibitor.
SOURCE: Reprinted by permission from Macmillan Publishers Ltd. Bennett and Rose, 2010.

The high rate of viral production (10^9 particles/day) coupled with the error rate of the critical viral enzyme reverse transcriptase (1/genome) means that an enormous number of viral variants are produced each day in an infected individual. Although many of these variants are likely to be defective, only a single virus with a mutation conferring resistance to a specific antiretroviral agent can lead to a population of resistant virus. The possibility that a population of resistant virus will be established is minimized by the use of a combination of antiretroviral agents. In the setting of multiple drugs, a series of mutations is required for resistance to emerge. Resistance was a major problem in treating patients with HIV

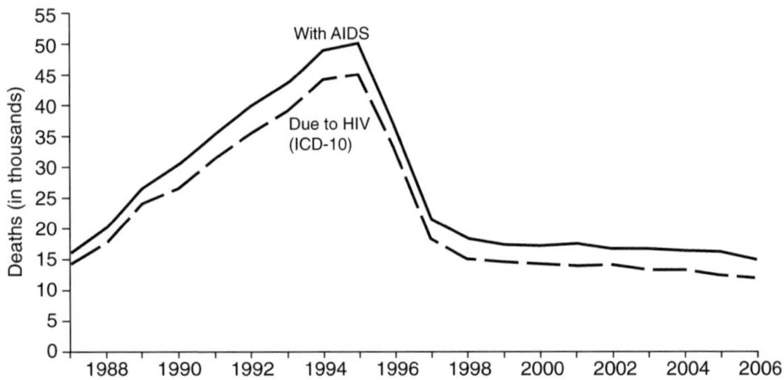

FIGURE 2-2 Estimated numbers of U.S. AIDS case reports and death certificates in which HIV disease was selected as the underlying cause of death, 1987–2006.
SOURCE: Centers for Disease and Control and Prevention, 2007.

infection when single-drug or dual-drug therapy was used. Now it is less of a problem with the use of potent combination regimens (Bangsberg et al., 2000, 2003, 2004). Although only some viruses are resistant to all current antiretroviral drugs, it is possible that such strains will become more prevalent in the future. CD4 count and viral load are currently the leading laboratory indicators of the progression of HIV infection (see Chapter 3). Other independent indicators include hemoglobin and direct markers of inflammation and coagulation.

Treatment Side Effects

Although they save lives, antiretrovirals have a variety of side effects, some of which can be permanently disabling. Further complicating the picture is the fact that some side effects from treatment resemble manifestations of HIV/AIDS; as a result, clinicians may have trouble determining whether the root cause of the symptom is the antiretroviral or the underlying disease. Given the array of antiretrovirals currently available (see Table C-2 for a list of current HIV/AIDS antiretrovirals and potential side effects), one is often able to switch to an alternative regimen to attempt to distinguish a side effect from a disease manifestation. Some of the formerly common side effects from treatment are now relatively rare. For example, pancreatitis and kidney stones are no longer common complications of HIV/AIDS therapy.

Under certain circumstances, patients continue to be disabled by HIV/AIDS, despite advances in treatment and the opportunity to choose alternate medications (Klimas et al., 2008). Although currently the overall outlook is much brighter for patients with HIV infection than it was in 1981, not all patients respond to medication, including those:

- Who do not have access to state-of-the-art treatment;
- Who are infected with multidrug-resistant viruses;
- Who are unable to adhere to treatment regimens; or
- Who have a relatively small number of usually irreversible complications, such as progressive multifocal leukoencephalopathy.

Furthermore, patients with comorbidities, such as depression, diabetes, and cardiovascular disease, must manage multiple medical therapies (Stoff et al., 2004). The resulting use of multiple medications may lead to further complications and drug interactions. Finally, individuals continue to enter medical care with advanced HIV disease (indicated by low CD4 counts) and suffer from an array of HIV-associated conditions that will likely result in disability for more than one year.

Medication Adherence

Adherence to antiretroviral therapy is widely accepted as crucial to successful outcomes. The level of adherence is reflected by both the suppression of plasma levels of HIV (Aloisi et al., 2002; Lanièce et al., 2003; Nieuwkerk and Oort, 2005) and the individual's overall quality of life (Mannheimer et al., 2005). Nonadherence to combination antiretroviral therapy regimens, which is common among HIV-positive individuals, compromises clinical effectiveness and is an antecedent to the development of viral resistance (Abel and Painter, 2003; Aloisi et al., 2002; Chesney et al., 2000). It is also associated with increased risk of mortality (Lima et al., 2009). A systematic review of 72 developed-country studies and 12 developing-country studies identified barriers to adherence common to both settings, including fear of disclosure, substance abuse, forgetfulness, suspicion of treatment, complicated regimens, number of pills, quality of life, work and family responsibilities, falling asleep, and lack of access to medications (Mills et al., 2006).

IMPROVEMENTS IN FUNCTIONING AND CAPACITY TO RETURN TO WORK

In most cases, HIV/AIDS is no longer a near-term fatal disease. In these situations, following initiation and stabilization on therapy, patients with HIV infection may engage in a full range of activities, including employment (Goldman and Bao, 2004). Return to work is an important social and economic milestone for HIV-infected individuals and their families, and a contribution to society as a whole (Hergenrather et al., 2005). Although no national employment statistics are available for people living with HIV/AIDS in the United States, nearly 70 percent are between ages 25 and 49, the average working ages (CDC, 2008). In 2000, slightly more than 60 percent of working-age Americans with disabilities were employed full- or part-time, compared to nearly 80 percent of nondisabled Americans (U.S. Census Bureau, 2003).

Moving from disability status to employment leads to increased, if not complete, independence in the community. Individuals who maintain part- or full-time employment achieve improved physical and mental health due to their improved economic status. Psychological well-being may also improve due to individuals' ability to engage in a standard activity deemed valuable by society (Braveman and Keilhofner, 2006).

For individuals with HIV/AIDS, the decision to work may be influenced by a number of factors. These factors may include personal beliefs that shape behaviors, either motivating return to work or impeding employment. The opinions of various groups, such as family, friends, or the treating physician, may also positively or negatively influence a person's decision to work. Empirical research has not shown that any one of these groups' opinions has a greater effect on the individual's decision to work than another. Due to the myriad factors to consider when deciding to work, individuals welcome guidance from trusted social networks (Hergenrather et al., 2004).

In studies examining return-to-work patterns for people with HIV/AIDS, the most often cited motivation to consider employment was financial need (Arns et al., 2004; Martin et al., 2006; Rabkin et al., 2004). Sociodemographic indicators are also strongly associated with increased likelihood of returning to work. For example, men are more likely to work than women, and younger individuals are more likely to work than older adults (Brooks et al., 2004; Burns et al., 2006). Other motivators leading individuals to consider returning to the workplace include positive support from family and friends, and, in some cases, explicit encouragement to seek employment (Hergenrather et al., 2004; Martin et al., 2004). Common barriers to employment include lower socioeconomic status, less education, and limited work experience (Braveman and Keilhofner, 2006). Perceived lack of flexible schedules to accommodate adherence to prescribed treatment or lack of sensitive workplace environments may also impede an individual's decision to return to work (Hergenrather et al., 2004).

Not everyone with HIV/AIDS who is capable of employment actually returns to work. The overall patterns by which patients continue, resume, or suspend employment after learning their HIV status vary. Often patients stop working for a brief time when they first learn of their diagnosis. This is frequently in the setting of a secondary infection that prompted diagnostic testing. Once patients are successfully on a stable therapeutic regimen, they may achieve a balanced health status and desire to resume their work activities.

However, treatment-related complications and the challenges of managing their health condition may limit full participation in daily activities for some individuals living with HIV/AIDS. Therefore, many individuals remain on Social Security disability despite physical indicators of positive health status such as higher CD4 count, low viral load, or the absence of AIDS-defining illnesses or other infections (Burns et al., 2006). In particular, neurocognitive impairment associated with HIV infection has been shown to have a significant association with the rate of unemployment among affected individuals, despite the absence of physical symptoms due to HIV (Heaton et al., 2010).

REFERENCES

Abel, E., and L. Painter. 2003. Factors that influence adherence to HIV medications: Perceptions of women and health care providers. *Journal of the Association of Nurses in AIDS Care* 14(4):61–69.

Aloisi, M. S., C. Arici, R. Balzano, P. Noto, R. Piscopo, G. Filice, F. Menichetti, A. Monforte, G. Ippolito, and E. Girardi. 2002. Behavioral correlates of adherence to antiretroviral therapy. *Journal of Acquired Immune Deficiency Syndromes* 31(Suppl 3):S145–S148.

Arns, P., D. Martin, and R. Chernoff. 2004. Psychosocial needs of HIV-positive individuals seeking workforce re-entry. *AIDS Care* 16(3):377–386.

Bangsberg, D. R., F. M. Hecht, E. D. Charlebois, A. R. Zolopa, M. Holodniy, L. Sheiner, J. D. Bamberger, M. A. Chesney, and A. Moss. 2000. Adherence to protease inhibitors, HIV-1 viral load, and development of drug resistance in an indigent population. *AIDS* 14(4):357–366.

Bangsberg, D. R., E. D. Charlebois, R. M. Grant, M. Holodniy, S. G. Deeks, S. Perry, K. N. Conroy, R. Clark, D. Guzman, A. Zolopa, and A. Moss. 2003. High levels of adherence do not prevent accumulation of HIV drug resistance mutations. *AIDS* 17(13):1925–1932.

Bangsberg, D. R., A. R. Moss, and S. G. Deeks. 2004. Paradoxes of adherence and drug resistance to HIV antiretroviral therapy. *Journal of Antimicrobial Chemotherapy* 53(5): 696–699.

Bennett, N. J., and F. B. Rose. 2010. HIV disease. *emedicine.com*, http://emedicine.medscape.com/article/211316-overview (accessed June 18, 2010).

Braveman, B., and G. Keilhofner. 2006. HIV/AIDS and employment: The continuing challenge. *Work* 27(3):205–207.

Brooks, R. A., D. J. Martin, D. J. Ortiz, and R. C. Veniegas. 2004. Perceived barriers to employment among persons living with HIV/AIDS. *AIDS Care* 16(6):756–766.

Buchacz, K., R. K. Baker, F. J. Palella Jr., J. S. Chmiel, K. A. Lichtenstein, R. M. Novak, K. C. Wood, J. T. Brooks, and the HOPS Investigators. 2010. AIDS-defining opportunistic illnesses in U.S. patients, 1994–2007: A cohort study. *AIDS* 24(10):1549–1559.

Burns, S. M., L. R. L. Young, and S. Maniss. 2006. Predictors of employment and disability among people living with HIV/AIDS. *Rehabilitation Psychology* 51(2):127–134.

CDC (Centers for Disease Control and Prevention). 2001. *First report of AIDS.* Atlanta, GA: Centers for Disease Control and Prevention, U.S. Department of Health and Human Services.

CDC. 2007. *HIV/AIDS surveillance report: Cases of HIV infection and AIDS in the United States and Dependent Areas, 2007*. Atlanta, GA: Centers for Disease Control and Prevention, U.S. Department of Health and Human Services.

CDC. 2008. HIV prevalence estimates—United States, 2006. *Morbidity and Mortality Weekly Report* 57(39):1073–1076.

Chesney, M. A., J. R. Ickovics, D. B. Chambers, A. L. Gifford, J. Neidig, B. Zwickl, and A. W. Wu. 2000. Self-reported adherence to antiretroviral medications among participants in HIV clinical trials: The AACTG adherence instruments. *AIDS Care* 12(3):255–266.

Egger, M., M. May, G. Chêne, A. N. Phillips, B. Ledergerber, F. Dabis, D. Costagliola, A. D'Arminio Monforte, F. de Wolf, P. Reiss, J. D. Lundgren, A. C. Justice, S. Staszewski, C. Leport, R. S. Hogg, C. A. Sabin, M. J. Gill, B. Salzberger, and J. A. C. Sterne. 2002. Prognosis of HIV-1-infected patients starting highly active antiretroviral therapy: A collaborative analysis of prospective studies. *The Lancet* 360(9327):119–129.

Fama, R., M. J. Rosenbloom, B. N. Nichols, A. Pfefferbaum, and E. V. Sullivan. 2009. Working and episodic memory in HIV infection, alcoholism, and their comorbidity: Baseline and 1-year follow-up examinations. *Alcoholism: Clinical and Experimental Research* 33(10):1815–1824.

Goldman, D. P., and Y. Bao. 2004. Effective HIV treatment and the employment of HIV(+) adults. *Health Services Research* 39:1691–1712.

Grant, I. 2008. Neurocognitive disturbances in HIV. *International Review of Psychiatry* 20(1):33–47.

Hall, H., R. Song, P. Rhodes, J. Prejean, Q. An, L. M. Lee, J. Karon, R. Brookmeyer, E. H. Kaplan, M. T. McKenna, and R. S. Janssen. 2008. Estimation of HIV incidence in the United States. *Journal of the American Medical Association* 300(5):520–529.

Heaton, R., D. Clifford, D. Franklin Jr., S. Woods, C. Ake, F. Vaida, R. Ellis, S. Letendre, T. Marcotte, J. Atkinson, M. Rivera-Mindt, O. Vigil, M. Taylor, A. Collier, C. Marra, B. Gelman, J. McArthur, S. Morgello, D. Simpson, J. McCutchan, I. Abramson, A. Gamst, C. Fennema-Notestine, T. Jernigan, J. Wong, and I. Grant for The CHARTER Study Group. 2010 (in press). HIV-associated neurocognitive disorders persist in the era of potent antiretroviral therapy. *Neurology*.

Hergenrather, K. C., S. D. Rhodes, and G. Clark. 2004. Employment-seeking behavior of persons with HIV/AIDS: A theory-based approach. *Journal of Rehabilitation* 70(4):22–32.

Hergenrather, K. C., S. D. Rhodes, and G. Clark. 2005. The employment perspectives study: Identifying factors influencing the job-seeking behavior of persons living with HIV/AIDS. *AIDS Education & Prevention* 17(2):131–142.

Hogg, R., J. A. C. Sterne, V. Lima, S. Grabar, M. Battegay, M. Bonarek, A. D'Arminio Monforte, A. Esteve, M. J. Gill, A. Justice, A. Hayden, F. Lampe, A. Mocroft, M. J. Mugavero, S. Staszewski, J. C. Wasmuth, A. van Sighem, M. Kitahata, J. Guest, M. Egger, and M. May. 2008. Life expectancy of individuals on combination antiretroviral therapy in high-income countries: A collaborative analysis of 14 cohort studies. *The Lancet* 372:293–299.

Kirk, J. B., and M. B. Goetz. 2009. Human immunodeficiency virus in an aging population, a complication of success. *Journal of the American Geriatrics Society* 57(11):2129–2138.

Klimas, N., A. O'Brien Koneru, and M. A. Fletcher. 2008. Overview of HIV. *Psychosomatic Medicine* 70(5):523–530.

Lanièce, I., M. Ciss, A. Desclaux, K. Diop, F. Mbodj, B. Ndiaye, O. Sylla, E. Delaporte, and I. Ndoye. 2003. Adherence to HAART and its principal determinants in a cohort of Senegalese adults. *AIDS* 17(Suppl 3):S103–S108.

Lima, V. D., R. Harrigan, D. R. Bangsberg, R. S. Hogg, R. Gross, B. Yip, and J. Montaner. 2009. The combined effect of modern highly active antiretroviral therapy regimens and adherence on mortality over time. *Journal of Acquired Immune Deficiency Syndromes* 50(5):529–536.

Mannheimer, S., J. Matts, E. Telzak, M. Chesney, C. Child, A. Wu, and G. Friedland. 2005. Quality of life in HIV-infected individuals receiving antiretroviral therapy is related to adherence. *AIDS Care* 17(1):10–22.

Martin, D. J., P. G. Arns, R. A. Chernoff, and M. Steckart. 2004. Working with HIV/AIDS: Who attempts workforce reentry following disability? *Journal of Applied Rehabilitation Counseling* 35(3):28–38.

Martin, D. J., M. J. Steckart, and P. G. Arns. 2006. Returning to work with HIV/AIDS: A qualitative study. *Work* 27(3):209–219.

Mills, E. J., J. B. Nachega, I. Buchan, J. Orbinski, A. Attaran, S. Singh, B. Rachlis, P. Wu, C. Cooper, L. Thabane, K. Wilson, G. H. Guyatt, and D. R. Bangsberg. 2006. Adherence to antiretroviral therapy in Sub-Saharan Africa and North America: A meta-analysis. *Journal of the American Medical Association* 296(6):679–690.

Nieuwkerk, P. T., and F. J. Oort. 2005. Self-reported adherence to antiretroviral therapy for HIV-1 infection and virologic treatment response: A meta analysis. *Journal of Acquired Immune Deficiency Syndromes* 38(4):445–448.

Pence, B. W., W. C. Miller, K. Whetten, J. J. Eron, and B. N. Gaynes. 2006. Prevalence of DSM-IV-defined mood, anxiety, and substance use disorders in an HIV clinic in the Southeastern United States. *Journal of Acquired Immune Deficiency Syndromes* 42(3):298–306.

Rabkin, J. G., M. McElhiney, S. J. Ferrando, W. Van Gorp, and S. Hsing. 2004. Predictors of employment of men with HIV/AIDS: A longitudinal study. *Psychosomatic Medicine* 66(1):72–78.

Satriano, J., A. Berkman, and R. H. Remien. 2005. Acquired immune deficiency syndrome and human immunodeficiency virus. In *Medical aspects of disability, 3rd ed. A handbook for the rehabilitation professional*, edited by H. H. Zaretsky, E. F. Richter III, and M. G. Eisenberg. New York: Springer Publishing Co.

Stoff, D. M., L. Mitnick, and S. Kalichman. 2004. Research issues in the multiple diagnoses of HIV/AIDS, mental illness and substance abuse. *AIDS Care* 16(Suppl 1):S1–S5.

U.S. Census Bureau. 2003. *Disability status: 2000. Census 2000 brief.* Washington, DC: U.S. Census Bureau.

Valcour, V. G., C. M. Shikuma, M. R. Watters, and N. C. Sacktor. 2004. Cognitive impairment in older HIV-1-seropositive individuals: Prevalence and potential mechanisms. *AIDS* 18(Suppl 1):S79–S86.

Vance, D. E., and T. C. Struzick. 2007. Addressing risk factors of cognitive impairment in adults aging with HIV: A social work model. *Journal of Gerontological Social Work* 49(4):51–77.

Vlassova, N., A. Angelino, and G. Treisman. 2009. Update on mental health issues in patients with HIV infection. *Current Infectious Disease Reports* 11(2):163–169.

Vranceanu, A. M., S. A. Safren, M. Lu, W. M. Coady, P. R. Skolnik, W. H. Rogers, and I. B. Wilson. 2008. The relationship of post-traumatic stress disorder and depression to antiretroviral medication adherence in persons with HIV. *AIDS Patient Care and STDs* 22(4):313–321.

3

Low CD4 Count as an Indicator of Disability

The committee sought to identify a laboratory marker or set of markers that could be used to make decisions about functional impairment and disability. However, after carefully reviewing data from several large multinational HIV/AIDS cohorts and related publications, the committee found no direct associations between laboratory measures and the level of disability. In the absence of such evidence, the committee considered measures predictive of disease progression, morbidity, and mortality, which, in the expert assessment of the committee, could be taken as surrogate markers of disability.

Two laboratory markers, CD4 count and HIV-1 viral load, are a routine part of HIV clinical care and recommended by all primary care guidelines. They are inexpensive and widely available. The results are present in medical records and available in the disability determination process. Of the two, CD4 count is most appropriate for consideration in the determination of HIV disability. The CD4 count is a direct marker of the stage of HIV-induced immune deficiency and of the near-term risk of morbidity and mortality.

INDICATORS OF DISEASE PROGRESSION

AIDS was first recognized when clinicians diagnosed previously healthy individuals with rare cancers or opportunistic infections such as Kaposi's sarcoma or *Pneumocystis jirovecii* pneumonia. In these early cases, it was noted that patients had severe depletion of the helper or CD4+ subtype of T-lymphocytes (CD4 cells), which in part explained their susceptibility to opportunistic infections and cancers. Shortly thereafter a novel retrovirus, now called HIV, was discovered as the cause of AIDS. Laboratory measures were later determined to correspond with severity of disease and the rate of clinical progression. The two measures most commonly used to stage HIV infection are the absolute number of CD4 cells per cubic millimeter (mm^3) of blood and the quantity of HIV RNA molecules per milliliter (mL) of plasma, also known as viral load.

The CD4 count indicates the degree of immune depletion or immunodeficiency. The remaining immunologic reserve, reflected in the CD4 count, is highly predictive of near-term risk of opportunistic diseases and mortality. The viral load, on the other hand, indicates the production rate of HIV virions and expected rate of subsequent CD4 cell destruction. Although CD4 count is the central means of staging the disease in HIV infection, the viral load is the most accurate means of following the success or failure of antiretroviral therapy. Researchers and clinicians have used both of these tests to determine prognosis. In the absence of combination antiretroviral therapy, Mellors et al. (1996) demonstrated that the combination of the viral load and CD4 count could be used together to determine prognosis and survival and to some extent as indicators guiding the optimal point to recommend the initiation of antiretroviral therapy (see Figure 3-1).

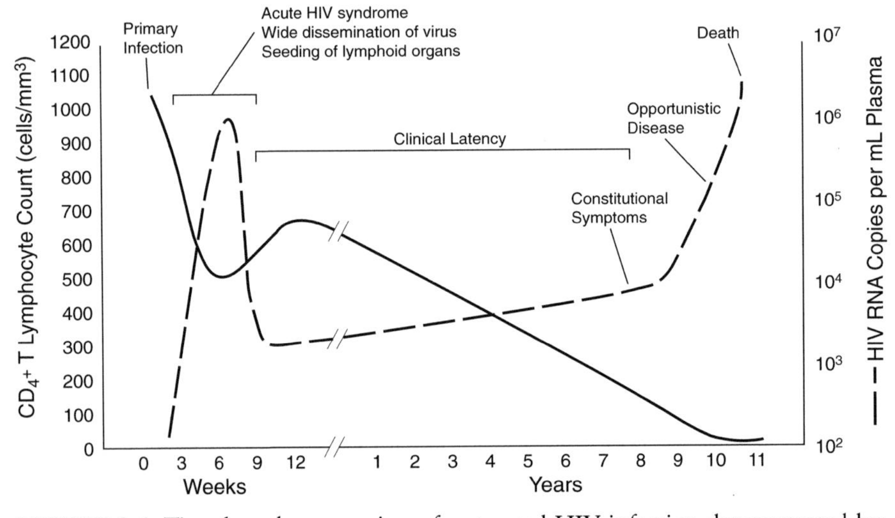

FIGURE 3-1 Time-based progression of untreated HIV infection demonstrated by CD4 count and viral load.
SOURCE: Image reprinted with permission from eMedicine.com, 2010, http://emedicine.medscape.com/article/211316-overview. Adapted from Fauci and Pantaleo, 1996.

CD4 Count

The CD4+ T-cell count is the single best laboratory determinant of clinical outcomes (Egger et al., 2002). It is an important prognostic indicator of the remaining degree of immune function and is the single most important laboratory criterion for initiation of antiretroviral therapy in the patient with HIV infection. A typical healthy, HIV-negative person has a CD4 count greater than 500 cells/mm^3 (Klimas et al., 2008). CD4 cells are directly and indirectly destroyed by HIV infection, and a lower number or percentage correlates with increasing risk of morbidity and mortality. In the early days of the HIV epidemic, CD4 less than 200 cells/mm^3 was quickly established as the threshold below which serious or fatal opportunistic infections became common. The risk for certain opportunistic infections can be reduced by the prophylactic use of antibiotics. This use is recommended based on specific CD4 counts. For example, the risk of *Pneumocystis jirovecii* pneumonia rises steeply when the CD4 falls below 200 cells/mm^3, and daily treatment with trimethoprim/sulfamethoxazole is recommended for these individuals (Meyers et al., 2008).

In 1993, the Centers for Disease Control and Prevention added a CD4 of less than 200 cells/mm^3 as an AIDS-defining condition, which became a key issue before the development of effective antiretroviral therapy when the current HIV Infection Listings were published. As the CD4 count continues to fall, which it does inevitably in the absence of antiretroviral therapy, HIV-infected persons have an accelerated risk of a wide range of opportunistic diseases, all with serious morbidity, many rapidly fatal, unless immune deficiency is reversed with HIV suppression. In the time before current combination antiretroviral therapy, an HIV-infected adult with a CD4 $\leq$ 50 cells/mm^3 had approximately a 45 percent 12-month mortality rate without therapy (Yarchoan et al., 1991).

Table 3-1 shows dramatic improvements in 12-month mortality rates before and after combination antiretroviral therapy for three multinational cohorts (U.S. Military HIV Natural History Study [Department of Defense, or DoD], EuroSIDA [SIDA is the Spanish acronym for AIDS], and the North American AIDS Cohort Collaboration on Research and Design [NA ACCORD]), supporting the notion that mortality rates have changed over time with the introduction of combination antiretroviral therapy. More importantly, these data show a substantial difference in mortality between CD4 $\leq$ 50 cells/mm^3 and CD4 50–100 cells/mm^3, indicating that a CD4 threshold (at or below 50 cells/mm^3) independently predicts increased mortality.

The CD4 count usually rises with the initiation of potent combination antiretroviral therapy. The extent and rate of recovery may be limited in some individuals with a low CD4 cell nadir, which is associated with an

TABLE 3-1 12-Month Mortality Rates for Patients With HIV Infection as a Function of CD4 Strata, Before or After Combination Antiretroviral Therapy

			CD4 < 25		CD4 ≤ 50		CD4 51–100		CD4 101–200	
Cohort	N	Total Deaths	Pre-cART	Post-cART	Pre-cART	Post-cART	Pre-cART	Post-cART	Pre-cART	Post-cART
DoD	5,187	1,659	40	N/A	36	N/A	15	N/A	8	N/A
EuroSIDA	19,933	3,403	44	7	37	6	18	3	7	2
NA ACCORD	45,192	6,786	50	16	42	13	20	8	8	5

NOTE: cART = Combination antiretroviral therapy; N/A = Insufficient or no data. Precombination antiretroviral therapy is defined as before 1993 in the DoD and NA ACCORD cohorts and before 1997 in the EuroSIDA cohort. All cohorts defined postcombination antiretroviral therapy as after 2000.

SOURCES: Agan et al., 2010; Justice et al., 2010; Mocroft and the EuroSIDA Study Group, 2010.

increased incidence of the potentially disabling immune reconstitution inflammatory syndrome (IRIS). IRIS may develop in patients with HIV who also have coinfections or inflammatory diseases when beginning therapy (Hoffman et al., 2010). As the immune system responds to treatment and begins to restore to healthy levels, the first weeks on therapy typically include an increase in CD4 count and decrease in viral load (Hoffman et al., 2010). IRIS develops in 15 to 25 percent of patients when they start combination antiretroviral therapy (French et al., 2004; Jevtovi et al., 2005; Shelburne et al., 2006) and can be associated with substantial morbidity and even mortality. Research has shown CD4 of less than 100 cells/mm^3 to be an independent risk factor for the development of IRIS (Manabe et al., 2007).

When the CD4 count is low, patients remain at an increased risk of morbidity and mortality from AIDS-related conditions. Close monitoring is needed during this vulnerable period of at least 12 months or until successful antiretroviral management is established. The probability of achieving HIV suppression is reduced in those with a CD4 $\leq$ 50 cells/mm^3 at treatment initiation (Knobel et al., 2001) and at 48 weeks following the initiation of therapy. Patients who initiated therapy with CD4 $\leq$ 50 cells/mm^3 have an average CD4 of 167 cells/mm^3, compared to an average CD4 of 281 cells/mm^3 for those who started therapy with CD4 in the 51–200 cells/mm^3 range (Robbins et al., 2009). Because of its prognostic significance, CD4 count has become the central criterion for deciding when to recommend beginning antiretroviral therapy, and, along with HIV viral load, is universally used to monitor the outcomes of this treatment.

CD4 count determination is recommended by all guidelines of HIV management and essentially all patients diagnosed with HIV infection have results of this test available in their medical records. CD4 count is an inexpensive ($50 or less in most laboratories)[1] and reproducible test performed in numerous hospital and commercial laboratories. The significance of the CD4 count in staging and monitoring HIV disease is that it is a low-cost method of allowing clinicians to chart progression of disease and response to treatment. These measurements are easily obtained from medical records.

HIV-1 Viral Load

The number of copies of HIV-1 virions in the circulating blood (viral load) can be accurately measured by polymerase chain reaction or other nucleic acid detection methods. Most assays can accurately detect and reproducibly quantitate viral loads greater than 50 copies/mL. The viral load

[1] Personal communication, C. del Rio, Emory University, May 13, 2010.

in chronic infection is in the range of 8,000 to 60,000 copies/mL (Mellors et al., 2007). Each infected person has a relatively characteristic viral load or set point over the course of infection. Although the viral load has been used in the diagnosis of acute HIV infection before the appearance of serum HIV antibodies, its primary application is in monitoring response to antiretroviral therapy. Viral load is expected to decline rapidly once therapy is initiated and to drop to levels of less than 50 copies/mL after 12 to 24 weeks of treatment. The poorest responses to combination antiretroviral therapy are in those patients with CD4 less than 50 cells/mm^3, viral load greater than 100,000 copies/mL, and age greater than 50 when treatment is initiated (Egger et al., 2002). Once a goal of suppression of viral load ≤ 50 copies/mL is achieved, the test is repeated (every 3 to 6 months is recommended in most guidelines) to detect subsequent virologic failure. This is often a consequence of poor adherence to the prescribed medication.

Viral load, along with the CD4 count, is considered a routine test and part of the standard of care in all published guidelines for patients with HIV/AIDS. Like the CD4 count, this test is performed regularly throughout a patient's treatment regimen to determine treatment efficacy. The viral load is also relatively inexpensive (about $100 in most labs)[2] and is widely available. Unlike the CD4 count, the viral load does not directly indicate disease stage. Although the loss of CD4 cells is somewhat faster in those with very high viral loads, even that relationship is weak. The viral load is of crucial importance in monitoring response to antiretroviral therapy, but is not needed as part of disability assessment.

CD4 COUNT AS AN INDICATOR OF DISABILITY

Unfortunately, reproducible, standardized, and widely accepted measures of HIV functional impairment are limited. However, a strong relationship exists between advanced immune impairment and clinical outcomes, including mortality, although exceptions can occur. Laboratory markers of HIV infection are important indicators of the severity of disease. In the absence of direct measures of disability, the committee reviewed a variety of measures, notably CD4 count and viral load, to evaluate their efficacy in predicting morbidity, mortality, and treatment response. The committee concluded that viral load is a strong indicator of success of antiretroviral therapy, while CD4 is a strong indicator of disease progression. Therefore, CD4 is more appropriate in assessing disability than viral load.

Based on this review, the CD4 count was found to meet many of the principles identified in Chapter 1 for a listing and is already fully incorporated in current medical practice. Of the predictive measures considered, CD4 count is part of a routine standard of care for patients with HIV/AIDS,

[2]Personal communication, C. del Rio, Emory University, May 13, 2010.

commonly used, and an objective measure found easily in the medical record. All patients being medically managed for HIV infection should have serial CD4 count determinations in their medical records.

Findings from the literature and the data cohorts led the committee to find that a threshold can be drawn at CD4 $\leq$ 50 cells/mm^3 that is directly associated with morbidity and mortality. The committee concludes that CD4 $\leq$ 50 cells/mm^3 is a significant prognostic marker of poor outcome and, in the absence of direct data on functioning, of disability. CD4 $\leq$ 50 cells/mm^3 is associated with functional impairments severe enough to warrant it as a listings-level impairment. Such a low level of CD4 cells indicates a very advanced stage of HIV infection and increased morbidity and mortality over time. It is important to note that this does not require a claimant to have symptomatic HIV infection.

A claimant with a CD4 $\leq$ 50 cells/mm^3 ideally would receive treatment as part of his disability benefits, potentially improving his immunologic and functional status. After a period of time, if the claimant's CD4 count is greater than 50 cells/mm^3, the claim should be reevaluated to determine whether the person continues to be disabled according to other components of the HIV Infection Listings, including sublistings estimating functional status. Since antiretroviral treatment often allows clinical improvement over a period of 1 or 2 years, the committee believes claimants allowed under such a listing should be reevaluated periodically for disability status. The committee believes 3 years would allow for a sustained response and is the maximum practical period for Social Security Administration (SSA) reassessment. If the claimant's CD4 count exceeds the minimum threshold and the claimant is not disabled according to other sublistings, he should no longer receive disability benefits. However, in the event that the CD4 count drops below 50 cells/mm^3, his disability benefits should be reinstated.

RECOMMENDATION 1. SSA should use CD4 count as an indicator of disability. Specifically, CD4 $\leq$ 50 cells/mm^3 is an indicator that a claimant's HIV infection is disabling. This allowance should be reevaluated periodically by SSA.

REFERENCES

Agan, B., B. Hale, N. Crum-Cianflone, T. Whitman, A. Ganesan, G. Wortmann, A. Weintrob, V. Barthel, V. Marconi, M. Landrum, T. Ferguson, L. Eberly, A. Lifson, K. H. Hullsiek, G. Grandits, and N. Michael for the U.S. Military (Department of Defense) HIV Natural History Study. 2010 (unpublished). *Mortality by CD4 count or clinical diagnosis.*

Egger, M., M. May, G. Chêne, A. N. Phillips, B. Ledergerber, F. Dabis, D. Costagliola, A. D'Arminio Monforte, F. de Wolf, P. Reiss, J. D. Lundgren, A. C. Justice, S. Staszewski, C. Leport, R. S. Hogg, C. A. Sabin, M. J. Gill, B. Salzberger, and J. A. C. Sterne. 2002. Prognosis of HIV-1-infected patients starting highly active antiretroviral therapy: A collaborative analysis of prospective studies. *The Lancet* 360(9327):119–129.

Fauci, A. S., and G. Pantaleo. 1996. Immunopathogenic mechanisms of HIV infection. *Annals of Internal Medicine* 124(7):654–663.

French, M. A., P. Price, and S. F. Stone. 2004. Immune restoration disease after antiretroviral therapy. *AIDS* 18(12):1615–1627.

Hoffman, J., J. van Griensven, R. Colebunders, and M. McKellar. 2010. Role of the CD4 count in HIV management. *HIV Therapy* 4(1):27–39.

Jevtovi, D. J., D. Salemovi, J. Ranin, I. Pei, S. Derjav, and O. Djurkovi-Djakovi. 2005. The prevalence and risk of immune restoration disease in HIV-infected patients treated with highly active antiretroviral therapy. *HIV Medicine* 6(2):140–143.

Justice, A., S. J. Gange, J. P. Tate, L. P. Jacobson, K. Gebo, K. Althoff, M. Kitahata, M. Saag, M. Horberg, and R. Moore for the NA-ACCORD and VACS Project Teams. 2010 (unpublished). *Report to the Institute of Medicine committee evaluating disability criteria for those with HIV infection.*

Klimas, N., A. O'Brien Koneru, and M. A. Fletcher. 2008. Overview of HIV. *Psychosomatic Medicine* 70(5):523–530.

Knobel, H., A. Guelar, A. Carmona, M. Espona, A. González, J. L. López-Colomés, P. Saballs, J. L. Gimeno, and A. Díez. 2001. Virologic outcome and predictors of virologic failure of highly active antiretroviral therapy containing protease inhibitors. *AIDS Patient Care and STDs* 15(4):193–199.

Manabe, Y., J. Campbell, E. Sydnor, and R. Moore. 2007. Immune reconstitution inflammatory syndrome: Risk factors and treatment implications. *Journal of Acquired Immune Deficiency Syndromes* 46(4):456–462.

Mellors, J. W., C. R. Rinaldo Jr., P. Gupta, R. M. White, J. A. Todd, and L. A. Kingsley. 1996. Prognosis in HIV-1 infection predicted by the quantity of virus in plasma. *Science* 272(5265):1167–1170.

Mellors, J. W., J. B. Margolick, J. P. Phair, C. R. Rinaldo, R. Detels, L. P. Jacobson, and A. Munoz. 2007. Prognostic value of HIV-1 RNA, CD4 cell count, and CD4 cell count slope for progression to AIDS and death in untreated HIV-1 infection. *Journal of the American Medical Association* 297(21):2349–2350.

Meyers, D., T. Wolff, K. Gregory, L. Marion, V. Moyer, H. Nelson, D. Petitti, and G. F. Sawaya. 2008. USPSTF recommendations for STI screening. (Prepared for the U.S. Preventive Services Task Force.) *American Family Physician* 77:819–824, http://www.ahrq.gov/clinic/uspstf08/methods/stinfections.htm (accessed June 18, 2010).

Mocroft, A., and the EuroSIDA Study Group. 2010 (unpublished). *The incidence and probability of death in HIV-infected persons pre- and post-cART.* University College London.

Robbins, G. K., J. G. Spritzler, E. S. Chan, D. M. Asmuth, R. T. Gandhi, B. A. Rodriguez, G. Skowron, P. R. Skolnik, R. W. Shafer, and R. B. Pollard. 2009. Incomplete reconstitution of T-cell subsets on combination antiretroviral therapy in the AIDS Clinical Trials Group Protocol 384. *Clinical Infectious Diseases* 48(3):350–361.

Shelburne, S. A., M. Montes, and R. J. Hamill. 2006. Immune reconstitution inflammatory syndrome: More answers, more questions. *Journal of Antimicrobial Chemotherapy* 57(2):167–170.

Yarchoan, R., D. J. Venzon, J. M. Pluda, J. Lietzau, K. M. Wyvill, A. A. Tsiatis, S. M. Steinberg, and S. Broder. 1991. CD4 count and the risk for death in patients infected with HIV receiving antiretroviral therapy. *Annals of Internal Medicine* 115(3):184–189.

4

Imminently Fatal or Severely Disabling HIV-Associated Conditions

Even in the era of potent antiretroviral therapy, patients with HIV infection continue to develop very aggressive, generally untreatable conditions that are imminently fatal or severely disabling. Although much less common than in the early epidemic, these conditions resemble the AIDS-defining infections or cancers that were considered appropriate for disability allowance in the previous HIV Infection Listings. This chapter identifies and describes these conditions and discusses how the committee believes they should be addressed in the HIV Infection Listings.

IMMINENTLY FATAL OR SEVERELY DISABLING CONDITIONS

Although the treatment of HIV infection has improved greatly since the beginning of the epidemic with the development of combination antiretroviral therapy, some rare but very aggressive conditions occur that can rapidly lead to death or severe disability (see Box 4-1). These HIV-associated conditions are generally untreatable even with combination antiretroviral therapy, resulting in limited recovery. The average length of survival for people afflicted with these conditions ranges from 3 to 24 months. The probability that claimants with these conditions will die or be seriously disabled within a year is so high that the committee believes they deserve immediate disability. As opposed to allowances made based on low CD4 counts as discussed in Chapter 3, allowances resulting from these aggressive conditions would be permanent on verification of the condition and would not require reevaluation.

BOX 4-1
Immediately Fatal or Severely Disabling Conditions

Documented presence of one of the following conditions ought to be considered a permanent disability:

- HIV-associated dementia;
- Multicentric Castleman's disease;
- Kaposi's sarcoma involving the pulmonary parenchyma;
- Primary central nervous system lymphomas;
- Primary effusion lymphoma; or
- Progressive multifocal leukoencephalopathy.

HIV-Associated Dementia

HIV-associated dementia (also known as AIDS dementia complex, HIV dementia, or HIV encephalopathy) is part of the spectrum of HIV-associated neurocognitive disorders (HANDs), discussed in Chapter 5. It refers to severe impairment (measured as performance greater than two standard deviations below normal) in at least two cognitive domains that extremely limits everyday functioning (Antinori et al., 2007). The main features are disabling cognitive impairment accompanied by motor dysfunction, speech problems, and behavioral change. This results in an inability to carry out more than the most basic activities of daily living independently (e.g., eating, bathing, dressing) and an inability to work.

Before the introduction of combination antiretroviral therapy, the mean survival of patients with HIV-associated dementia was 3 to 6 months; marginal improvement lasting over several months may be gained through use of combination antiretroviral therapy (Tozzi et al., 2007). Incidence of HAND in developed countries has declined ten-fold as a result of combination antiretroviral therapy (Bhaskaran et al., 2008; Kaul, 2009). HIV-associated dementia by definition qualifies as a severely disabling condition and is observed in 5 percent or fewer of HIV-infected persons (Heaton et al., 2009).

HIV-associated dementia typically occurs after years of HIV infection and is associated with low CD4 levels and high plasma viral loads. Diagnosis can be made by a clinician based on a mental status evaluation assessing the domains of cognitive functioning.

Although HIV encephalopathy is currently considered under sublistings 14.08G and 114.08G, the term is no longer widely used in the treatment of adults infected with HIV. HIV-associated dementia is characterized by cognitive or motor dysfunction that limits ability to perform daily functions and therefore should be considered a severely disabling condition in Part A of the HIV Infection Listing.

Multicentric Castleman's Disease

Multicentric Castleman's disease (MCD) resembles advanced-stage non-Hodgkin's lymphoma, with diffuse nodal involvement and "B" symptoms, although the proliferative tissue is histologically inflammatory, but benign. MCD can affect the liver and spleen. It has been associated with high levels of the marker of immune activation interleukin-6.

Like Kaposi's sarcoma, multicentric Castleman's disease is associated with infection by the human herpesvirus-8 (HHV-8). Unlike Kaposi's, however, widespread availability of combination antiretroviral therapy has not led to decreased prevalence of this disease. The prognosis for multicentric Castleman's disease is poor, with an overall mortality rate of 44 percent (Mylona et al., 2008). However, advances in therapy have led to longer survival; a recent study of 21 patients found a 2-year survival rate of 95 percent with rituximab (Bower et al., 2007). Malignancies have been reported in 32 percent of patients (Bowne et al., 1999; Newlon et al., 2007). The disease occurs more frequently in men and in people ages 30 through 50. Although MCD is uncommon in pediatric populations, children may have better outcomes than adults (Newlon et al., 2007; Parez et al., 1999).

Diagnosing multicentric Castleman's disease has many uncertainties because it exhibits nonspecific characteristics and can mimic other neoplasms. Definitive diagnosis can be made by surgical resection and histopathologic findings showing B-cell proliferation. While the Epstein-Barr virus (EBV) is not consistently associated with MCD, HHV-8 infection is nearly universal. Combined chemotherapy is recommended for patients with good health status; however, those with poor health status should be considered for treatment with steroids and single-agent chemotherapy. Rituximab and antiretroviral therapy both may be effective (Stebbing et al., 2008; Sullivan et al., 2008).

Multicentric Castleman's disease is not specifically indicated in the current Listing of Impairments. However, given its severity in those infected with HIV, the disease should be considered in the HIV Infection Listings.

Kaposi's Sarcoma Involving the Pulmonary Parenchyma

Kaposi's sarcoma is a fatal condition when it manifests in the lungs, where it tends to grow as sheets of tumor tissue in the peribronchial and perivascular axial interstitial spaces. Chest radiographs typically show a patchy infiltrating process. The disease is commonly multifocal and pleural effusions are common. These are typically hemorrhagic, but cytologically benign. The most common symptoms are progressive dyspnea, nonproductive cough, and fever.

Even with the use of combination antiretroviral therapy, survival for pulmonary Kaposi's sarcoma has been shown to be 4 to 19 months (Hannon et al., 1998; Holkova et al., 2001; Palmieri et al., 2006). Approximately 20 percent of deaths related to pulmonary Kaposi's sarcoma are due to complications of the disease, such as upper airway obstruction or parenchymal destruction (Gasparetto et al., 2009; Restrepo et al., 2006).

Pulmonary Kaposi's sarcoma is diagnosed through a combination of tests (clinical, radiographic, and laboratory) and specifically by bronchoscopy and transbronchial biopsy (Aboulafia, 2000; Gasparetto et al., 2009).

Kaposi's sarcoma in the pulmonary parenchyma is currently considered as part of sublistings 14.08E2b and 114.08E2b. The committee concludes that due to the aggressive and fatal nature of pulmonary Kaposi's sarcoma, it needs to be retained in the HIV Infection Listings and should be considered a permanent disability.

Primary Central Nervous System Lymphomas

Primary central nervous system lymphomas are aggressive B-cell, non-Hodgkin's lymphomas arising within the central nervous system (CNS). Although uncommon, they are associated with advanced stages of HIV-induced immunodeficiency. The peripheral CD4 count is in the 0 to 50 cells/mm^3 range. EBV infection is almost invariably demonstrated in the CNS. Prognosis is extremely poor even with the initiation of combination antiretroviral therapy.

This therapy has resulted in decreased incidence and increased median survival for HIV-infected patients with primary CNS lymphomas (Bower et al., 2006). With antiretroviral therapy, 2-year survival increased to 29 percent (Biggar et al., 2005) with a median survival of 8 to 18 months (Diamond et al., 2006; Hoffmann et al., 2001).

Magnetic resonance imaging (MRI) or contrast-enhanced computed tomography (CT) usually show multiple lesions in almost any location, but usually deep in the white matter of the brain in the periventricular region.

Unlike lymphomas listed in 13.05 and 113.05, these lymphomas specifically impair people living with advanced stages of immunodeficiency. Therefore they should be considered under the HIV Infection Listings and should be provided permanent disability because of the severity of the disease.

Primary Effusion Lymphoma

Primary effusion lymphoma (PEL, also called body cavity lymphoma) is a rare, aggressive type of B-cell, non-Hodgkin's lymphoma arising within body cavities (e.g., pleural space, pericardium, peritoneum). The median survival for PEL is around 6 months. Prognosis is poor, even with combination chemotherapy. Death in patients with PEL is frequently associated with opportunistic infection, HIV-related complication, and progression of lymphoma (Chen et al., 2009). Primary effusion lymphoma accounts for 1 to 5 percent of AIDS-related lymphomas (Navarro and Kaplan, 2006).

PEL is associated with evidence of HHV-8 and EBV infection, although the involvement of these infections in its pathogenesis remains poorly understood. Patients with primary effusion lymphoma usually also have low CD4 counts. PEL is diagnosed by pathological analysis of the involved tissue and biopsies of body cavity-lining tissue (Chen et al., 2009).

Primary effusion lymphoma is a fatal condition. It is not specifically considered in the Malignant Neoplastic Diseases section of the Listing of Impairments (13.00 and 113.00) and is appropriate for inclusion in the HIV Infection Listings.

Progressive Multifocal Leukoencephalopathy

Progressive multifocal leukoencephalopathy (PML) is a rare disorder caused by polyomavirus JC. Asymptomatic primary infection in the CNS from polyomavirus JC occurs in childhood; antibodies can be found in 86 percent of all adults, where it is latent in the kidneys and lymphoid organs (Weber et al., 1997). In individuals with compromised immune systems, the virus reactivates, spreads to the brain, and has damaging inflammatory effects. PML occurs more frequently in people with AIDS than in others with compromised immune systems, perhaps because of how HIV affects brain tissue or interacts with polyomavirus JC (Berger, 2003). The most prominent symptoms, which evolve over several days to several weeks, are clumsiness; progressive weakness; and visual, speech, and sometimes personality changes (NINDS, 2010).

Untreated, PML results in death over a period of weeks to months. Nearly 5 percent of HIV-infected people develop PML prior to combination antiretroviral therapy (NINDS, 2010). Since the advent of potent antiretroviral therapy, the median survival of patients with PML has increased to 16 to 26 months (Berenguer et al., 2003; Falcó et al., 2008); 40 to 50 percent of patients survive PML (Antinori et al., 2003; De Luca et al., 2000), although most with significant neurologic sequelae. PML continues to occur in HIV-1-infected patients despite combination antiretroviral therapy. These patients may have a shorter median survival compared with patients who do not receive treatment (Wyen et al., 2004).

Diagnosis of PML includes brain biopsy, MRI with consistent white-matter lesions, and confirmation of the presence of polyomavirus JC (NINDS, 2010). There is no specific treatment for PML. Therapy with cytosine arabinoside, interferon-alfa, and cidofovir has not shown any benefit in the treatment of PML compared to antiretroviral therapy alone (De Luca et al., 2008).

PML is considered under the current 14.08D sublisting. Because of its aggressive nature in HIV-infected patients, it should be included in the HIV Infection Listings as a condition that warrants permanent disability.

PLACE IN THE DETERMINATION PROCESS

The rare conditions described above are generally untreatable and are fatal or extremely disabling. Because of the gravity of these conditions, the committee believes these claimants need to be considered separately from other HIV infection claimants. To expedite their claims, these claimants ought to receive permanent disability on confirmation of diagnosis. Supplemental Security Income applicants may qualify for presumptive disability on presentation at the Social Security Administration (SSA) field offices, which allows for immediate payment of benefits for up to 6 months as the claim goes through the five-step disability determination process.

It is worth noting that in 2007, SSA launched a program called "compassionate allowances" as a way of quickly identifying conditions that should be deemed permanently disabling and providing these claimants with disability benefits. Compassionate allowance cases require minimal objective medical evidence to determine the claimant disabled and eligible to receive benefits. Notably, PML is also one of less than 100 conditions identified by SSA as so serious that claimants receive a compassionate allowance.

Compassionate allowance cases progress through Steps 1 and 2 and either meet or equal the listings in Step 3 (see Figure 1-1). It is important to note that conditions identified as compassionate allowances are typically found in the Listing of Impairments under the appropriate body system. If the condition cannot be verified, the claim will proceed through Steps 4 and 5 of the determination process. The committee believes the conditions identified in this chapter are so severe that SSA may want to consider them as compassionate allowance conditions.

RECOMMENDATION 2. SSA should make disability determination allowances permanent for imminently fatal and/or severely disabling

HIV-associated conditions. These conditions may be appropriate as compassionate allowances. These include the following:

- **HIV-associated dementia;**
- **Multicentric Castleman's disease;**
- **Kaposi's sarcoma involving the pulmonary parenchyma;**
- **Primary central nervous system lymphomas;**
- **Primary effusion lymphoma; and**
- **Progressive multifocal leukoencephalopathy.**

REFERENCES

Aboulafia, D. M. 2000. The epidemiologic, pathologic, and clinical features of AIDS-associated pulmonary Kaposi's sarcoma. *Chest* 117(4):1128–1145.

Antinori, A., A. Cingolani, and P. Lorenzini. 2003. Clinical epidemiology and survival of progressive multifocal leukoencephalopathy in the era of highly active antiretroviral therapy: Data from the Italian registry investigative neuro AIDS (IRINA). *Journal for Neurovirology* 9(Suppl):1–25.

Antinori, A., G. Arendt, J. T. Becker, B. J. Brew, D. A. Byrd, M. Cherner, D. B. Clifford, P. Cinque, L. G. Epstein, K. Goodkin, M. Gisslen, I. Grant, R. K. Heaton, J. Joseph, K. Marder, C. M. Marra, J. C. McArthur, M. Nunn, R. W. Price, L. Pulliam, K. R. Robertson, N. Sacktor, V. Valcour, and V. E. Wojna. 2007. Updated research nosology for HIV-associated neurocognitive disorders. *Neurology* 69(18):1789–1799.

Berenguer, J., P. Miralles, J. Arrizabalaga, E. Ribera, F. Dronda, J. Baraia-Etxaburu, P. Domingo, M. Márquez, Francisco J. Rodriguez-Arrondo, F. Laguna, R. Rubio, J. L. Rodrigo, J. Mallolas, and V. de Miguel. 2003. Clinical course and prognostic factors of progressive multifocal leukoencephalopathy in patients treated with highly active antiretroviral therapy. *Clinical Infectious Diseases* 36(8):1047–1052.

Berger, J. R. 2003. Progressive multifocal leukoencephalopathy in acquired immunodeficiency syndrome: Explaining the high incidence and disproportionate frequency of the illness relative to other immunosuppresive conditions. *Journal of Neurovirology* 9(Suppl 1):38–41.

Bhaskaran, K., C. Mussini, A. Antinori, A. S. Walker, M. Dorrucci, C. Sabin, A. Phillips, and K. Porter. 2008. Changes in the incidence and predictors of human immunodeficiency virus-associated dementia in the era of highly active antiretroviral therapy. *Annals of Neurology* 63(2):213–221.

Biggar, R. J., E. A. Engels, S. Ly, A. Kahn, M. J. Schymura, J. Sackoff, P. Virgo, and R. M. Pfeiffer. 2005. Survival after cancer diagnosis in persons with AIDS. *Journal of Acquired Immune Deficiency Syndromes* 39(3):293–299.

Bower, M., T. Powles, M. Nelson, S. Mandalia, B. Gazzard, and J. Stebbing. 2006. Highly active antiretroviral therapy and human immunodeficiency virus-associated primary cerebral lymphoma. *Journal of the National Cancer Institute* 98(15):1088–1091.

Bower, M., T. Powles, S. Williams, T. N. Davis, M. Atkins, S. Montoto, C. Orkin, A. Webb, M. Fisher, M. Nelson, B. Gazzard, J. Stebbing, and P. Kelleher. 2007. Brief communication: Rituximab in HIV-associated multicentric Castleman disease. *Annals of Internal Medicine* 147(12):836–839.

Bowne, W. G., J. J. Lewis, and D. A. Filippa. 1999. The management of unicentric and multicentric Castleman's disease: A report of 16 cases and a review of the literature. *Cancer* 85(3):706–717.

Chen, S. Y., W. J. Moss, S. S. Pipkin, and W. McFarland. 2009. A novel use of AIDS surveillance data to assess the impact of initial treatment regimen on survival. *International Journal of STD & AIDS* 20(5):330–335.

De Luca, A., M. L. Giancola, A. Ammassari, S. Grisetti, M. G. Paglia, M. Gentile, A. Cingolani, R. Murri, G. Liuzzi, A. D'Arminio Monforte, and A. Antinori. 2000. The effect of potent antiretroviral therapy and JC virus load in cerebrospinal fluid on clinical outcome of patients with AIDS-associated progressive multifocal leukoencephalopathy. *Journal of Infectious Diseases* 182(4):1077–1083.

De Luca, A., A. Ammassari, P. Pezzotti, P. Cinque, J. Gasnault, J. Berenguer, S. Di Giambenedetto, A. Cingolani, Y. Taoufik, P. Miralles, C. M. Marra, and A. Antinori for Gesida 9/99, IRINA, ACTG 363 study groups. 2008. Cidofovir in addition to antiretroviral treatment is not effective for AIDS-associated progressive multifocal leukoencephalopathy: A multicohort analysis. *AIDS* 22(14):1759–1767.

Diamond, C., T. H. Taylor, T. Im, M. Miradi, M. Wallace, and H. Anton-Culver. 2006. Highly active antiretroviral therapy is associated with improved survival among patients with AIDS-related primary central nervous system non-Hodgkin's lymphoma. *Current HIV Research* 4(3):375–378.

Falcó, V., M. Olmo, S. V. del Saz, A. Guelar, J. R. Santos, M. Gutiérrez, D. Colomer, E. Deig, G. Mateo, M. Montero, E. Pedrol, D. Podzamczer, P. Domingo, and J. M. Llibre. 2008. Influence of HAART on the clinical course of HIV-1-infected patients with progressive multifocal leukoencephalopathy: Results of an observational multicenter study. *Journal of Acquired Immune Deficiency Syndromes* 49(1):26–31.

Gasparetto, T. D., E. Marchori, S. Lourenco, G. Zanetti, A. Domingues Vianna, A. A. Santos, and L. F. Nobre. 2009. Pulmonary involvement in Kaposi sarcoma: Correlation between imaging and pathology. *Orphanet Journal of Rare Diseases* 4(18).

Hannon, F. B., P. J. Easterbrook, S. Padley, F. Boag, R. Goodall, and R. H. Phillips. 1998. Bronchopulmonary Kaposi's sarcoma in 106 HIV-1 infected patients. *International Journal of STD & AIDS* 9(9):518–525.

Heaton, R. K., D. Franklin, D. Clifford, S. P. Woods, M. R. Mindt, O. Vigil, M. Taylor, T. Marcotte, J. H. Atkinson, and I. Grant. 2009. *HIV-associated neurocognitive impairment (NCI) remains prevalent in the era of combination antiretroviral therapy (cART): The CHARTER Study.* Paper presented at 16th Conference on Retroviruses and Opportunistic Infections, Montreal, Canada, February 8–11.

Hoffmann, C., S. Tabrizian, E. Wolf, C. Eggers, A. Stoehr, A. Plettenberg, T. Buhk, H.-J. Stellbrink, H.-A. Horst, H. Jäger, and T. Rosenkranz. 2001. Survival of AIDS patients with primary central nervous system lymphoma is dramatically improved by HAART-induced immune recovery. *AIDS* 15(16):2119–2127.

Holkova, B., K. Takeshita, D. M. Cheng, M. Volm, C. Wasserheit, R. Demopoulos, and A. Chanan-Khan. 2001. Effect of highly active antiretroviral therapy on survival in patients with AIDS-associated pulmonary Kaposi's sarcoma treated with chemotherapy. *Journal of Clinical Oncology* 19(18):3848–3851.

Kaul, M. 2009. HIV-1 associated dementia: Update on pathological mechanisms and therapeutic approaches. *Current Opinion in Neurology* 22(3):315–320.

Mylona, E. E., I. G. Baraboutis, L. J. Lekakis, O. Georgiou, V. Papastamopoulos, and A. Skoutelis. 2008. Multicentric Castleman's disease in HIV infection: A systematic review of the literature. *AIDS Reviews* 10(1):25–35.

Navarro, W. H., and L. D. Kaplan. 2006. AIDS-related lymphoproliferative disease. *Blood* 107(1):13–20.

Newlon, J. L., M. Couch, and J. Brennan. 2007. Castelman's disease: Three case reports and a review of the literature. *Ear, Nose & Throat Journal* 86(7):414–418.

NINDS (National Institute of Neurological Disorders and Stroke). 2010. *NINDS progressive multifocal leukoencephalopathy information page*, http://www.ninds.nih.gov/disorders/pml/pml.htm (accessed June 9, 2010).

Palmieri, C., T. Dhillon, C. Thirlwell, T. Newsom-Davis, A. M. Young, M. Nelson, B. G. Gazzard, and M. Bower. 2006. Pulmonary Kaposi sarcoma in the era of highly active antiretroviral therapy. *HIV Medicine* 7:291–293.

Parez, N., B. Bader-Meunier, C. C. Roy, and J. P. Dommergues. 1999. Paediatric Castleman disease: Report of seven cases and review of the literature. *European Journal of Pediatrics* 158(8):631–637.

Restrepo, C. S., S. Martinez, J. A. Lemos, J. A. Carrillo, D. F. Lemos, P. Ojeda, and P. Koshy. 2006. Imaging manifestations of Kaposi sarcoma. *RadioGraphics* 26:1169–1185.

Stebbing, J., L. Pantanowitz, F. Dayyani, R. J. Sullivan, M. Bower, and B. J. Dezube. 2008. HIV-associated multicentric Castleman's disease. *American Journal of Hematology* 83(6): 498–503.

Sullivan, R. J., L. Pantanowitz, C. Casper, J. Stebbing, and B. J. Dezube. 2008. Epidemiology, pathophysiology, and treatment of Kaposi sarcoma-associated herpesvirus disease: Kaposi sarcoma, primary effusion lymphoma, and multicentric Castleman disease. *Clinical Infectious Diseases* 47(9):1209–1215.

Tozzi, V., P. Balestra, R. Bellagamba, A. Corpolongo, M. F. Salvatori, U. Visco-Comandini, C. Vlassi, M. Giulianelli, S. Galgani, A. Antinori, and P. Narciso. 2007. Persistence of neuropsychological deficits despite long-term highly active antiretroviral therapy in patients with HIV-related neurocognitive impairment: Prevalence and risk factors. *Journal of Acquired Immune Deficiency Syndromes* 45(2):174–182.

Weber, T., C. Trebst, S. Frye, P. Cinque, L. Vago, C. J. Sindic, W. J. Schulz-Schaeffer, H. A. Kretzschmar, W. Enzensberger, G. Hunsmann, and W. Luke. 1997. Analysis of the systemic and intrathecal humoral immune response in progressive multifocal leukoencephalopathy. *Journal of Infectious Diseases* 176(1):250–254.

Wyen, C., C. Hoffmann, N. Schmeisser, A. Wohrmann, N. Qurishi, J. Rockstroh, S. Esser., A. Reike, B. Ross, T. Lorenzen, K. Schmitz, W. Stenzel, B. Salzberger, and G. Fatkenheuer. 2004. Progressive multifocal leukencephalopathy in patients on highly active antriretroviral therapy: Survival and risk factors of death. *Journal of Acquired Immune Deficiency Syndromes* 37(2):1263–1268.

5

HIV-Associated Conditions Without Listings Elsewhere

The course of HIV and the compounding effects of its comorbidities and treatment are sometimes difficult to predict, complicating decisions about whether people are able to work and for what period of time. A number of potentially severe HIV-associated conditions can be disabling, even though they are not imminently fatal. These impairments can be the result of the disease itself, adverse effects of HIV treatments, comorbid diseases, or from the treatment of those conditions.

Some concurrent conditions are covered in the Listing of Impairments, but others are not. The committee considered the two groups separately because a current listing provides these claimants with a path to being deemed disabled. If a current listing does not exist for conditions that can be truly disabling, a path to receive disability benefits will need to be identified. HIV-associated conditions without listings mentioned elsewhere in the Listing of Impairments are discussed in this chapter. Conditions covered elsewhere in the Listing of Impairments are discussed in Chapter 6.

THE IMPORTANCE OF FUNCTIONING IN DETERMINING DISABILITY

As discussed later in this chapter, the committee believes that in the era of potent antiretroviral therapy, the presence of an opportunistic infection or a manifestation of HIV alone is insufficient to declare a person unable to work. For instance, adverse effects of treatment can affect one's ability to work (e.g., interferon therapy for hepatitis C leads to malaise and fever), but the extent to which these residual conditions impair functioning is unknown. Therefore, even though the literature is unclear, the committee believes, based on its expertise, the combination of clinical severity and limited functional capacity can allow for an appropriate determination of disability to be made. The severity of the conditions in Box 5-1 can be more appropriately determined by coupling objective tests of medical impairment with an assessment of functioning.

The committee examined the literature for widely accepted, valid measures of functioning to determine which measures of functioning should be used (see Appendix D). As discussed in Chapter 1, few such measures were identified, none of which are commonly found in a claimant's medical record. The current 14.08K sublisting, as well as other listings in the immune and mental disorders body systems, incorporates three measures of functioning: (1) limitation of activities of daily living; (2) limitation in maintaining social functioning; and (3) limitation in completing tasks in a timely manner due to deficiencies in concentration, persistence, or pace. The committee found disability examiners to be familiar with the requirements, generally to like this sublisting, and to be fairly comfortable using it. This is supported by the fact that sublisting 14.08K provides the second most

BOX 5-1
List of HIV-Associated Conditions Without Current Listings Elsewhere in the Listing of Impairments

Comorbidities induced by HIV and its treatment currently without listings elsewhere include, but are not limited to:

- Diarrhea;
- Distal sensory polyneuropathy;
- HIV-associated neurocognitive disorders;
- HIV-associated wasting syndrome;
- Kaposi's sarcoma;
- Lipoatrophy or lipohypertrophy; and
- Osteoporosis.

These conditions should be considered in the HIV Infection Listing when diagnosed in a person with established HIV infection and marked limitation in functioning in one or more of the following areas:

- Ability to perform activities of daily living;
- Maintenance of social functioning; and/or
- Completion of tasks in a timely manner due to deficiencies in concentration, persistence, or pace.

Symptoms such as fatigue, malaise, and pain also should be considered if found to limit functioning.

allowances in the HIV Infection Listing (see Figure 1-2). In the absence of a single, widely used measure of functioning for people living with HIV/AIDS, the committee believes these three measures should be retained in a revised listing.

RECOMMENDATION 3. SSA should continue to include measures of functional capacity in the HIV Infection Listings and update these measures with research advances.

Although opportunistic infections now occur, albeit at a lower rate, they can still be associated with early mortality. Based on data received from the NA ACCORD and EuroSIDA databases (Justice et al., 2010; Mocroft and the EuroSIDA Study Group, 2010), the committee believes that the majority of HIV-infected people with severe opportunistic infections would be captured by a CD4 $\leq$ 50 cells/mm^3 listing, as discussed in Chapter 3. Disability assessment could also be triggered by poor functional status based on the above three measures of functioning; such allowances could "equal" a listing or be determined at a later stage.

CONDITIONS CURRENTLY WITHOUT LISTINGS

Advances in treatment have reduced the frequency of many opportunistic infections and manifestations currently in the HIV Infection Listings. These infections and manifestations are generally less common, no longer necessarily permanently debilitating, or less predictive of disability than they were in 1993 when the HIV Infection Listings were developed. It is now uncommon for patients to present with these manifestations to the point that they are both unresponsive to standard therapy *and* completely disabled. For example, diarrhea attributed to HIV infection that is resistant to treatment and lasting for more than 12 months is extremely uncommon today. These manifestations can become persistent as a result of late-stage AIDS that is untreated or unresponsive to treatment due to increased drug resistance or nonadherence with persistent viremia. The committee assumes that allowances for these conditions would be made based on the notion that HIV-associated conditions would be chronic, as the SSA definition of disability requires that the impairment last for a minimum of 12 months or result in death. Other unlisted conditions could conceivably be considered as medically equaling the Listings.

Diarrhea

Two major causes of diarrhea are associated with HIV: opportunistic infections (e.g., cryptosporidiosis, microsporidiosis) and adverse reactions to medications. HIV infection complicated by the opportunistic infections that were causes of debilitating diarrhea in the era prior to combination antiretroviral therapy are now relatively rare as a result of this therapy. Now the more common cause of diarrhea is adverse reactions to medicines, which show variable rates depending on the drug.

Severe cases of diarrhea can lead to dehydration and malnutrition, and have been found to significantly reduce quality of life in areas such as physical functioning, social functioning, and fatigue (Siddiqui et al., 2007). The Nutrition for Healthy Living Cohort found 28 percent of 671 patients had chronic diarrhea. This was more common in those with an AIDS-defining illness than HIV-positive patients in earlier stages of disease (Knox et al., 2000). The current incidence of chronic diarrhea is higher in the HIV-infected population than the general population, but can often be managed by changes in the anti-HIV regimen or by symptomatic treatment using diphenoxylate, loperamide, curcumin, or mesalamine.

Despite these advances, a small number of patients still have chronic and sometimes debilitating diarrhea from an opportunistic infection that cannot be effectively treated or diarrhea as an adverse reaction to antiretroviral agents that cannot be changed due to limited options (Esser et al., 2007; Monkemuller et al., 2000; Siddiqui et al., 2007; Tinmouth et al., 2007; Tramarin et al., 2004).

Although acute diarrhea continues to be a serious ailment affecting the lives of many infected with HIV, it usually resolves spontaneously or with treatment. Acute diarrhea does not meet the statutory definition of disability where a condition must last for 12 months or result in death. Chronic diarrhea is defined by the committee as a change in bowel habit with at least three loose or watery stools (i.e., take the form of the container) lasting for at least 3 weeks and unresponsive to standard treatment. Treatment protocols vary based on the cause of diarrhea and the stage of HIV infection. Many microbial pathogens can be treated with antibiotics, and some require combination antiretroviral therapy with immune recovery. Some patients benefit from "nonspecific therapy" such as loperamide.

Diarrhea is not specifically mentioned in other parts of the Listing of Impairments. Although cases of HIV patients with diarrhea that lasts for at least 12 months or result in death are rare, some do exist in late presenters or as a result of toxicity to HIV treatment. Therefore, the committee determined diarrhea should be included in the HIV Infection Listings when associated with marked limitation in functioning.

Distal Sensory Polyneuropathy

Peripheral neuropathy is a disease of the peripheral nervous system, associated with pain, weakness, and sensations such as burning and numbness. This can lead to nerve damage and can reduce quality of life. For example, patients may have difficulty walking, persistent pain, and absence of sensation. Many forms of HIV-associated peripheral neuropathy exist, with the most common among HIV patients being distal sensory polyneuropathy.

Prevalence is increasing, with more than one-third of HIV patients having symptomatic distal sensory polyneuropathy, and up to an additional one-third without symptoms (Gonzalez-Duarte et al., 2007; Schifitto et al., 2005); another study found 58 percent of HIV-infected patients with signs of peripheral neuropathy (Ellis et al., 2008). Symptoms include sensations of burning, hypersensitivity to touch, and tingling and various types of pain, mostly in the extremities, which compromise quality of life, cause decline in everyday function, and can lead to unemployment (Ellis et al., 2010). Incidence has been shown to both decrease and remain the same with the use of combination antiretroviral therapy (Gonzalez-Duarte et al., 2007; Lichtenstein et al., 2005). More advanced HIV disease, exposure to combination antiretroviral therapy, and older age all contribute to increased frequency of neuropathy (Ellis et al., 2008). The drugs that were most frequently implicated (ddI, d4T, and ddC) are now used infrequently (ddI and d4T) or no longer made (ddC). This condition is generally irreversible and sometimes requires aggressive pain management, including use of narcotics.

With a wide range of symptoms, peripheral neuropathy is difficult to diagnose, requiring a neurologic examination. The exact etiology of distal sensory polyneuropathy is unknown, but as indicated above, it is associated with HIV infection, antiretroviral therapy, or possibly comorbid conditions such as hepatitis C coinfection (Ellis et al., 2008).

Peripheral neuropathy is assessed under Listing 11.14 of the neurologic body system. However, this Listing refers to motor functioning, as opposed to sensory functioning, which is found to afflict HIV patients. For this reason, distal sensory polyneuropathy that is associated with marked functional impairment should be considered as part of revised HIV Infection Listings.

HIV-Associated Neurocognitive Disorders

HIV infection frequently results in neurological complications, some of the most frequent of which are neurocognitive. HIV-associated neurocognitive disorders (HAND) are characterized by a decline in cognitive functioning affecting multiple domains (see Box 5-2).

Despite modern combination antiretroviral therapies, HAND has been reported in approximately 40 percent of those with HIV infection (Antinori et al., 2007; Heaton et al., 2010). HAND is prevalent in more advanced

BOX 5-2
Most Commonly Affected Domains of Cognitive Functioning

- Memory;
- Attention and speed of information processing;
- Executive functioning; and
- Psychomotor performance.

stages of HIV disease (e.g., in approximately 50 percent of those individuals who meet the criteria for AIDS) and tends to be more severe in those with the greatest immune compromise (e.g., current CD4 less than 50 cells/mm^3, nadir CD4 less than 200 cells/mm^3, and high viremia) (Heaton et al., 2010). HAND outcomes vary, with some cases improving, especially with long-term viral suppression and immune reconstitution. Other cases manifest static impairment, and others develop a fluctuating or declining course. Periodic reassessments of status are therefore desirable.

Three levels of HAND have been defined (Antinori et al., 2007):

- *HIV-associated dementia (HAD)*, introduced in Chapter 4, refers to severe impairment in at least two cognitive domains (see Box 5-2) that markedly or extremely affect everyday functioning. Commonly the individual is unable to carry out more than the most basic activities of daily living independently (e.g., eating, bathing, dressing). Typically the diagnosis can be made by a clinician based on a mental status evaluation, assessing the domains of cognitive functioning. If neuropsychological testing is carried out, HAD can be identified by performance that falls 2 standard deviations or more below expected in at least two cognitive functioning domains.
- *HIV-associated mild neurocognitive disorder (HIV MND)* refers to presentations with at least two areas of neurocognitive compromise, but the severity is less than with HAD. The effect on everyday functioning is less severe than with HAD; typically the individual manages basic activities of daily living, but needs some assistance or accommodation in more demanding activities. These include most forms of employment and schooling. Assistance or accommodation is also needed in more complex home tasks such as financial management. If neuropsychological testing is performed, HIV MND is defined by performance between 1 and less than 2 standard deviations below the mean in at least two cognitive functioning domains.

- *HIV-associated asymptomatic neurocognitive impairment (HIV ANI)* exists when mild cognitive decline, ascertained by neuropsychological performance 1 to less than 2 standard deviations below expectation, is documented, but there is no documentation of impairment in everyday functioning. Some cases report exerting greater effort to maintain performance, but do not require other accommodation. This category is listed for completeness, but HIV ANI does not qualify for Social Security disability.

In the case of MND, which may be observed in about 25 percent of HIV-infected persons (Heaton et al., 2010), there is not total disability. However, mild to moderate disability of MND may combine with other sources of functional impairment (e.g., severe neuropathy, marked mood change, severe fatigue due to treatment, or comorbid conditions such as hepatitis C) to produce an overall picture of severe functional impairment. Because these conditions are specific to HIV, HIV-associated mild neurocognitive disorder should be included in the HIV Infection Listings when marked functional limitations can be demonstrated.

HIV-Associated Wasting Syndrome

"HIV wasting" is an AIDS-defining condition that is defined as an involuntary loss of more than 10 percent baseline body weight that is accompanied by chronic fever, fatigue, or diarrhea for at least 30 days (CDC, 1992). Although this is the definition most often used in the literature, it may lead to underreporting of AIDS in the more recent era of combination antiretroviral therapy (Siddiqui et al., 2009).

Involuntary weight loss in patients with HIV infection has shown a consistent correlation with morbidity and mortality. This weight loss has been reported in patients treated with combination antiretroviral therapy, including patients who have HIV suppression and CD4 counts above 200 cells/mm^3, although this combination is unusual (Mangili et al., 2006; Tang et al., 2002; Uhlenkott et al., 2008).

HIV-associated wasting syndrome is defined by the committee as an involuntary weight loss of 10 percent and a body mass index (BMI) less than 18.5 (the BMI that is the standard metric used to define malnutrition). The use of a 10 percent involuntary reduction in body weight is based on multiple reports that consistently show a correlation between death and this level of weight loss. These include reports in the postcombination antiretroviral therapy era.

The causes of involuntary weight loss are not specified, but they have been studied extensively and appear to be "multifactorial." The main causes are inadequate caloric intake and altered metabolism. Contributing factors include: HIV that is untreated or unresponsive to treatment (the pre-combination therapy experience), opportunistic infections and tumor, malabsorption due to "AIDS enteropathy," depression, gastrointestinal adverse reactions to antiretroviral agents or other treatments (including decreased intake and lipoatrophy), hypogonadism, protein energy dysmetabolism, and cytokine dysregulation (Mangili et al., 2006).

Outside of the HIV Infection Listings, weight loss due to any digestive disorder is described under Listings 5.08 and 105.08 in the Digestive System. Because of the increased risk of mortality and a potential impact on quality of life and functioning, the committee concludes that HIV wasting syndrome should be included in the HIV Infection Listings to the extent that they cover substantial involuntary weight loss that markedly impairs functioning.

Kaposi's Sarcoma

In HIV-infected persons, Kaposi's sarcoma (KS) is uniformly associated with coinfection with human herpesvirus-8 (HHV-8). KS is definitively diagnosed by biopsy, and histologically KS is characterized by vascular proliferation and a vigorous inflammatory reaction. In early stages, it is debated whether KS is a true malignancy, but this seems clearer in more advanced disease. It arises from endothelial tissues and can affect any region of the body except the central nervous system. KS is especially common in some body regions and organs. Areas commonly affected include the skin, the oral pharynx, the conjuctiva, and the gastrointestinal tract. Some patients have lymphatic obstruction with chronic leg edema. Lesions in the digestive system can occasionally bleed; involvement of the pulmonary parenchyma, often with associated pleural effusions, is symptomatic and rapidly fatal (see Chapter 4). Advanced Kaposi's sarcoma in any region can cause death, although this is very uncommon with the availability of antiretroviral therapy, except when there is pulmonary involvement.

It is important to note that there is increased social stigma because the lesions are visible. The lesions can cause particular difficulty in the workplace for the person who has them. Additionally, larger lesions can cause chronic pain. For these reasons the committee specifically identified KS and not other opportunistic infections.

The risk of morbidity and mortality of Kaposi's sarcoma has been reduced dramatically since the beginning of the epidemic, largely as a result of combination antiretroviral therapy (Bower et al., 2009; Grabar et al., 2008; Mocroft et al., 2004). In one study, the percentage of KS in HIV-infected Americans fell from 1980 to 1989 (63.9 percent) and from 1996 to 2002 (30 percent) (Engels et al., 2006). An 85 percent decline in risk of death was found between precombination antiretroviral therapy (1993 to 1995) and postcombination antiretroviral therapy (2001 to 2003) eras in a large cohort of men in France (Grabar et al., 2008). In the postcombination therapy era, the overall 5-year survival for Kaposi's sarcoma patients on combined therapy was 91 percent in one British report (Bower et al., 2009).

Cutaneous KS is typically a treatable condition that responds to the initiation of antiretroviral therapy, usually completely. With more advanced-stage disease, or in those with incomplete response to antiretroviral therapy, systemic chemotherapy can be helpful to control the condition, and some topical agents occasionally are used as well. KS can, however, remain a serious and disabling condition despite treatment, especially in cases exhibiting visceral disease or bulky cutaneous involvement.

Based on the expertise of the committee, it was determined that Kaposi's sarcoma (currently Listings 14.08E2 and 114.08E2) and the social stigma attached to it can be disabling. Squamous cell carcinoma and lymphomas are part of the Malignant Neoplastic Diseases Listings (13.00 and 113.00), which include recurrent disease following antineoplastic therapy. These Listings do not address Kaposi's sarcoma, which can respond to antiretroviral therapy. KS that severely limits an individual's ability to work should therefore be included in the HIV Infection Listings.

Lipoatrophy or Lipohypertrophy

Disabling disorders involving adipose tissues in people living with HIV/AIDS are collectively known as lipodystrophy and present as either lipoatrophy or lipohypertrophy. Lipoatrophy (fat wasting) refers to the reduction of subcutaneous body fat, particularly in the face and distal extremities. Although less disabling, lipohypertrophy refers to an increase of body fat in the central abdomen, breasts in women, and the dorsoclavicular fat pad (buffalo hump) (Cabrero et al., 2010; Fichtenbaum, 2009). These disorders are primarily cosmetic; however, in rare instances they can result in permanent disfigurement and pain, or both, and can reduce a person's ability to walk, stand, or sit if they manifest on the pads of feet or the buttocks. Importantly, they can also negatively impact the quality of a patient's life due to depression, fears of stigma, and reduced social functioning. This is particularly true if the disorder occurs in the face (Crane et al., 2008; Guaraldi et al., 2008).

Although the etiology of lipoatrophy and lipohypertrophy are not well understood, lipoatrophy is thought to be caused by thymidine nucleoside reverse transcriptase inhibitors. The most frequent cause is stavudine (d4T), which is no longer commonly used. Nevertheless, once the characteristic changes in the face have occurred, they are generally irreversible except with cosmetic surgery. Lipohypertrophy may be caused by protease inhibitors or a refeeding process. As with lipoatrophy, discontinuation or change in treatments has not been shown to be very effective in reversing changes that have already taken place (Cabrero et al., 2010).

No consensus definition or standard, objective measure defining lipoatrophy or lipohypertrophy exists. Both are diagnosed on a clinical basis, often through patient self-reports confirmed by clinicians. As a result, the prevalence of both lipoatrophy and lipohypertrophy in HIV-infected people is difficult to measure and ranges widely. Contrast-enhanced computed tomography (CT) scans and magnetic resonance imaging (MRIs) can be used to quantify the amount of fat reduction or development, although these procedures are costly. One study suggests that more than 45 percent of HIV-positive people have experienced lipoatrophy and more than 25 percent have experienced lipohypertrophy (Cabrero et al., 2010). Another found the prevalence of fat atrophy and central fat deposition to be 30 and 44 percent, respectively (Jacobson et al., 2005). However, many of these cases may not be disabling. Furthermore, an analysis of the Swiss HIV Cohort Study suggests that the prevalence of lipodystrophy has decreased continuously since 2003 (Nguyen et al., 2008).

Both lipoatrophy and lipohypertrophy are conditions specific to the treatment of HIV/AIDS and are not found in other sections of the Listing of Impairments; therefore, they should be considered under the HIV Infection Listings when associated with marked functional limitation, including stigma that can be limiting in the workplace.

Osteoporosis

First documented in the late 1990s, the etiology of osteoporosis in HIV/AIDS patients remains poorly understood today. Osteoporosis is a disease characterized by the loss of bone mass over time and can lead to fragility and a high risk of fracture. This is of particular concern for bones in the hips and spine, which have the potential to cause pain and affect a person's ability to ambulate.

Evidence shows that osteoporosis occurs at a higher rate in HIV-infected populations as compared to seronegative populations. Additionally, a review of the literature suggests the prevalence of osteoporosis ranges from 3 to 21 percent (Paccou et al., 2009); another study found a prevalence of 33 percent (Cazanave et al., 2008). Although a higher percent of HIV-infected patients suffer from osteopenia (characterized by a less severe level of bone loss), osteoporosis (the more severe condition) can ultimately lead to a reduction in quality of life.

Defined by the World Health Organization (WHO), osteoporosis occurs when bone density is 2.5 standard deviations below average, also known as having a T-score of less than –2.5. Bone density is commonly determined through dual X-ray absorptiometry (DEXA) and WHO's Fracture

Risk Assessment Tool. Hypothesized to be caused both by the virus and antiretroviral treatments (Brown et al., 2009; Fichtenbaum, 2009), there is no conclusive evidence in the literature about the true etiology of osteoporosis. Nonetheless, HIV-induced bone loss has been ascribed to reductions in lymphocyte activity and increases in bone-absorbing cytokines, among others. Other risk factors include low body weight, smoking, vitamin D deficiency, and living for long periods of time with HIV (Fichtenbaum, 2009). Osteoporosis also has been theorized to result from antiretroviral treatment.

Although bone damage is considered under the Musculoskeletal System of the Listing of Impairments, it does not address osteoporosis. For this reason and because severe disability can result from HIV infection complicated by osteoporosis, the committee believes it should be included in the HIV Infection Listings when associated with marked functional limitation.

HIV-ASSOCIATED CONDITIONS IN THE LISTINGS

HIV/AIDS is no longer a nearly fatal disease, but a number of serious conditions can cause disability, even in the era of potent antiretroviral therapy. The committee suggests that a listing be developed that identifies the HIV-associated conditions currently without listings elsewhere in the Listing of Impairments. The committee concludes that an assessment of functioning should be completed in disability claims that present with (1) HIV-associated conditions; (2) adverse effects of treatment for HIV or comorbid conditions; or (3) other significant, documented symptoms (e.g., fatigue, malaise, pain). To account for the unpredictable nature of HIV and its treatment, allowances made under these parameters should be considered a disability for 3 years following the last documentation of the manifestation, adverse effects, or symptoms. This time period reflects the fact that HIV is now viewed as a generally manageable chronic disease. The immunologic and functional status of many HIV claimants is likely to improve once they are engaged in care and are receiving therapy. It should be noted that the benefits of therapy may decrease as comorbidities continue to develop, therefore requiring regular reevaluation.

RECOMMENDATION 4. Comorbidities induced by HIV infection or adverse effects of treatment should be considered disabling if they markedly limit functioning in one or more of the following areas: ability to perform activities of daily living; maintenance of social functioning; or completion of tasks in a timely manner due to deficiencies in concentration, persistence, or pace. This includes, but is not limited to, the following conditions:

- **Diarrhea;**

- **Distal sensory polyneuropathy;**
- **HIV-associated neurocognitive disorders;**
- **HIV-associated wasting syndrome;**
- **Kaposi's sarcoma;**
- **Lipoatrophy or lipohypertrophy; and**
- **Osteoporosis.**

Symptoms such as fatigue, malaise, and pain should also be considered if found to limit functioning. Periodically, SSA should reevaluate claims made using these comorbidities, consistent with the reevaluation of other disability allowances.

REFERENCES

Antinori, A., G. Arendt, J. T. Becker, B. J. Brew, D. A. Byrd, M. Cherner, D. B. Clifford, P. Cinque, L. G. Epstein, K. Goodkin, M. Gisslen, I. Grant, R. K. Heaton, J. Joseph, K. Marder, C. M. Marra, J. C. McArthur, M. Nunn, R. W. Price, L. Pulliam, K. R. Robertson, N. Sacktor, V. Valcour, and V. E. Wojna. 2007. Updated research nosology for HIV-associated neurocognitive disorders. *Neurology* 69(18):1789–1799.

Bower, M., J. Weir, N. Francis, T. Newsom-Davis, S. Powles, T. Crook, M. Boffito, B. Gazzard, and M. Nelson. 2009. The effect of HAART in 254 consecutive patients with AIDS-related Kaposi's sarcoma. *AIDS* 23(13):1701–1706.

Brown, T. T., G. A. McComsey, M. S. King, R. B. Qaqish, B. M. Bernstein, and B. A. Da Silva. 2009. Loss of bone mineral density after antiretroviral therapy initiation, independent of antiretroviral regimen. *Journal of Acquired Immune Deficiency Syndromes* 51(5):554–561.

Cabrero, E., L. Griffa, and A. Burgos. 2010. Prevalence and impact of body physical changes in HIV patients treated with highly active antiretroviral therapy: Results from a study on patient and physician perceptions. *AIDS Patient Care and STDs* 24(1):5–13.

Cazanave, C., M. Dupon, V. Lavignolle-Aurillac, N. Barthe, S. Lawson-Ayayi, N. Mehsen, P. Mercié, P. Morlat, R. Thiébaut, F. Dabis, and Groupe d'Epidémiologie Clinique du SIDA en Aquitaine. 2008. Reduced bone mineral density in HIV-infected patients: Prevalence and associated factors. *AIDS* 22(3):395–402.

CDC (Centers for Disease Control and Prevention). 1992. 1993 revised classification system for HIV infection and expanded surveillance case definition for AIDS among adolescent and adults. *Morbidity and Mortality Weekly Report* 41(RR–17).

Crane, H. M., C. Grunfeld, R. D. Harrington, K. K. Uldall, P. S. Ciechanowski, and M. M. Kitahata. 2008. Lipoatrophy among HIV-infected patients is associated with higher levels of depression than lipohypertrophy. *HIV Medicine* 9(9):780–786.

Ellis, R. J., J. Marquie-Beck, P. Delaney, T. Alexander, D. B. Clifford, J. C. McArthur, D. M. Simpson, C. Ake, A. C. Collier, B. B. Gelman, J. McCutchan, S. Morgello, and I. Grant. 2008. Human immunodeficiency virus protease inhibitors and risk for peripheral neuropathy. *Annals of Neurology* 64(5):566–572.

Ellis, R. J., D. Rosario, D. B. Clifford, J. C. McArthur, D. Simpson, T. Alexander, B. B. Gelman, F. Vaida, A. Collier, C. M. Marra, B. Ances, J. H. Atkinson, R. H. Dworkin, S. Morgello, and I. Grant for The CHARTER Study Group. 2010. Continued high prevalence and adverse clinical impact of human immunodeficiency virus-associated sensory neuropathy in the era of combination antiretroviral therapy: The CHARTER Study. *Archives of Neurology* 67(5):552–558.

Engels, E. A., R. M. Pfeiffer, J. J. Goedert, P. Virgo, T. S. McNeel, S. M. Scoppa, and R. J. Biggar for the HIV/AIDS Cancer Match Study. 2006. Trends in cancer risk among people with AIDS in the United States 1980–2002. *AIDS* 20(12):1645–1654.

Esser, S., D. Helbig, U. Hillen, J. Dissemond, and S. Grabbe. 2007. Side effects of HIV therapy. *Journal der Deutschen Dermatologischen Gesellschaft* 5(9):745–754.

Fichtenbaum, C. J. 2009. Metabolic abnormalities associated with HIV infection and antiretroviral therapy. *Current Infectious Disease Reports* 11(1):84–92.

Gonzalez-Duarte, A., K. Cikurel, and D. M. Simpson. 2007. Managing HIV peripheral neuropathy. *Current HIV/AIDS Reports* 4(3):114–118.

Grabar, S., E. Lanoy, C. Allavena, M. Mary-Krause, M. Bentata, P. Fischer, A. Mahamat, C. Rabaud, and D. Costagliola. 2008. Causes of the first AIDS-defining illness and subsequent survival before and after the advent of combined antiretroviral therapy. *HIV Medicine* 9(4):246–256.

Guaraldi, G., R. Murri, G. Orlando, C. Giovanardi, N. Squillace, M. Vandelli, B. Beghetto, G. Nardini, M. De Paola, R. Esposito, and A. W. Wu. 2008. Severity of lipodystrophy is associated with decreased health-related quality of life. *AIDS Patient Care and STDs* 22(7):577–585.

Heaton, R., D. Clifford, D. Franklin Jr., S. Woods, C. Ake, F. Vaida, R. Ellis, S. Letendre, T. Marcotte, J. Atkinson, M. Rivera-Mindt, O. Vigil, M. Taylor, A. Collier, C. Marra, B. Gelman, J. McArthur, S. Morgello, D. Simpson, J. McCutchan, I. Abramson, A. Gamst, C. Fennema-Notestine, T. Jernigan, J. Wong, and I. Grant for The CHARTER Study Group. 2010 (in press). HIV-associated neurocognitive disorders persist in the era of potent antiretroviral therapy. *Neurology.*

Jacobson, D. L., T. Knox, D. Spiegelman, S. Skinner, S. Gorbach, and C. Wanke. 2005. Prevalence of, evolution of, and risk factors for fat atrophy and fat deposition in a cohort of HIV-infected men and women. *Clinical Infectious Diseases* 40(12):1837–1845.

Justice, A., S. J. Gange, J. P. Tate, L. P. Jacobson, K. Gebo, K. Althoff, M. Kitahata, M. Saag, M. Horberg, and R. Moore for the NA-ACCORD and VACS Project Teams. 2010 (unpublished). *Report to the Institute of Medicine committee evaluating disability criteria for those with HIV infection.*

Knox, T. A., D. Spiegelman, S. C. Skinner, and S. Gorbach. 2000. Diarrhea and abnormalities of gastrointestinal function in a cohort of men and women with HIV infection. *American Journal of Gastroenterology* 95(12):3482–3489.

Lichtenstein, K., C. Armon, A. Baron, A. Moorman, K. C. Wood, and S. Holmberg. 2005. Modification of the incidence of drug-associated symmetrical peripheral neuropathy by host and disease factors in the HIV outpatient study cohort. *Clinical Infectious Diseases* 40(1):148–157.

Mangili, A., D. H. Murman, A. M. Zampini, and C. A. Wanke. 2006. HIV/AIDS: Nutrition and HIV infection: Review of weight loss and wasting in the era of highly active antiretroviral therapy from the nutrition for healthy living cohort. *Clinical Infectious Diseases* 42(6):836–842.

Mocroft, A., and the EuroSIDA Study Group. 2010 (unpublished). *The incidence and probability of death in HIV-infected persons pre- and post-cART.* University College London.

Mocroft, A., O. Kirk, N. Clumeck, P. Gargalianos-Kakolyris, H. Trocha, N. Chentsova, F. Antunes, H.-J. Stellbrink, A. N. Phillips, and J. D. Lundgren. 2004. The changing pattern of Kaposi sarcoma in patients with HIV, 1994–2003. *Cancer* 100(12):2644–2654.

Monkemuller, K. E., S. A. Call, A. J. Lazenby, and C. M. Wilcox. 2000. Declining prevalence of opportunistic gastrointestinal disease in the era of combination antiretroviral therapy. *American Journal of Gastroenterology* 95(2):457–462.

Nguyen, A., A. Calmy, V. Schiffer, E. Bernasconi, M. Battegay, M. Opravil, J.-M. Evison, P. Tarr, P. Schmid, T. Perneger, and B. Hirschel. 2008. Lipodystrophy and weight changes: Data from the Swiss HIV cohort study, 2000–2006. *HIV Medicine* 9(3):142–150.

Paccou, J., N. Viget, I. Legrout-Gérot, Y. Yazdanpanah, and B. Cortet. 2009. Bone loss in patients with HIV infection. *Joint Bone Spine* 76(6):637–641.

Schifitto, G., M. P. McDermott, J. C. McArthur, K. Marder, N. Sacktor, D. R. McClernon, K. Conant, B. Cohen, L. G. Epstein, K. Kieburtz, and the NEAD Consortium. 2005. Markers of immune activation and viral load in HIV-associated sensory neuropathy. *Neurology* 64(5):842–848.

Siddiqui, J., A. L. Phillips, E. S. Freedland, A. R. Sklar, T. Darkow, and C. R. Harley. 2009. Prevalence and cost of HIV-associated weight loss in a managed care population. *Current Medical Research & Opinion* 25(5):1307–1317.

Siddiqui, U., E. J. Bini, K. Chandarana, J. Leong, S. Ramsetty, D. Schiliro, and M. Poles. 2007. Prevalence and impact of diarrhea on health-related quality of life in HIV-infected patients in the era of highly active antiretroviral therapy. *Journal of Clinical Gastroenterology* 41(5):484–490.

Tang, A. M., J. Forrester, D. Spiegelman, T. A. Knox, E. Tchetgen, and S. L. Gorbach. 2002. Weight loss and survival in HIV-positive patients in the era of highly active antiretroviral therapy. *Journal of Acquired Immune Deficiency Syndromes* 31(2):230–236.

Tinmouth, J., G. Tomlinson, G. Kandel, S. Walmsley, H. A. Steinhart, and R. Glazier. 2007. Evaluation of stool frequency and stool form as measures of HIV-related diarrhea. *HIV Clinical Trials* 8(6):421–428.

Tramarin, A., N. Parise, S. Campostrini, D. D. Yin, M. J. Postma, R. Lyu, R. Grisetti, A. Capetti, A. M. Cattelan, M. T. Di Toro, A. Mastroianni, E. Pignattari, V. Mondardini, G. Calleri, E. Raise, and F. Starace for the Palladio Study Group. 2004. Association between diarrhea and quality of life in HIV-infected patients receiving highly active antiretroviral therapy. *Quality of Life Research* 13(1):243–250.

Uhlenkott, M. C., S. E. Buskin, E. M. Kahle, E. Barash, and D. M. Aboulafia. 2008. Causes of death in the era of highly active antiretroviral therapy: A retrospective analysis of a hybrid hematology–oncology and HIV practice and the Seattle/King County adult/adolescent spectrum of HIV-related diseases project. *The American Journal of the Medical Sciences* 336(3):217–223.

6

HIV-Associated Conditions With Listings Elsewhere

As discussed in Chapter 2, a new set of medical conditions associated with HIV infection has emerged in recent years. These conditions are also seen in the general population and include cardiovascular disease and malignancies. In the United States, these and other conditions have become the leading cause of morbidity and mortality for persons living with HIV infection. Chapter 5 reviewed HIV-associated conditions currently not covered elsewhere in the Listing of Impairments. In contrast, some comorbid conditions occurring with increased frequency or at an earlier age among people living with HIV are already mentioned elsewhere in the Listings. In these instances, the Social Security Administration (SSA) has processes in place to deal with claimants affected by multiple conditions. One procedure called cross-referencing allows claims to be decided based on the specific requirements of an existing listing.

CONDITIONS COVERED ELSEWHERE IN THE LISTINGS

The prevalence of disabling chronic conditions already included in the Listing of Impairments separately from the HIV Infection Listings (see Box 6-1) is growing among HIV-infected populations and will likely increase as people live longer with HIV infection. Although HIV infection increases the risk for developing these conditions and in some instances accelerates the rate of disease progression, the comorbid conditions in Box 6-1 are generally not clinically distinct and can be evaluated adequately using the current listing criteria.

BOX 6-1
List of HIV-Associated Conditions With Current Listings Elsewhere in the Listing of Impairments

HIV-associated conditions that have current listings in the Listing of Impairments, not covered in the HIV Infection Listings, include the following, but are not limited to:

- Cardiovascular disease;
- Chronic kidney disease, including HIV-associated nephropathy;
- Diabetes;
- Hepatitis; and
- Malignancies, not otherwise specified in the report.

Cardiovascular Disease

An increased risk for cardiovascular disease in HIV-infected populations as compared with HIV-negative populations has been well documented (Currier et al., 2008). Cardiovascular disease is the leading cause of death of Americans. It is also a leading cause of death in those infected with HIV, with an analysis of the Data Collection on Adverse Events of Anti-HIV Drugs Study finding that 11 percent of HIV-positive people die from a cardiovascular condition (Smith and the D:A:D Study, 2009). The risk factors for cardiovascular disease in HIV-infected populations are the same as those in the general population, including smoking, older age, diabetes, male gender, and other prior cardiovascular conditions (Currier et al., 2008; Glass et al., 2006). Increasingly, HIV infection itself is considered a cardiovascular disease risk factor, probably as or more important than the conventional ones.

The exact mechanisms and extent of the relationship between HIV and cardiovascular disease are not well understood. Hypotheses suggest increased cardiovascular disease can be related to HIV infection and, to a lesser extent, combination antiretroviral therapies. A review of cohort studies indicated that HIV-infected adults are at higher risk of cardiovascular disease than adults without HIV (Currier et al., 2008). The presence of HIV can lead to changes in lipid profiles that are themselves cardiovascular disease risk factors, such as low HDL-C and high triglyceride levels (Aberg, 2009). HIV is also implicated in chronic inflammation, which can be a cause of endothelial dysfunction, a risk factor for atherosclerosis (de Saint Martin et al., 2007). While the risk of developing cardiovascular disease is elevated in conjunction with HIV infection, the disease profile and impact on disability is similar to that in uninfected individuals.

Studies of the effects of antiretroviral agents on cardiovascular disease risk are mixed. A literature review concluded that combination antiretroviral therapy has only a modest effect on increased cardiovascular risk (Aberg, 2009). The association of protease inhibitors with metabolic disturbances is complex—effects might be attributed to the specific drug and might not be applicable to the entire drug class. For example, indinavir and lopinavir-ritonavir have been shown to increase risk of myocardial infarction in 12 and 13 percent of patients, respectively (Worm et al., 2010), whereas the whole class of protease inhibitors was found to affect 16 percent of patients (The D:A:D Study Group, 2007). The nucleoside reverse transcriptase inhibitors abacavir and didanosine were also associated with an increased risk of myocardial infarction (Worm et al., 2010). One study found an increased risk of hypertension in patients taking nonnucleoside reverse transcriptase inhibitors as compared to HIV-positive patients not on antiretroviral treatment (Wilson et al., 2009).

Cardiovascular disease is a significant cause of disability among Americans and is covered by SSA's Listing of Impairments under the Cardiovascular System (Listings 4.00 and 104.00). Cardiovascular disease is also a significant comorbidity of HIV infection. The committee concludes that HIV-infected claimants with disability due to cardiovascular disease should be considered under the Cardiovascular System Listings.

Chronic Kidney Disease, Including HIV-Associated Nephropathy

Chronic kidney disease includes HIV-associated nephropathy and end-stage renal disease (Gupta et al., 2005; Lucas et al., 2007; Szczech et al., 2004a; Winston et al., 2008). About 30 percent of HIV patients experience abnormal kidney functioning. Defined in Listing 6.00 as kidney damage or a glomerular filtration rate ≤ 60 mL/min for 3 or more months (National Kidney Foundation, 2002), chronic kidney disease can leave people at greater risk for faster progression to AIDS-defining illnesses and death (Szczech et al., 2004b). The disease is similar between seropositive and seronegative populations. Although the literature about the relationship between chronic kidney disease and HIV and its treatment is still developing, the incidence of chronic kidney disease appears to be slowing. Incidence of chronic kidney disease decreased significantly after the introduction of combination antiretroviral therapy. Although prevalence increased, this increase is potentially due to longer survival times (Lucas et al., 2007).

Chronic kidney failure is diagnosed through screening urine analysis, calculated estimates of renal function (e.g., creatinine clearance, glomerular filtration rate), and kidney biopsy. These tests are recommended by the Infectious Disease Society of America's *Guidelines for the Management of Chronic Kidney Disease in HIV-Infected Patients* (Gupta et al., 2005).

In addition to HIV infection, renal functioning can be impaired by diabetes and hypertension. Hepatitis C is also a risk factor for chronic kidney disease. Nephrotoxicity can be induced by HIV treatments, such as indinivir and tenofovir (Izzedine et al., 2005; Szczech et al., 2004a; Winston et al., 2008).

Renal failure in HIV patients is also known as HIV-associated nephropathy, which is characterized by significant proteinuria and quick advancement to end-stage renal disease due to scarring of blood vessels in the kidneys. Today, HIV-associated nephropathy remains an aggressive disease, especially when it advances to the point of requiring dialysis. One-year survival has increased from 25 to 75 percent (Winston et al., 2008). While one study found the overall prevalence of HIV-associated nephropathy to be 6.9 percent (Shahinian et al., 2000), the true prevalence is unknown. HIV-associated nephropathy is definitively diagnosed only by kidney biopsy, but they are performed relatively infrequently. Kidney biopsies have shown that the condition is present in approximately 40 to 60 percent of specimens taken from HIV-infected individuals (Szczech et al., 2004a).

Disability due to impaired renal functioning is described in and adjudicated based on the Genitourinary Impairment Listings (6.00 and 106.00), although the more current term is chronic kidney disease. Because HIV and its treatments do not result in a form of chronic kidney disease distinct from the Genitourinary Impairment Listings, it ought to be cross-referenced to those listings. HIV-associated nephropathy is not specifically mentioned in the Genitourinary Impairment Listings, but because it has the same end result as renal failure it is adequately covered by those listings. Furthermore, SSA may wish to consider adopting changes to the aforementioned guidelines for managing chronic kidney disease in HIV patients in the future as a method of keeping up with advances in treatment.

Diabetes

Diabetes is a metabolic disease characterized by high blood glucose levels and leading eventually to multisystem complications, such as kidney failure, cardiovascular disease, retinopathy, and neuropathy. Diabetes is diagnosed through blood glucose tests. The American Diabetes Association has set diagnostic standards that include the following as meeting the definition of diabetes: 2-hour plasma glucose ≥ 200 mg/dL, fasting glucose ≥ 126 mg/dL, or hemoglobin A1C ≥ 6.5 percent (American Diabetes Association, 2009; The International Expert Committee, 2009).

The number of people with concomitant diabetes and HIV has increased since the introduction of combination antiretroviral therapy. The prevalence of diabetes among men infected with HIV in the Multicenter AIDS Cohort Study was 14 percent, significantly greater than among uninfected controls, and was associated with a nadir CD4 cell count under 300 cells/mm^3 (Winston et al., 2008). In the Swiss HIV Cohort Study, the risk for developing diabetes was associated with protease inhibitors and nucleoside reverse transcriptase inhibitor therapy (Ledergerber et al., 2007). In contrast, the Women's Interagency HIV Study failed to document increased risk for diabetes associated with HIV infection, although among HIV-infected women, longer duration of nucleoside-based therapy was associated with greater risk (Tien et al., 2007). This finding contrasts with an earlier analysis of data from the same cohort, which concluded that protease inhibitors were associated with a three-fold increased rate of self-reported diabetes (Justman et al., 2003).

Although the complete picture of metabolic dysfunction in the setting of HIV infection remains to be described, clearly people with HIV infection are at risk for developing diabetes as a result of preexisting factors such as diet, environment, and genetics, in addition to the effects of HIV and its treatment.

Diabetes is listed as part of the Endocrine System in the Listing of Impairments (specifically Listing 9.08), which lists neuropathy, acidosis, and retinitis proliferans as the conditions under which allowances should be made. Listing 109.08 requires recurrent acidosis, hypoglycemia, retarded growth, and reduced renal functioning for juvenile diabetes. Claimants with both HIV and diabetes should be cross-referenced to Listings 9.08 and 109.08.

Hepatitis

Hepatitis is a general term referring to a variety of diseases leading to inflammation of the liver cells, the hepatocytes. Hepatitis ranges from an asymptomatic, self-limited condition to a fulminant, rapidly fatal disease. Chronic hepatitis can lead to liver fibrosis called cirrhosis, hepatocellular carcinoma, and chronic impairment of liver function. Hepatitis can be caused by infections, drugs, and collagen-vascular diseases, but the most common causes of HIV infection follow coinfection with the hepatitis B or C viruses (HBV and HCV, respectively). Also important are cases of liver injury from drugs used in HIV management either as a direct drug toxicity or as part of an inflammatory response to the restored immune system following the introduction of antiretroviral drugs. Hepatitis B is most commonly diagnosed through blood tests for the hepatitis B surface antigen, hepatitis B virus DNA, and hepatitis B early antigen. Tests to detect the presence of hepatitis C viral RNA are used to diagnose hepatitis C.

Findings indicate that HIV has been shown to accelerate progression to cirrhosis and hepatocellular cancer in hepatitis C-coinfected patients and that coinfected patients may not respond as well to treatment of hepatitis

C (Soriano et al., 2002; Sulkowski, 2004). Whether combination antiretroviral therapy improves liver function in those coinfected with either HBV or HCV remains unclear, but it does slow hepatitis progression. Coinfection is also an indication to initiate HIV therapy at an early stage of HIV infection.

Hepatitis is discussed in the Digestive System Listings (specifically, chronic liver disease is covered in Listings 5.05 and 105.05). The committee suggests editorial changes be made within 5.00 and 105.00, the introductory text that describes chronic viral hepatitis infections (specifically 5.00D4 and 105.00D4), to better reflect the current state of hepatitis care. This includes stating that HIV infection may accelerate the clinical course of viral hepatitis infection and patients infected with HIV may have a poorer response to treatment instead of simply stating that it may affect the clinical course of disease; including hepatitis B virus DNA as a method of diagnosing hepatitis B infection; revising "hepatitis B envelope antigen" to "hepatitis B early antigen" or "hepatitis B 'e' antigen"; adding "hepatocellular carcinoma" to end-stage liver disease and cirrhosis as a condition with increased risk of progression; and removing "combination of interferon injections" as a method of suppressing hepatitis B virus. Because HIV and hepatitis coinfection does not necessarily redefine the level of disability but instead causes people to reach the same level of disease severity more quickly, cross-referencing to Listings 5.05 and 105.05 is appropriate for HIV-infected claimants also living with hepatitis.

Malignancies Not Otherwise Specified

Cancers in people living with HIV/AIDS can be fatal and can lead to high levels of morbidity. These conditions have been classified into two groups: AIDS-defining cancers and non-AIDS–defining cancers. AIDS-defining cancers, as identified by the Centers for Disease Control and Prevention, are Kaposi's sarcoma, invasive cervical cancer, and non-Hodgkin's lymphoma, both those arising within the central nervous system (CNS) and ones arising peripheral to that site. Non-AIDS–defining cancers are all other cancers that manifest in HIV-infected persons. Some malignancies are specifically discussed in prior chapters—primary CNS lymphomas (Chapter 4), Kaposi's sarcoma (Chapters 4 and 5), and primary effusion lymphoma (Chapter 4)—because of the aggressive nature of the condition or because they are still relatively common clinical conditions despite the wide use of antiretroviral therapy.

Since the development of potent combination antiretroviral therapy, the incidence of AIDS-defining cancers has dramatically decreased (Brodt et al., 1997; Buchacz et al., 2010; Grulich et al., 2001; Rabkin et al., 1993). However, non-AIDS–defining cancers are increasingly common, whether simply reflecting the now aging cohort of HIV-infected persons benefiting from HIV therapy or growing at an increased rate caused by HIV infection and immune deficiency or inflammation or even as an adverse effect of antiretroviral drugs. The standardized incidence rate for all non-AIDS–defining cancers is about twice that of the general population, although this is an area of active, ongoing investigation (Powles et al., 2009; Shiels et al., 2009).

The most common non-AIDS–defining cancers include cancers of the anus, liver, lung, oropharynx, and Hodgkin's lymphoma (Nguyen et al., 2010; Patel et al., 2008; Powles et al., 2009). Generally, the severity of these cancers is not increased as a result of HIV coinfection and they respond comparably to chemotherapeutic management. One exception is Hodgkin's lymphoma, which may be more aggressive in HIV/AIDS patients (Powles et al., 2009). The risk factors for these cancers depend on the type of malignancy. For example, smoking is a major risk factor for lung cancer, both in the general population and in the HIV-positive population; this can be attributed in part to higher smoking rates in the HIV-positive population and longer duration of tobacco exposure (Nguyen et al., 2010). Interestingly, most cancers that appear to have an increased incidence in HIV-infected persons have a second viral infection as a potential cause, including oropharyngeal cancer (Epstein-Barr virus), anal cancer (human papillomavirus), and hepatocellular cancer (HBV, HCV).

The effect of combination antiretroviral therapy on the increased risk of non-AIDS–defining cancers is unclear. Nonnucleoside reverse transcriptase inhibitors may be associated with an increased risk of Hodgkin's lymphoma (Powles et al., 2009), and an increase in cancer was reported with an early CCR5 inhibitor, but the literature is limited about the effects of specific classes of antiretroviral therapy on developing malignancies. Combination antiretroviral therapy may improve survival for some types of cancers, but this is not yet well supported in the literature (Nguyen et al., 2010).

Malignancies not otherwise specified in this report can be disabling and are important to consider in the management of HIV/AIDS. These malignancies are generally not unique from malignancies in noninfected individuals. These conditions follow the same standard treatment regimens as in the general population. Therefore, the committee concludes that malignancies should be considered under the Malignant Neoplastic Diseases Listings (13.00 and 113.00).

COMORBIDITY IN THE LISTINGS

SSA has specific processes in place to deal with claimants affected by multiple conditions. A process called cross-referencing can be used at the Listings step, where the claim is "referred" to an existing listing and the decision is made based on the specific requirements of that listing. For example, a claimant coinfected with HIV and hepatitis can currently be adjudicated under either Listing 5.05, chronic liver disease, or Listing 14.08K, repeated manifestations of HIV. If the primary impairment is hepatitis and the claimant does not meet the 14.08K listing, the claim can be referred to 5.05. In this case, the claim is adjudicated in the same way as a hepatitis claim without HIV is, *regardless of the claimant's HIV diagnosis*, unless the condition is also part of the HIV Infection Listings.

Upon assessment of the criteria currently in the Listing of Impairments for these other infections, the committee determined that these were appropriate for assessing disability for individuals with HIV coinfection. Because the condition is not usually clinically distinct and can be captured adequately by other disability listings, the committee concluded that HIV coinfection with one of the conditions listed in Box 6-1 should be cross-referenced to other listings.

RECOMMENDATION 5. SSA should cross-reference the following HIV-associated conditions to existing listings:

- **Cardiovascular disease (Listings 4.00 and 104.00);**
- **Chronic kidney disease, including HIV-associated nephropathy (Listing 6.00 and 106.00);**
- **Diabetes (Listings 9.08 and 109.08);**
- **Hepatitis (Listings 5.05 and 105.05); and**
- **Malignancies (Listings 13.00 and 113.00), not otherwise specified in the report.**

This recommendation differs from Recommendation 4 in two ways. First, the duration of these allowances should follow the durations identified by the other sublistings. However, if the literature is found to show that HIV coinfection causes changes to the disease not effectively captured in other disability listings, SSA may want to consider adding the disease to the HIV Infection Listings. Second, unlike conditions in Recommendation 4, the conditions discussed in this chapter are not linked to functional criteria to allow for the conditions to be easily cross-referenced.

REFERENCES

Aberg, J. A. 2009. Cardiovascular complications in HIV management: Past, present, and future. *Journal of Acquired Immune Deficiency Syndromes* 50(1):54–64.

American Diabetes Association. 2009. Standards of medical care in diabetes—2009. *Diabetes Care* 32(Suppl 1):S13–S61.

Brodt, H. R., B. S. Kamps, P. Gute, B. Knupp, S. Staszewski, and E. B. Helm. 1997. Changing incidence of AIDS-defining illnesses in the era of antiretroviral combination therapy. *AIDS* 11(14):1731–1738.

Buchacz, K., R. K. Baker, F. J. J. Palella, J. S. Chmiel, K. A. Lichtenstein, R. M. Novak, K. C. Wood, J. T. Brooks, and the HOPS Investigators. 2010. AIDS-defining opportunistic illnesses in US patients, 1994–2007: A cohort study. *AIDS* 24(10):1549–1559.

Currier, J. S., J. D. Lundgren, A. Carr, D. Klein, C. A. Sabin, P. E. Sax, J. T. Schouten, and M. Smieja for Working Group 2. 2008. Epidemiological evidence for cardiovascular disease in HIV-infected patients and relationship to highly active antiretroviral therapy. *Circulation* 118(2):e29–e35.

The D:A:D Study Group. 2007. Class of antiretroviral drugs and the risk of myocardial infarction. *New England Journal of Medicine* 356(17):1723–1735.

de Saint Martin, L., E. Pasquier, O. Vandhuick, B. Arnaud, S. Vallet, J. Duchemin, V. Bellein, and L. Bressollette. 2007. Correlations between carotid IMT, Factor VIII activity level and metabolic disturbances: A cardiovascular risk factor in the HIV positive persons. *Current HIV Research* 5(3):361–364.

Glass, T., C. Ungsedhapand, M. Wolbers, R. Weber, P. Vernazza, M. Rickenbach, H. Furrer, E. Bernasconi, M. Cavassini, B. Hirschel, M. Battegay, and H. Bucher. 2006. Prevalence of risk factors for cardiovascular disease in HIV-infected patients over time: The Swiss HIV cohort study. *HIV Medicine* 7(6):404–410.

Grulich, A. E., Y. Li, A. M. McDonald, P. K. Correll, M. G. Law, and J. M. Kaldor. 2001. Decreasing rates of Kaposi's sarcoma and non-Hodgkin's lymphoma in the era of potent combination anti-retroviral therapy. *AIDS* 15(5):629–633.

Gupta, S. K., J. A. Eustace, J. A. Winston, I. I. Boydstun, T. S. Ahuja, R. A. Rodriguez, K. T. Tashima, M. Roland, N. Franceschini, F. J. Palella, J. L. Lennox, P. E. Klotman, S. A. Nachman, S. D. Hall, and L. A. Szczech. 2005. Guidelines for the management of chronic kidney disease in HIV-infected patients: Recommendations of the HIV Medicine Association of the Infectious Diseases Society of America. *Clinical Infectious Diseases* 40(11):1559–1585.

The International Expert Committee. 2009. International expert committee report on the role of the A1C assay in the diagnosis of diabetes. *Diabetes Care* 32(7):1327–1334.

Izzedine, H., V. Launay-Vacher, and G. Deray. 2005. Antiviral drug-induced nephrotoxicity. *American Journal of Kidney Diseases* 45(5):804–817.

Justman, J. E., L. Benning, A. Danoff, H. Minkoff, A. Levine, R. M. Greenblatt, K. Weber, E. Piessens, E. Robison, and K. Anastos. 2003. Protease inhibitor use and the incidence of diabetes mellitus in a large cohort of HIV-infected women. *Journal of Acquired Immune Deficiency Syndromes* 32(3):298–302.

Ledergerber, B., H. Furrer, M. Rickenbach, R. Lehmann, L. Elzi, B. Hirschel, M. Cavassini, E. Bernasconi, P. Schmid, M. Egger, and R. Weber. 2007. Factors associated with the incidence of type 2 diabetes mellitus in HIV-infected participants in the Swiss HIV cohort study. *Clinical Infectious Diseases* 45(1):111–119.

Lucas, G. M., S. H. Mehta, M. G. Atta, G. D. Kirk, N. Galai, D. Vlahov, and R. D. Moore. 2007. End-stage renal disease and chronic kidney disease in a cohort of African-American HIV-infected and at-risk HIV-seronegative participants followed between 1988 and 2004. *AIDS* 21(18):2435–2443.

National Kidney Foundation. 2002. *K/DOQI clinical practice guidelines for chronic kidney disease: Evaluation, classification, and stratification*, http://www.kidney.org/professionals/kdoqi/guidelines/doqi_upex.html (accessed March 2, 2010).

Nguyen, M. L., K. J. Farrell, and C. J. Gunthel. 2010. Non-AIDS–defining malignancies in patients with HIV in the HAART era. *Current Infectious Disease Reports* 12(1):46–55.

Patel, P., D. L. Hanson, P. S. Sullivan, R. M. Novak, A. C. Moorman, T. C. Tong, S. D. Holmberg, and J. T. Brooks. 2008. Incidence of types of cancer among HIV-infected persons compared with the general population in the United States, 1992–2003. *Annals of Internal Medicine* 148(10):728–736.

Powles, T., D. Robinson, J. Stebbing, J. Shamash, M. Nelson, B. Gazzard, S. Mandelia, H. Moller, and M. Bower. 2009. Highly active antiretroviral therapy and the incidence of non-AIDS–defining cancers in people with HIV infection. *Journal of Clinical Oncology* 27(6):884–890.

Rabkin, C. S., R. J. Biggar, M. S. Baptiste, T. Abe, B. A. Kohler, and P. C. Nasca. 1993. Cancer incidence trends in women at high risk of human immunodeficiency virus (HIV) infection. *International Journal of Cancer* 55(2):208–212.

Shahinian, V., S. Rajaraman, M. Borucki, J. Grady, W. M. Hollander, and T. S. Ahuja. 2000. Prevalence of HIV-associate nephropathy in autopsies of HIV-infected patients. *American Journal of Kidney Diseases* 35:884–888.

Shiels, M. S., S. R. Cole, G. D. Kirk, and C. Poole. 2009. A meta-analysis of the incidence of non-AIDS cancers in HIV-infected individuals. *Journal of Acquired Immune Deficiency Syndromes* 52(5):611–622.

Smith, C., and Data Collection on Adverse Events of Anti-HIV Drugs (D:A:D) Study. 2009. *Association between modifiable and non-modifiable risk factors and specific causes of death in the HAART era: The data collection on adverse events of anti-HIV drugs study.* Paper presented at Conference on Retroviruses and Opportunistic Infections Montreal, Canada, February 8–11.

Soriano, V., M. Sulkowski, C. Bergin, A. Hatzakis, P. Cacoub, C. Katlama, A. Cargnel, S. Mauss, D. Dieterich, S. Moreno, C. Ferrari, T. Poynard, and J. Rockstroh. 2002. Care of patients with chronic hepatitis C and HIV co-infection: Recommendations from the HIV–HCV international panel. *AIDS* 16(6):813–828.

Sulkowski, M. S. 2004. Hepatitis C virus infection in HIV-infected patients. *Current HIV/AIDS Reports* 1(3):128–135.

Szczech, L. A., S. K. Gupta, R. Habash, A. Guasch, R. Kalayjian, R. Appel, T. A. Fields, L. P. Svetkey, K. H. Flanagan, P. E. Klotman, and J. A. Winston. 2004a. The clinical epidemiology and course of the spectrum of renal diseases associated with HIV infection. *Kidney International* 66(3):1145–1152.

Szczech, L. A., D. R. Hoover, J. G. Feldman, M. H. Cohen, S. J. Gange, L. Goozé, N. R. Rubin, M. A. Young, X. Cai, Q. Shi, W. Gao, and K. Anastos. 2004b. Association between renal disease and outcomes among HIV-infected women receiving or not receiving antiretroviral therapy. *Clinical Infectious Diseases* 39(8):1199–1206.

Tien, P. C., M. F. Schneider, S. R. Cole, A. M. Levine, M. Cohen, J. Dehovitz, M. Young, and J. E. Justman. 2007. Antiretroviral therapy exposure and incidence of diabetes mellitus in the Women's Interagency HIV Study. *AIDS* 21(13):1739–1745.

Wilson, S., G. Scullard, S. Fidler, J. Weber, and N. Poulter. 2009. Effects of HIV status and antiretroviral therapy on blood pressure. *HIV Medicine* 10(6):388–394.

Winston, J., G. Deray, T. Hawkins, L. Szczech, C. Wyatt, and B. Young. 2008. Kidney disease in patients with HIV infection and AIDS. *Clinical Infectious Diseases* 47(11):1449–1457.

Worm, S. W., C. Sabin, R. Weber, P. Reiss, W. El-Sadr, F. Dabis, S. De Wit, M. Law, A. D. Monforte, N. Friis-Møller, O. Kirk, E. Fontas, I. Weller, A. Phillips, and J. Lundgren. 2010. Risk of myocardial infarction in patients with HIV infection exposed to specific individual antiretroviral drugs from the 3 major drug classes: The data collection on adverse events of anti-HIV drugs (D:A:D) study. *Journal of Infectious Diseases* 201(3):318–330.

7

Concepts Specific to Children With HIV/AIDS

HIV infection in children is given unique consideration in practice and research due to the distinct ways the virus is transmitted and how therapy affects the maturing body. The majority of children with HIV infection were infected by their mother via perinatal transmission during pregnancy or delivery, or postpartum through breastfeeding. Perinatal transmission was first recognized in 1985. The number of new cases increased steadily until its peak in the early 1990s. The identification of HIV infection during pregnancy and use of antiretroviral therapy during pregnancy and postpartum to the infant specifically to reduce transmission has been a remarkable success in preventing new HIV infections in children. Through aggressive testing and prophylaxis implementation, the incidence of perinatal HIV infection declined throughout the 2000s. In 2007, the estimated number of new HIV infections among children under age 13 in the 34 states and 5 territories with name-based reporting was 159, a decline from 2004 of 25 percent (CDC, 2009). However, because of increased survival of perinatally infected children, in 2007, nearly 15,500 U.S. children under age 13 lived in the United States (CDC, 2009).

Prior to the availability of antiretroviral therapy, many perinatally infected infants died before their second birthday. As noted below, survival is now markedly improved and many perinatally infected children are aging into adolescence and young adulthood. Understanding of the consequences of early HIV infection in this population is a rapidly evolving field and is the main focus of the majority of current research in pediatric HIV. Consideration of disabilities in this population will need ongoing review to take advantage of new information and findings as they become available.

SURVIVAL AND PROGNOSIS

Children have benefited from advances in treatment in the same patterns as adults. The Pediatric Spectrum of Disease Cohort has clearly demonstrated this improvement as a function of birth year and correlates with the available antiretroviral treatments. Clinical trials to approve antiretrovirals for children were on a delayed timetable compared to adults. By 1994, most children were on a therapy regimen of one or two antiretrovirals. In 1997, combination antiretroviral therapy of two or three drugs, usually including a protease inhibitor, became standard. The birth cohort of 1997 to 2001 had a significantly higher survival than earlier birth cohorts. The benefits of combination antiretroviral therapy beyond reduced mortality include improved functioning of the immune system and reduced complications from comorbid and opportunistic disease (McConnell et al., 2005).

Because of reductions in new infections and improvements in therapy leading to improved survival for infected infants and children, the median age of surviving perinatally infected children was 14.8 years in 2007 and continues to increase. Additionally, the median age of death has increased from 7.2 years in 1994 to 18.2 years in 2006 (Patel et al., 2008).

Successful antiretroviral therapy in young infants and children is challenged by the limited number of agents available as a liquid or powder formulation. Liquid formulations can also require special storage conditions and are often unpalatable. Children with HIV infection have benefited from legislation aimed at expanding available agents for children. Many new agents are being used in children a little over one year from the date they become available for use in adults.

Despite these successes, perinatally infected children who are aging up into adolescence are challenged by decreasing options for therapy. Many of these children received each new antiretroviral when it became available and had sequential courses of mono or dual therapy, resulting in the presence of multiple resistance mutations, especially to the nucleoside reverse transcriptase inhibitor class of agents. These resistance mutations often necessitate the use of complex regimens that further challenge medication adherence (Rakhmanina et al., 2008).

Complications of Perinatal HIV in Growing Children and Adolescents

Although antiretroviral treatment improves prognosis, complications associated with HIV infection and its treatments may occur. Complications include growth abnormalities, developmental and pubertal delay, abnormal metabolic profiles and fat distribution, decreased bone mineral density, and increased mental health disorders. Furthermore, as these perinatally infected children age into adolescence and young adulthood and become sexually active, they are at risk of sexually transmitted diseases and pregnancy. Aside from the increased risk of resistance mutations necessitating more complex antiretroviral regimens, few data are available to detect differences in these complications between birth cohorts that received sequential therapy and those that benefited from combination antiretroviral therapy soon after birth.

Growth

Delayed growth was a common finding in perinatally infected children who were documented to have lower Z scores for health and weight compared to normal values. Slower growth in these children was associated with higher HIV viral loads. With the availability of combination antiretroviral regimens, there were small improvements in height and weight Z scores demonstrated in the PACTG 219C and other international cohorts (Buchacz et al., 2001; Hirschfeld, 1996; Steiner et al., 2001; Verweel et al., 2002). Not surprisingly, the children who demonstrated virologic suppression had better gains than the ones who did not.

In addition to delayed growth, delayed pubertal development has also been reported. Puberty was delayed in HIV-infected girls by 21 months and boys by 15 months. Children with more severe immunosuppression were more likely to experience delayed puberty (Buchacz et al., 2003; de Martino et al., 2001).

Similar to adults with HIV infection, perinatally infected children can also develop lipoatrophy or lipohypertrophy, or a combination of both. These abnormalities can occur in 10 to 33 percent of children and adolescents and can be associated with increases in cholesterol, triglycerides, and insulin resistance. Fat redistribution often becomes apparent during puberty (Aurpibul et al., 2007; Carter et al., 2006; Ene et al., 2007; Lapphra et al., 2005; Rosso et al., 2007; Taylor et al., 2004; Verkauskiene et al., 2006).

The physical appearance of perinatally infected children can be influenced by these aberrations in growth, pubertal development, and fat distribution. Because early adolescent development is characterized by the rapid physiologic body changes of puberty with a heightened awareness of their body image and concern for physical attraction, perinatally infected children may have altered self-images.

Metabolic

Metabolic abnormalities in cholesterol, triglycerides, and insulin that may have long-term effects on cardiac health also have been observed in perinatally HIV-infected children. Abnormal lipid profiles have been reported in 13 to 83 percent of children and are more frequent with the use of protease inhibitors and greater with the use of boosted protease inhibitors. This also occurs in children at a younger age and those who are more adherent and have undetectable viral loads (Tassiopoulos et al., 2008). Insulin resistance has been reported in up to 13 percent and hyperinsulinemia in 60 percent (Carter et al., 2006; Ergun-Longmire et al., 2006; Farley et al., 2005; Lapphra et al., 2005). In addition to metabolic abnormalities, at least three studies have now shown increased intima medial thickness in the carotids of HIV-infected children and adolescents. Older age, protease inhibitor therapy, and duration of antiretroviral therapy appear to increase the risk; however, there was no association with lipid abnormalities or diet. Elevations of inflammatory markers have also been seen (Charakida et al., 2005; Giuliano et al., 2008; McComsey et al., 2007). Taken together, these findings may implicate significant cardiac abnormalities and risk for earlier cardiac disease in this population.

Neurologic

Neurological manifestations of HIV infections are seen more frequently in children than in adults. In the early years of the epidemic, 50 to 90 percent of HIV-infected children showed signs of progressive central nervous system disorders (Lindsey et al., 2007; Singh et al., 2010), which include HIV-associated encephalopathy manifested by limitations in cognitive, language, motor, and behavior functioning. Children can experience delayed acquisition of new developmental milestones or rapid loss of previously attained milestones. Motor abnormalities include hypertonicity, which results in abnormally rigid muscle tone, and hyperreflexia, which are overactive or overresponsive reflexes. The presence of neurologic symptoms can contribute to disability in children by affecting the main domains of childhood functional equivalence recognized by the Social Security Administration—acquiring and using information; attending and completing tasks; interacting and relating with others; moving about and manipulating objects; caring for yourself; and maintaining health and physical well-being. The institution of antiretroviral therapy has resulted in significant improvements in neurologic findings (Faye et al., 2004; Pizzo et al., 1988). Because neurodevelopment is most rapid in the early years of life, earlier HIV treatment may reduce HIV encephalopathy. In the French Perinatal Cohort, HIV-infected infants receiving combination antiretroviral therapy before age 6 months had less encephalopathy compared with those for whom this therapy was initiated after age 6 months (Faye et al., 2004).

Developmental testing has been performed in a subset of the Children with HIV Early Antiretroviral Therapy trial in South Africa. In this clinical trial, HIV-infected infants were randomized to early (beginning within the first 12 weeks of life) as compared to delayed (beginning with clinical or

CD4 indications) combination antiretroviral therapy. Infants in the early therapy group had improved overall and locomotor scores using the Griffiths Mental Development test compared to the delayed group (Laughton et al., 2009). Even in the era of combination antiretroviral therapy, neurological manifestations still present serious challenges for children.

Adherence and Behavioral Challenges

As previously discussed, treatment adherence is a challenge among HIV-infected populations, and is problematic because of the potential of viral mutations resulting in resistance to antiretrovirals. Although children share many of the structural and social barriers to adherence as adults, adherence can be particularly challenging in children due to (1) the frequency of doses or (2) the number of pills to administer per dose, which can create a burden on caregivers who are responsible for ensuring very young children receive their treatment. Furthermore, the treatments available in liquid form are often not palatable. In addition, many perinatally infected children aging into adolescence demonstrate independence and rebellion via nonadherence.

Other behavioral issues associated with adolescence, including sexual debut, have been studied in perinatally infected children. Surprisingly, in one U.S. study, 40 percent of perinatally infected youth ages 9 to 16 reported having unprotected sex (Mellins et al., 2009). Pregnancies have also begun to occur in perinatally infected young women. In the PACTG 219C cohort, 38 of 638 girls became pregnant (6 percent, first pregnancy rate of 18.8/1,000 person years). Thirty-two of these resulted in live births; 29 were HIV uninfected, 1 was HIV infected, and 2 were of unknown status (Brogly et al., 2007).

There is a growing body of literature examining the mental health status of perinatally HIV-infected children. However, isolating the role of HIV infection remains difficult because many of the risk factors associated with mental health disorders overlap with those for HIV (e.g., poverty, disrupted home life, history of mental illness, substance abuse) (Jeremy et al., 2005). Rigorous study designs using validated instruments are just beginning to become available. Mellins et al. (2009) have demonstrated that infected children have greater risk of developing any psychiatric condition, predominantly attention deficit hyperactivity disorder, compared to uninfected control subjects. No differences in risk for developing anxiety or mood disorders or substance abuse were observed. The presence of a mental health disorder was associated with sex and drug use risk behaviors. The use of psychotropic medications is common in HIV-infected youth, with approximately one third receiving some medications in 2003, most commonly antidepressants, stimulants, and antipsychotics (Wiener et al., 2006).

It is now becoming necessary to transition aging up youth to adult care providers. As with many chronic diseases, this can be challenging due to reluctance to leave pediatric and adolescent clinics. Successful transitioning necessitates initiating discussion long before the move occurs and creating an individualized plan. Independence must be encouraged and facilitated, and adolescents need to be educated about their disease state and how to maneuver adult health care systems. A successful transition has the fewest "gaps" in services and results in no decline in HIV-disease status (Judd et al., 2007; Spiegel and Futterman, 2009; Vijayan et al., 2009; Wiener et al., 2007).

RATIONALE FOR LISTING RECOMMENDATIONS FOR PEDIATRIC PATIENTS

Children receiving benefits under Part B (114.08) are required to be reviewed under Part A (14.08) when they reach age 18. Given that many adolescents will be transitioning to adult care around this time, it is especially critical for comprehensive records to be available for disability reassessment. If not readily available, records should be sought from both current and previous providers.

To allow for a smooth transition, the committee recommends that the listing specific to children should follow as closely as possible to the Listing in Part A of the SSA Listing of Impairments.

RECOMMENDATION 6. SSA should ensure that the HIV Infection Listings in Parts A and B of the SSA Listing of Impairments are constructed similarly. However, conditions specific to children not found in adults should also be listed in Part B, including age-appropriate CD4 and developmental criteria, neurological manifestations of HIV infection, and HIV-related growth disturbance.

Listings Based on Age-Specific CD4 Criteria

As discussed in Chapter 3, CD4 count has a strong relationship with outcomes in adults. Based on these findings, the committee has recommended a listing based on CD4 count in adults. Similarly, outcome measures such as CD4 count and percentage, viral load, and number of hospitalizations help to characterize morbidity associated with HIV infection in children. The significance of prognostic measures differs in pediatric patients from those of adults. CD4 count and percentage in healthy, non-HIV-infected infants and young children are significantly higher than those observed in non-HIV-infected adults. As children mature, CD4 counts fluctuate irregularly, slowly declining to correspond with adult values by the time children reach age 5 (Working Group on Antiretroviral Therapy, 2009). Accordingly, CD4 percentage has been most often used as a valid predictive value of a growing child's immune status. The HIV Pediatric Prognostic Markers Collaborative Study assessed laboratory and clinical data from 3,941 HIV-infected children and demonstrated the prognostic value of CD4 percentage and HIV RNA copy number. As in adults, as CD4 declined, there was evidence of HIV progression (Dunn, 2003). Although HIV RNA copy number was also predictive of HIV progression, it was not as strong a predictor as CD4 percentage. This group also studied the predictive value of CD4 count for disease progression and found that patterns in children ages 4 to 5 or older were similar to that observed in adults (HIV Paediatric Prognostic Markers Collaborative Study, 2006).

Because of the differences in CD4 count and percentage and prognosis between children and adults, Recommendation 1 for adults needs to be modified for children. It is desirable to keep the recommendation as similar as possible, and documentation should be easily abstracted from the medical record. Count, percentage, or both may be available in medical records, but research indicates CD4 percentage has little or no prognostic value over and above that of CD4 count (Dunn, 2010). Thus, even though the pediatric guidelines emphasize there is stronger predictability using CD4 percentage in children less than age 4 (Working Group on Antiretroviral Therapy, 2009), CD4 count may be more acceptable at any age (Dunn, 2010). Based on approximate equivalency for the various age groups for HIV disease progression and death, the committee recommends the age-specific CD4 count and percentage criteria for children depicted in Table 7-1 (Dunn, 2010; Dunn et al., 2008).

As in adults, the committee believes claimants allowed under such a listing should be reevaluated periodically for disability status in accordance with the usual SSA process.

Imminently Fatal or Severely Disabling HIV-Associated Conditions

The specific conditions listed in Recommendation 2 in Chapter 4 (HIV-associated dementia, multicentric Castleman's disease, Kaposi's sarcoma

TABLE 7-1 Proposed Disabling CD4 Count Ranges for Children

Age Range	Suggested CD4 Count	Suggested CD4 Percentage
< 1 year	≤ 500 cells/mm^3	< 15 percent
1–5 years	≤ 200 cells/mm^3	< 15 percent
> 5 years	≤ 50 cells/mm^3	N/A

NOTE: N/A = not applicable.

involving the pulmonary parenchyma, primary central nervous system lymphomas, primary effusion lymphoma, and progressive multifocal leukoencephalopathy) are rare in children, but have been reported. Accordingly, a similar listing should be included in the pediatric HIV Infection Listing. Modifications should include the replacement of HIV-associated dementia with the current listing for neurological manifestations of HIV infection (currently 114.08G). Even in the era of combination antiretroviral therapy, neurological manifestations still present serious challenges for children. Therefore, neurological manifestations in children and adolescents should be maintained under Part B. The presence of neurological manifestations in children serves as an indicator of disease severity and progression resulting in higher mortality rates among those children who have been diagnosed with early onset (Mitchell, 2001). Neurological manifestations can be characterized by the following:

- *Impaired brain growth.* Impaired brain growth is the decrease in serial measurements of head circumference velocity and is typically seen in children under age 2 (Mintz, 1996). This condition can lead to microcephaly or brain atrophy. Older children who develop impaired brain growth do so at a slower rate, and it is similar to that seen in adults (Mitchell, 2001).
- *Progressive motor dysfunction.* Progressive motor dysfunction is when motor milestones are not achieved. It is possible to have once attained these milestones, but lose the ability to perform them, resulting in the impairment of fine and gross motor skills (Mintz, 1996).
- *Loss of previously acquired or delay of developmental milestones and intellectual ability.* This is the plateau of acquisition or a regression of age-appropriate neurodevelopmental milestones, which can be standard developmental scales or neuropsychological tests. Such loss is often seen more in school-age children, thus labeling them as "at risk" (Mitchell, 2001).

In addition, growth development is an important indicator of children's health and is seen as one of the most sensitive indicators of disease progression (Hirschfeld, 1996). Growth disturbance or failure to grow has been associated with rapid progression from asymptomatic HIV infection to AIDS in children, thus leading to shorter survival (Baylor International Pediatric AIDS Initiative, 2010). As a result, the committee concluded that the current listing for growth disturbance (currently 114.08H) should be retained in Part B.

HIV-Associated Comorbidities Currently Without Listings

Similar to adults, many of these comorbidities also occur in children, including those related to HIV infection itself and to medications used to treat HIV. Because of these similarities, the committee recommends a parallel listing for children. However, the listing should be modified to remove HIV-associated wasting syndrome and neurocognitive disorder, which are similar to the current listings 114.08F and 114.08G and recommended to be retained as discussed above. In addition, functional assessments in children must be age and developmentally appropriate. The listing in Part B would therefore include the following conditions:

- Diarrhea;
- Distal sensory polyneuropathy;
- Kaposi's sarcoma;
- Lipoatrophy or lipohypertrophy; and
- Osteoporosis.

Recommendation 4 in adults, which focuses on comorbidities, should be modified to replace activities of daily living, maintenance of social functioning, and completion of tasks in a timely manner with current Part B listings that address developmental and emotional disorders of newborn and younger infants (currently paragraphs A–E of 112.12) and organic mental disorders (currently paragraphs B1–2 of 112.02).

HIV-Associated Comorbidities Currently With Listings

While the conditions contained in Recommendation 5 are not common in children (cardiovascular disease, chronic kidney disease, diabetes, hepatitis, and malignancies), they do occur and may become more evident as perinatally infected children continue to age. Additionally, there are current pediatric listings for these conditions that would be applicable. Therefore, the committee recommends that Recommendation 5 should also apply to the Part B HIV Infection Listing.

Lymphocytic Interstitial Pneumonia/Pulmonary Lymphoid Hyperplasia Complex

The committee decided the lymphoid interstitial pneumonia/pulmonary lymphoid hyperplasia complex (current 114.08J) should be removed from the HIV Infection Listing. Lymphocytic interstitial pneumonia/pulmonary lymphoid hyperplasia complex is an HIV-associated disease with no known etiology. It was commonly observed in HIV-infected children before the availability of combination antiretroviral therapy. In 1987, the Centers for Disease Control and Prevention (CDC) classified lymphocytic interstitial pneumonia/pulmonary lymphoid hyperplasia complex as a category C (severely symptomatic) AIDS-defining illness in children (Lynch et al., 2001). However, studies have since shown that it is not associated with shorter survival in HIV-infected children and that the presence of lymphocytic interstitial pneumonia/pulmonary lymphoid hyperplasia complex is actually seen as having improved the survival rates (de Martino et al., 1991; Lynch et al., 2001). This finding has prompted changes to the way the complex is considered. For example, in 1994 the CDC redefined the classification as a category B (moderately symptomatic) AIDS-defining illness in children (CDC, 1994).

REFERENCES

Aurpibul, L., T. Puthanakit, B. Lee, A. Mangklabruks, T. Sirisanthana, and V. Sirisanthana. 2007. Lipodystrophy and metabolic changes in HIV-infected children on non-nucleoside reverse transcriptase inhibitor-based antiretroviral therapy. *Antiviral Therapy* 12(8): 1247–1254.

Baylor International Pediatric AIDS Initiative. 2010. In *HIV curriculum for the health professional*, edited by G. Waggonner. Houston, TX: Baylor College of Medicine. http://bayloraids.org/curriculum/files/complete_highres.pdf (accessed April 20, 2010).

Brogly, S. B., D. H. Watts, N. Ylitalo, E. L. Franco, G. R. Seage III, J. Oleske, M. Eagle, and R. Van Dyke. 2007. Reproductive health of adolescent girls perinatally infected with HIV. *American Journal of Public Health* 97(6):1047–1052.

Buchacz, K., J. S. Cervia, J. C. Lindsey, M. D. Hughes, G. R. Seage III, W. M. Dankner, J. M. Oleske, and J. Moye. 2001. Impact of protease inhibitor-containing combination antiretroviral therapies on height and weight growth in HIV-infected children. *Pediatrics* 108(4):e72.

Buchacz, K., A. D. Rogol, J. C. Lindsey, C. M. Wilson, M. D. Hughes, G. R. Seage III, J. M. Oleske, A. S. Rogers, and the Pediatric AIDS Clinical Trials Group 219 Study Team. 2003. Delayed onset of pubertal development in children and adolescents with perinatally acquired HIV infection. *Journal of Acquired Immune Deficiency Syndromes* 33(1):56–65.

Carter, R. J., J. Wiener, E. J. Abrams, J. Farley, S. Nesheim, P. Palumbo, and M. Bulterys for the Perinatal AIDS Collaborative Transmission Study—HIV Follow-up after Perinatal Exposure Group. 2006. Dyslipidemia among perinatally HIV-infected children enrolled in the PACTS-HOPE cohort, 1999–2004: A longitudinal analysis. *Journal of Acquired Immune Deficiency Syndromes* 41(4):453–460.

CDC (Centers for Disease Control and Prevention). 1994. Revised classification system for HIV-infection in children less than 13 years of age. *Morbidity and Mortality Weekly Report* 43:1–10.

CDC. 2009. *Cases of HIV Infection and AIDS in the United States and Dependent Areas, 2007, Table 1.* http://www.cdc.gov/hiv/topics/surveillance/resources/reports/2007report/pdf/table1.pdf (accessed May 7, 2010).

Charakida, M., A. E. Donald, H. Green, C. Storry, M. Clapson, M. Caslake, D. T. Dunn, J. P. Halcox, D. M. Gibb, N. J. Klein, and J. E. Deanfield. 2005. Early structural and functional changes of the vasculature in HIV-infected children: Impact of disease and antiretroviral therapy. *Circulation* 112(1):103–109.

de Martino, M., P.-A. Tovo, L. Galli, C. Gabiano, S. Cozzani, C. Gotta, G. Scarlatti, A. Fiocchi, P. Cocchi, P. Marchisio, R. Canino, A. Mautone, F. Chiappe, A. Campelli, R. Consolini, G. Izzi, A. Laverda, S. Alberti, A. E. Tozzi, and M. Duse. 1991. Prognostic significance of immunologic changes in 675 infants perinatally exposed to human immunodeficiency virus. *The Journal of Pediatrics* 119(5):702–709.

de Martino, M., P.-A. Tovo, L. Galli, C. Gabiano, F. Chiarelli, M. Zappa, G. C. Gattinara, D. Bassetti, V. Giacomet, E. Chiappini, M. Duse, S. Garetto, and D. Caselli for the Italian Register for HIV Infection in Children. 2001. Puberty in perinatal HIV-1 infection: A multicentre longitudinal study of 212 children. *AIDS* 15(12):1527–1534.

Dunn, D. 2003. Short-term risk of disease progression in HIV-1-infected children receiving no antiretroviral therapy or zidovudine monotherapy: A meta-analysis. *Lancet* 362(9396): 1605–1611.

Dunn, D. 2010. Discordance between CD4 cell count and CD4 cell percentage: Implications for when to start antiretroviral therapy in HIV-1 infected children. *AIDS* 24(8): 1213–1217.

Dunn, D., P. Woodburn, T. Duong, J. Peto, A. Phillips, D. Gibb, and K. Porter. 2008. Current CD4 cell count and the short-term risk of AIDS and death before the availability of effective antiretroviral therapy in HIV-infected children and adults. *Journal of Infectious Diseases* 197(3):398–404.

Ene, L., T. Goetghebuer, M. Hainaut, A. Peltier, V. Toppet, and J. Levy. 2007. Prevalence of lipodystrophy in HIV-infected children: A cross-sectional study. *European Journal of Pediatrics* 166(1):13–21.

Ergun-Longmire, B., K. Lin-Su, A. M. Dunn, L. Chan, K. Ham, C. Sison, J. Stavola, and M. G. Vogiatzi. 2006. Effects of protease inhibitors on glucose tolerance, lipid metabolism, and body composition in children and adolescents infected with human immunodeficiency virus. *Endocrine Practice* 12(5):514–521.

Farley, J., P. Gona, M. Crain, J. Cervia, J. Oleske, G. Seage, and J. Lindsey for the Pediatric AIDS Clinical Trials Group Study 219C Team. 2005. Prevalence of elevated cholesterol and associated risk factors among perinatally HIV-infected children (4–19 years old) in Pediatric AIDS Clinical Trials Group 219C. *Journal of Acquired Immune Deficiency Syndromes* 38(4):480–487.

Faye, A., J. Le Chenadec, C. Dollfus, I. Thuret, D. Douard, G. Firtion, E. Lachassinne, M. Levine, J. Nicolas, F. Monpoux, J. Tricoire, C. Rouzioux, M. Tardieu, M. J. Mayaux, and S. Blanche. 2004. Early versus deferred antiretroviral multidrug therapy in infants infected with HIV type 1. *Clinical Infectious Diseases* 39(11):1692–1698.

Giuliano, I., S. de Freitas, M. de Souza, and B. Caramelli. 2008. Subclinic atherosclerosis and cardiovascular risk factors in HIV-infected children: PERI study. *Coronary Artery Disease* 19(3):167–172.

Hirschfeld, S. 1996. Dysregulation of growth and development in HIV-infected children. *Journal of Nutrition* 126(Suppl 10):2641S–2650S.

HIV Paediatric Prognostic Markers Collaborative Study. 2006. Predictive value of absolute CD4 cell count for disease progression in untreated HIV-1–infected children. *AIDS* 20(9):1289–1294.

Jeremy, R. J., S. Kim, M. Nozyce, S. Nachman, K. McIntosh, S. I. Pelton, R. Yogev, A. Wiznia, G. M. Johnson, P. Krogstad, and K. Stanley for the Pediatric AIDS Clinical Trials Group 338, and 377 Study Teams. 2005. Neuropsychological functioning and viral load in stable antiretroviral therapy-experienced HIV-infected children. *Pediatrics* 115(2):380–387.

Judd, A., K. Doerholt, P. A. Tookey, M. Sharland, A. Riordan, E. Menson, V. Novelli, E. G. H. Lyall, J. Masters, G. Tudor-Williams, T. Duong, and D. M. Gibb for the Collaborative HIV Paediatric Study and the National Study of HIV in Pregnancy and Childhood. 2007. Morbidity, mortality, and response to treatment by children in the United Kingdom and Ireland with perinatally acquired HIV infection during 1996–2006: Planning for teenage and adult care. *Clinical Infectious Diseases* 45(7):918–924.

Lapphra, K., N. Vanprapar, W. Phongsamart, P. Chearskul, and K. Chokephaibulkit. 2005. Dyslipidemia and lipodystrophy in HIV-infected Thai children on highly active antiretroviral therapy (HAART). *Journal of the Medical Association of Thailand* 88(7):956–966.

Laughton, B., D. Grove, M. Kidd, P. Springer, E. Dobbels, B. Janse Van Rensburg, A. Violari, A. Babiker, S. A. Madhi, P. Jean-Phillippe, D. M. Gibb, and M. F. Cotton. 2009. Early antiretroviral therapy is associated with improved neurodevelopmental outcome in HIV infected infants: Evidence from the CHER (children with HIV early antiretroviral therapy) trial. Paper read at the 5th International AIDS Society Conference on HIV Pathogenesis and Treatment Cape Town, South Africa, July 19–22.

Lindsey, J. C., K. M. Malee, P. Brouwers, and M. D. Hughes. 2007. Neurodevelopmental functioning in HIV-infected infants and young children before and after the introduction of protease inhibitor-based highly active antiretroviral therapy. *Pediatrics* 119(3): e681–e693.

Lynch, J. L., J. G. Blickman, D. C. terMeulen, F. E. Babl, C. H. Moloney, and S. I. Pelton. 2001. Radiographic resolution of lymphocytic interstitial pneumonitis (LIP) in children with human immunodeficiency virus (HIV): Not a sign of clinical deterioration. *Pediatric Radiology* 31:299–303.

McComsey, G. A., M. O'Riordan, S. L. Hazen, D. El-Bejjani, S. Bhatt, M.-L. Brennan, N. Storer, J. Adell, D. A. Nakamoto, and V. Dogra. 2007. Increased carotid intima media thickness and cardiac biomarkers in HIV infected children. *AIDS* 21(8):921–927.

McConnell, M., R. H. Byers, T. Frederick, V. Peters, K. Dominguez, T. Sukalac, A. Greenberg, H.-W. Hsu, T. Rakusan, I. Ortiz, S. K. Melville, and M. G. Fowler for the Pediatric Spectrum HIV Disease Consortium. 2005. Trends in antiretroviral therapy use and survival rates for a large cohort of HIV-infected children and adolescents in the United States, 1989–2001. *Journal of Acquired Immune Deficiency Syndromes* 38(4):488–494.

Mellins, C. A., K. S. Elkington, J. A. Bauermeister, E. Brackis-Cott, C. Dolezal, M. McKay, A. Wiznia, M. Bamji, and E. J. Abrams. 2009. Sexual and drug use behavior in perinatally HIV-infected youth: Mental health and family influences. *Journal of the American Academy of Child and Adolescent Psychiatry* 48(8):810–819.

Mintz, M. 1996. Neurological and developmental problems in pediatric HIV infection. *Journal of Nutrition* 126(Suppl 10):2663S–2673S.

Mitchell, W. 2001. Neurological and developmental effects of HIV and AIDS in children and adolescents. *Mental Retardation and Developmental Disabilities Research Reviews* 7(3):211–216.

Patel, K., M. A. Hernán, P. L. Williams, J. D. Seeger, K. McIntosh, R. B. Van Dyke, and G. R. Seage III. 2008. Long-term effectiveness of highly active antiretroviral therapy on the survival of children and adolescents with HIV infection: A 10-year follow-up study. *Clinical Infectious Diseases* 46(4):507–515.

Pizzo, P. A., J. Eddy, J. Falloon, F. M. Balis, R. F. Murphy, H. Moss, P. Wolters, P. Brouwers, P. Jarosinski, M. Rubin, S. Broder, R. Yarchoan, A. Brunetti, M. Maha, S. Nusinoff-Lehrman, and D. G. Poplack. 1988. Effect of continuous intravenous infusion of zidovudine (AZT) in children with symptomatic HIV infection. *New England Journal of Medicine* 319(14):889–896.

Rakhmanina, N. Y., E. V. Capparelli, and J. N. van den Anker. 2008. Personalized therapeutics: HIV treatment in adolescents. *Clinical Pharmacology & Therapeutics* 84(6):734–740.

Rosso, R., A. Parodi, G. d'Annunzio, F. Ginocchio, L. Nicolini, C. Torrisi, M. P. Sormani, R. Lorini, C. Viscoli, and M. Vignolo. 2007. Evaluation of insulin resistance in a cohort of HIV-infected youth. *European Journal of Endocrinology* 157(5):655–659.

Singh, K., W. Sambisa, S. Munyati, B. Chandiwana, A. Chingono, R. Monash, and S. Weir. 2010. Targeting HIV interventions for adolescent girls and young women in Southern Africa: Use of the PLACE methodology in Hwange District, Zimbabwe. *AIDS and Behavior* 14(1):200–208.

Spiegel, H. M. L., and D. C. Futterman. 2009. Adolescents and HIV: Prevention and clinical care. *Current HIV/AIDS Reports* 6(2):100–107.

Steiner, F., C. Kind, C. Aebi, C.-A. Wyler-Lazarevitch, J.-J. Cheseaux, C. Rudin, L. Molinari, and D. Nadal. 2001. Growth in human immunodeficiency virus type 1-infected children treated with protease inhibitors. *European Journal of Pediatrics* 160(10):611.

Tassiopoulos, K., P. L. Williams, G. R. Seage, M. Crain, J. Oleske, and J. Farley for the International Maternal Pediatric Adolescent AIDS Clinical Trials 219C Team. 2008. Association of hypercholesterolemia incidence with antiretroviral treatment, including protease inhibitors, among perinatally HIV-infected children. *Journal of Acquired Immune Deficiency Syndromes* 47(5):607–614.

Taylor, P., C. Worrell, S. M. Steinberg, R. Hazra, S. Jankelevich, L. V. Wood, S. Zwerski, R. Yarchoan, and S. Zeichner. 2004. Natural history of lipid abnormalities and fat redistribution among human immunodeficiency virus-infected children receiving long-term, protease inhibitor-containing, highly active antiretroviral therapy regimens. *Pediatrics* 114(2):e235–e242.

Verkauskiene, R., C. Dollfus, M. Levine, A. Faye, S. Deghmoun, M. Houang, D. Chevenne, J.-L. Bresson, S. Blanche, and C. Levy-Marchal. 2006. Serum adiponectin and leptin concentrations in HIV-infected children with fat redistribution syndrome. *Pediatric Research* 60(2):225–230.

Verweel, G., A. van Rossum, N. G. Hartwig, T. Wolfs, H. J. Scherpbier, and R. de Groot. 2002. Treatment with highly active antiretroviral therapy in human immunodeficiency virus type 1-infected children is associated with a sustained effect on growth. *Pediatrics* 109(2):e25.

Vijayan, T., A. L. Benin, K. Wagner, S. Romano, and W. A. Andiman. 2009. We never thought this would happen: Transitioning care of adolescents with perinatally acquired HIV infection from pediatrics to internal medicine. *AIDS Care Psychological and Socio-Medical Aspects of AIDS/HIV* 21(10):1222–1229.

Wiener, L., H. Battles, C. Ryder, and M. Pao. 2006. Psychotropic medication use in human immunodeficiency virus-infected youth receiving treatment at a single institution. *Journal of Child and Adolescent Psychopharmacology* 16(6):747–753.

Wiener, L. S., M. Zobel, H. Battles, and C. Ryder. 2007. Transition from a pediatric HIV intramural clinical research program to adolescent and adult community-based care services: Assessing transition readiness. *Social Work in Health Care* 46(1):1–19.

Working Group on Antiretroviral Therapy and Medical Management of HIV-Infected Children. 2009. *Guidelines for the use of antiretroviral agents in pediatric HIV-infection.* http://aidsinfo.nih.gov/ContentFiles/PediatricGuidelines.pdf (accessed May 20, 2010).

8

Maximizing the Utility of the HIV Infection Listings

Previous chapters identified ways to redesign the HIV Infection Listings, with the goal of reliably and validly identifying people who are disabled in the context of current medical practice. With improvements in treatment, HIV/AIDS is now a chronic disease with improved patient longevity. The success of the HIV Infection Listings will depend on how they are used; this chapter recommends approaches to ensure its proper and effective implementation.

INTRODUCTORY TEXT

The committee determined that the introductory text (14.00 and 114.00) should be reviewed separately from the sublistings (14.08A to 14.08K and 114.08A to 114.08L), and should be revised based on changes made to them.

The introductory text precedes each body system, or section, of the Listing of Impairments and contains varying amounts of detail for each body system. The purpose of the introductory text is to clearly explain how the listings in each section are to be implemented. The intended audience is broad and includes claimants and their families, the general public, disability examiners, medical consultants, and adjudicators. Currently the introductory text for the HIV Infection Listings is woven throughout the Immune System Disorders Listing.

The committee heard from disability examiners and medical consultants that the introductory text for the HIV Infection Listings provides helpful guidance for implementing the listings. At the same time, many indicated it was confusing, disjointed, and difficult to read.

Reflect Changes in the Listings

The committee concluded that the introductory text should be revised to reflect the changes made in the HIV Infection Listings. If the Social Security Administration (SSA) decides to adopt the four categories described in Chapters 3 through 7 (i.e., CD4 $\leq$ 50 cells/mm^3, imminently fatal or severely disabling HIV-associated conditions, HIV-associated conditions without listings elsewhere in the Listing of Impairments, and HIV-associated conditions with listings elsewhere), brief explanations of each category should be included in the introductory text. Current concepts in HIV, such as those identified in Chapter 2, also need to be incorporated into the introductory text.

Simplify Language

The current introductory text of the HIV Infection Listings is long, not well organized, and highly technical. Detailed clinical descriptions pertain mostly to disability examiners and medical consultants, while the general discussion about what qualifies as a disabling condition is most useful for patients, their families, and advocates. In an effort to make the introductory text more audience appropriate and better organized, the committee suggests reorganizing the text to focus on the broad, general issues and to put the highly technical discussions into a different section.

One example is the discussion of how HIV is diagnosed. A way to simplify this would be to adopt the Department of Health and Human Services (HHS) guidelines for diagnosing HIV infection instead of including specific diagnostic methods in the introductory text. If SSA decides it is necessary to include diagnostic methods in the introduction, it should follow the HHS guidelines. Adopting guidelines from HHS and professional societies about the management of HIV infection would allow for the introduction to stay more current, and would require fewer updates as the management of HIV infection evolves.

To this end, the committee believes it would be prudent to separate the technical details from the basic overview of the HIV Infection Listings. The introductory text should be split into two pieces: general principles and technical overview.

General Principles

The general principles portion would be aimed at the general public and explain how the Listings are organized. A short opening section describing the evolution of HIV from an almost uniformly fatal disease to a chronic, complex, largely treatable disease is needed to provide some context for changes made to the Listings. This section needs to:

- Acknowledge that the ability to manage HIV infection has improved considerably, but a number of severe complications associated with HIV infection can persist and can be disabling;
- Address the possible adverse effects of treatment, which can become chronic and disabling; and
- Recognize that CD4 $\leq$ 50 cells/mm^3 is a surrogate marker of immune function in HIV-infected individuals and can indicate chronic disability and generally poor outcomes (e.g., progressive disability).

Technical Overview

The technical overview portion envisioned by the committee would describe specifics about the sublistings to help disability examiners, medical consultants, and adjudicators make decisions based on the HIV Infection Listings. This portion would include definitions and specific clinical details of disease manifestations. Although the language will be necessarily technical, it needs to be written in a clear and simple manner.

The committee recognizes the desire for the sublistings to avoid repetition of the introduction, but it learned that the introductory text and sublistings are not always used together. Therefore, definitions of the manifestations identified in previous chapters should be considered for inclusion in both the sublistings and the introduction.

Make User Friendly

To facilitate use of the Listing of Impairments, a cross-index ought to be developed that includes hyperlinks to the Internet version of the Listings. This would make them more user friendly for the public.

RECOMMENDATION 7. SSA should rewrite the introductory text for Parts A and B of the SSA Listing of Impairments by:

a. Simplifying and reorganizing the text to address the appropriate audiences; and

b. Consolidating all HIV references into one section.

REEVALUATING THE LISTINGS

Understanding of the effects of HIV disease and its associated conditions and treatment is continuously evolving. As HIV-infected persons are living longer on effective treatment regimens, new sources of illness are likely to develop. For example, the effects of HIV and treatments on cardiovascular disease and cognition are now emerging. To best meet claimants' needs, the Listings ought to continuously reflect advances in the clinical understanding of how HIV and its treatments affect health.

Potential Areas for Future Revisions

In future revisions, reflecting changes in the management and care of HIV infection will be important. Areas of particular concern for future assessments include long-term adverse events of treatment, newly emerging clinical manifestations of HIV infection, and consequences of nonadherence and resistance to antiretroviral therapies. SSA ought to monitor these issues and others that may potentially be added to the HIV Infection Listings as appropriate.

First, the long-term impacts of HIV and its treatment are still largely unknown because HIV disease did not become a chronic, manageable infection until combination antiretroviral therapies were widely introduced in the mid-1990s. Identifying all the effects from antiretroviral therapies could take many years as people use established and new combinations of them. Adverse effects of treatment with the potential to prevent people from performing daily activities will continue to evolve and may need to be addressed in the HIV Infection Listings.

Second, as discussed in previous chapters, HIV infection affects multiple body systems. With the evolution into a chronic disease with improved longevity, new disease conditions may arise that could cause severe impairments. For example, the impact of HIV on increasing risk of cardiovascular disease was not recognized until recently, and the impact of HIV infection on neurocognitive function with long-term survival is largely unknown. It is also possible that some impairments may also lessen or even disappear over time as new therapies are developed.

Finally, because HIV is perpetually replicating and evolving, complications of nonadherence and resistance is another issue to consider in future revisions of the HIV Infection Listings. Resistance can result from a number of causes, such as nonadherence and individual pharmacodynamics, which can lead to severe adverse health outcomes similar to those that occurred before widespread use of combination antiretroviral therapy. As the nature of treatment evolves, new patterns of resistance are likely to emerge. Transmitted resistance may also become an important factor to consider due to its potential to reduce treatment options.

Revision Process

SSA will need to create HIV Infection Listings that are both flexible enough and broad enough to reflect advances in HIV therapy. Although additions and revisions to the Listings will likely be needed, removal of some sublistings may also become necessary. The Listings also will need periodic revision to add, remove, or modify criteria to maintain its currency.

The committee understands that a process is in place for SSA to revise all the listings. This process typically involves evaluating an entire body system at one time and evaluating individual listings on a less frequent basis. However, given the rapidly evolving science of HIV disease and the pace of therapeutic advances in modern medicine, SSA may consider employing a more focused process that continuously assesses specific conditions.

USE OF DATA

Data can be very informative in making the HIV Infection Listings as effective as possible. SSA collects detailed data on each claim submitted and to an extent uses these data to inform its process. The data SSA collected about the HIV Infection Listings were very helpful to the committee in understanding how they are used. For example, the total number of allowances and denials for each sublisting showed that only a handful of claims were adjudicated under 14.08J in 2009, bringing into question the need to include it in a revision of the Listings. Patterns in the data also indicate that *Pneumocystis* pneumonia (PCP) infection accounts for more than 20 percent of all HIV allowances since 1999. Because PCP can now generally be treated effectively, this criterion is outdated; this suggests that many claimants continue to qualify for disability based on a history of ever having had PCP and not necessarily on current ability to work.

Specific data about the number of allowances that equal each sublisting could also be used to determine which sublistings may require modification. For instance, nearly half of 14.08K allowances medically equaled the Listing, suggesting it may be too narrow or out of date. Other analyses of equals allowances could reveal that a condition not in that listing is becoming increasingly prevalent. Similarly, if the number of medical–vocational allowances for a specific sublisting is high, it may indicate that the sublisting is too strict, forcing cases that should be allowed in Step 3 (the Listings Step) to be decided in the more time intensive and costly Steps 4 and 5. These data collected by SSA are key to identifying patterns that can inform the relevancy of the Listings and can provide a framework for revisions.

Currently, SSA's data are not available for public use. Making deidentified data publicly accessible and available for relevant analysis could result in improved timeliness and applicability of the HIV Infection Listings. The process of making these deidentified data accessible for improved scholarship could follow a process similar to that of the Centers for Medicare and Medicaid Services or the National Institutes of Health.

RECOMMENDATION 8. SSA should use its database to maximize the utility of the HIV Infection Listings by:

- **a. Collecting and analyzing data to evaluate their effectiveness; and**
- **b. Making data more widely accessible for outside analysis to better inform their currency and efficiency.**

INFORMATION: MEDICAL RECORDS AND SSA DISABILITY FORMS

The initial information SSA uses to adjudicate a claim is generally acquired through the medical record, SSA disability application forms, and supplemental documents submitted by health professionals. Although most information used at the Listings Step is found in the medical record, this information is not always complete or of high enough quality to adequately make a determination. The medical record is developed by health professionals primarily to follow a person's health history, not extent of disability, but the poor quality of record keeping is part of the problem. As a result, SSA must use more resources to seek additional information. Many Disability Determination Services have developed forms specifically to supplement HIV claims so that disability examiners and medical consultants have adequate information at the beginning of a decision process, saving time and resources. This reflects a need for SSA's application forms to be updated.

The committee expects that the forms will be updated to reflect revisions to the Listings and include measures of impairment, disability, and functioning. The forms should also be responsive to the decision-making needs of disability examiners and medical consultants.

ACCEPTABLE SOURCES OF INFORMATION

The information that SSA uses to make its decisions often comes from a claimant's "treating source," which includes "acceptable medical sources" and "other sources"[1] who can provide relevant information regarding a claimant's impairment. As described in Chapter 1, "acceptable medical sources" are limited to physicians, osteopaths, optometrists, psychologists, podiatrists, and speech-language pathologists. The opinions of these clinicians are often given controlling weight over "other sources."

"Other sources" are defined as those who can help provide supporting opinions in areas such as prognosis and physical and mental restrictions. When such sources have more meaningful and informative interactions with the claimant, these opinions receive equal weight or can outweigh those of acceptable medical sources.

Overall, SSA's regulations and rules make it seem that the opinions of "other sources" are not as important as those of the "treating source." Other sources may not be appropriate with respect to diagnosing HIV infec-

---

[1] Other sources are defined by SSA to "include public and private agencies; nonmedical sources such as schools, parents and caregivers, social workers and employers; and other practitioners such as naturopaths, chiropractors, and audiologists" (http://www.ssa.gov/disability/professionals/bluebook/evidentiary.htm).

tion and its manifestations, but their expertise can be particularly important when assessing whether a claimant meets a sublisting with a functional requirement (e.g., ability to perform activities of daily living). The opinions of other practitioners may be more appropriate in determining the severity of a claimant's disability, including other allied health professionals, such as advanced-practice nurses and rehabilitation counselors.

When evaluating a claimant's level of functioning and ability to work, a broader base of expertise may be needed to ensure that the most informed health professional is assessing the claim, as expressed in SSR 06-03p.[2] In these situations, the opinions of other practitioners have equal or greater applicability to the disability decision than those of the professionals listed as "acceptable medical sources." The committee concludes that SSA should consider including a wide array of licensed health professionals as acceptable medical sources (e.g., nurses, dentists, allied health professionals) for determining the functional effects of impairments.

TRAINING OF DISABILITY EXAMINERS AND MEDICAL CONSULTANTS

The committee recognizes that training of disability examiners and medical consultants is critical to implementing the HIV Infection Listings. Disability examiners and medical consultants are an important part of ensuring the effectiveness of the Listings and can provide critical feedback about how well the Listings are functioning. Disability examiners and medical consultants are rarely HIV specialists, but they have the most responsibility for implementing the Listings. They are challenged not only by the need to keep up to date with a quickly evolving disease, but also by large case loads that require knowledge of a wide variety of conditions and body systems.

The HIV Infection Listings can only be broadly effective if they are applied consistently across the country. However, training of disability examiners and medical consultants occur at the state level and can lead to regional differences in interpretation of the Listings. Training curriculums vary by state, usually requiring an 8- to 12-week course for disability examiners and an approximately 12-week process for medical consultants. Other on-the-job training often follows the formal training course. The National Association for Disability Examiners offers a voluntary certification program, and training conferences are held nationally. However, no

[2]SSR 06-03p is a ruling called "Considering Opinions and Other Evidence from Sources Who Are Not 'Acceptable Medical Sources' in Disability Claims; Considering Decisions on Disability by Other Governmental and Nongovernmental Agencies," which explains SSA's policy on opinions from nonacceptable medical sources.

mandatory national training curriculum exists to ensure that disability examiners and medical consultants interpret listings consistently across states and regions.

Training provides these personnel with the necessary background to accurately determine whether a claim meets or equals a listing. For example, the disability examiner/medical consultant team must be confident in its ability to interpret a listing and apply it to determine that a claimant has a limitation on activities of daily living, maintains social functioning, and completes tasks in a timely manner (the functional criteria in the current 14.08K sublisting). This information can be subjective and is not easily derived from the medical record. If the team is not able to accurately identify these limitations, cases that should be determined at Step 3 may unnecessarily progress to Steps 4 and 5, resulting in inefficiencies. By the same token, an incorrect allowance may be made at Step 3. Training on the technical details of the HIV Infection Listings and the most current advances in HIV medicine are essential to correctly interpreting and applying the Listings. As in continuing medical education, continuing training of medical examiners and disability examiners is also expected to enhance the professionalism and reduce turnover of these key personnel.

RESEARCH ON FUNCTIONAL ASSESSMENT AND RETURN TO WORK

As discussed in Chapter 5 and Appendix D, the committee believes assessment of functional capacity is necessary for identifying the severity of a person's disability. Ideally, an objective predictive measure of HIV-related employment disability would be available to assess whether a claimant would be able to work. Such a measure could be coupled with evidence of a claimant's medical condition to determine the severity of disability at Step 3.

The current knowledge base about functioning and return to work for people living with HIV/AIDS is limited, though research is likely to expand as they live longer. Areas of needed research include (1) how medical, psychosocial, financial/legal, and vocational factors impact functional limitations, and (2) how well a person's ability to function is impacted by the fit between the person and his work environment (Conyers and Braveman, 2010). Conclusive research about valid measures of functioning and returning to work could greatly improve the HIV Infection Listings.

REFERENCE

Conyers, L., and B. Braveman. 2010. *HIV/AIDS and employment*. Paper presented at Workshop of the IOM Committee on Social Security HIV Disability Criteria, Irvine, CA.

Appendix A

Current HIV Infection Listings (14.08 and 114.08)

CURRENT LISTING OF IMPAIRMENTS

Part A

The following sections in Part A are applicable to individuals age 18 and over and to children under age 18 where criteria are appropriate.

Section
1.00 Musculoskeletal System
2.00 Special Senses and Speech
3.00 Respiratory System
4.00 Cardiovascular System
5.00 Digestive System
6.00 Genitourinary Impairments
7.00 Hematological Disorders
8.00 Skin Disorders
9.00 Endocrine System
10.00 Impairments That Affect Multiple Body Systems
11.00 Neurological
12.00 Mental Disorders
13.00 Malignant Neoplastic Diseases
14.00 Immune System Disorders

HIV Infection Listing Introductory Text

14.00A. *What disorders do we evaluate under the immune system disorders listings?*
1. *We evaluate immune system disorders that cause dysfunction in one or more components of your immune system.*

a. The dysfunction may be due to problems in antibody production, impaired cell mediated immunity, a combined type of antibody/cellular deficiency, impaired phagocytes, or complement deficiency.

b. Immune system disorders may result in recurrent and unusual infections, or inflammation and dysfunction of the body's own tissues. Immune system disorders can cause a deficit in a single organ or body system that results in extreme (that is, very serious) loss of function. They can also cause lesser degrees of limitations in two or more organs or body systems, and when associated with symptoms or signs, such as severe fatigue, fever, malaise, diffuse musculoskeletal pain, or involuntary weight loss, can also result in extreme limitation.

c. We organize the discussions of immune system disorders in three categories: autoimmune disorders; immune deficiency disorders, excluding human immunodeficiency virus (HIV) infection; and HIV infection.

2. *Autoimmune disorders (14.00D).* Autoimmune disorders are caused by dysfunctional immune responses directed against the body's own tissues, resulting in chronic, multisystem impairments that differ in clinical manifestations, course, and outcome. They are sometimes referred to as rheumatic diseases, connective tissue disorders, or collagen vascular disorders. Some of the features of autoimmune disorders in adults differ from the features of the same disorders in children.

3. *Immune deficiency disorders, excluding HIV infection (14.00E).* Immune deficiency disorders are characterized by recurrent or unusual infections that respond poorly to treatment, and are often associated with complications affecting other parts of the body. Immune deficiency disorders are classified as either *primary* (congenital) or *acquired.* Individuals with immune deficiency disorders also have an increased risk of malignancies and of having autoimmune disorders.

4. *Human immunodeficiency virus (HIV) infection (14.00F).* HIV infection may be characterized by increased susceptibility to opportunistic infections, cancers, or other conditions, as described in 14.08.

B. *What information do we need to show that you have an immune system disorder?* Generally, we need your medical history, a report(s) of a physical examination, a report(s) of laboratory findings, and in some instances, appropriate medically acceptable imaging or tissue biopsy reports to show that you have an immune system disorder. Therefore, we will make every reasonable effort to obtain your medical history, medical findings, and results of laboratory tests. We explain the information we need in more detail in the sections below.

C. *Definitions*
1. *Appropriate medically acceptable imaging* includes, but is not limited to, angiography, X-ray imaging, computerized axial tomography (CAT scan) or magnetic resonance imaging (MRI), with or without contrast material, myelography, and radionuclear bone scans. "Appropriate" means that the technique used is the proper one to support the evaluation and diagnosis of the impairment.

2. *Constitutional symptoms or signs*, as used in these listings, means severe fatigue, fever, malaise, or involuntary weight loss. *Severe fatigue* means a frequent sense of exhaustion that results in significantly reduced physical activity or mental function. *Malaise* means frequent feelings of illness, bodily discomfort, or lack of well-being that result in significantly reduced physical activity or mental function.

3. *Disseminated* means that a condition is spread over a considerable area. The type and extent of the spread will depend on your specific disease.

4. *Dysfunction* means that one or more of the body regulatory mechanisms are impaired, causing either an excess or deficiency of immunocompetent cells or their products.

5. *Extra-articular* means "other than the joints"; for example, an organ(s) such as the heart, lungs, kidneys, or skin.

6. *Inability to ambulate effectively* has the same meaning as in 1.00B2b.

7. *Inability to perform fine and gross movements effectively* has the same meaning as in 1.00B2c.

8. *Major peripheral joints* has the same meaning as in 1.00F.

9. *Persistent* means that a sign(s) or symptom(s) has continued over time. The precise meaning will depend on the specific immune system disorder, the usual course of the disorder, and the other circumstances of your clinical course.

10. *Recurrent* means that a condition that previously responded adequately to an appropriate course of treatment returns after a period of remission or regression. The precise meaning, such as the extent of response or remission and the time periods involved, will depend on the specific disease or condition you have, the body system affected, the usual course of the disorder and its treatment, and the other facts of your particular case.

11. *Resistant to treatment* means that a condition did not respond adequately to an appropriate course of treatment. Whether a response is adequate or a course of treatment is appropriate will depend on the specific disease or condition you have, the body system affected, the usual course of the disorder and its treatment, and the other facts of your particular case.

12. *Severe* means medical severity as used by the medical community. The term does not have the same meaning as it does when we use it in connection with a finding at the second step of the sequential evaluation processes in §§404.1520, 416.920, and 416.924.

D. *Refers to autoimmune disorders excluding HIV.*

E. *Refers to immune deficiency disorders excluding HIV.*

F. *How do we document and evaluate human immunodeficiency virus (HIV) infection?* Any individual with HIV infection, including one with a diagnosis of acquired immune deficiency syndrome (AIDS), may be found disabled under 14.08 if his or her impairment meets the criteria in that listing or is medically equivalent to the criteria in that listing.

1. *Documentation of HIV infection.* The medical evidence must include documentation of HIV infection. Documentation may be by laboratory evidence or by other generally acceptable methods consistent with the prevailing state of medical knowledge and clinical practice. When you have had laboratory testing for HIV infection, we will make every reasonable effort to obtain reports of the results of that testing. However, we will not purchase laboratory testing to establish whether you have HIV infection.

a. *Definitive documentation of HIV infection.* A definitive diagnosis of HIV infection is documented by one or more of the following laboratory tests:

(i) HIV antibody tests. HIV antibodies are usually first detected by an ELISA screening test performed on serum. Because the ELISA can yield false-positive results, confirmation is required using a more definitive test, such as a Western blot or an immunofluorescence assay.

(ii) Positive "viral load" (VL) tests. These tests are normally used to quantitate the amount of the virus present, but also document HIV infection. Such tests include the quantitative plasma HIV RNA, quantitative plasma HIV branched DNA, and reverse transcriptase-polymerase chain reaction (RT-PCR).

(iii) HIV DNA detection by polymerase chain reaction (PCR).

(iv) A specimen that contains HIV antigen (for example, serum specimen, lymphocyte culture, or cerebrospinal fluid).

(v) A positive viral culture for HIV from peripheral blood mononuclear cells (PBMCs).

(vi) Other tests that are highly specific for detection of HIV and that are consistent with the prevailing state of medical knowledge.

b. *Other acceptable documentation of HIV infection.* We may also document HIV infection without the definitive laboratory evidence described in 14.00F1a, provided that such documentation is consistent with the prevailing state of medical knowledge and clinical practice and is consistent with the other evidence in your case record. If no definitive laboratory evidence is available, we may document HIV infection by the medical history, clinical and laboratory findings, and diagnosis(es) indicated in the medical evidence. For example, we will accept a diagnosis of HIV infection without definitive laboratory evidence of the HIV infection if you have an opportunistic disease that is predictive of a defect in cell-mediated immunity (for example, toxoplasmosis of the brain, *Pneumocystis* pneumonia (PCP)), and there is no other known cause of diminished resistance to that disease (for example, long-term steroid treatment, lymphoma). In such cases, we will make every reasonable effort to obtain full details of the history, medical findings, and results of testing.

2. *CD4 tests.* Individuals who have HIV infection or other disorders of the immune system may have tests showing a reduction of either the absolute count or the percentage of their T-helper lymphocytes (CD4 cells). The extent of immune suppression correlates with the level or rate of decline of the CD4 count. Generally, when the CD4 count is below $200/mm^3$ (or below 14 percent of the total lymphocyte count), the susceptibility to opportunistic infection is greatly increased. Although a reduced CD4 count alone does not establish a definitive diagnosis of HIV infection, a CD4 count below 200 does offer supportive evidence when there are clinical findings, but not a definitive diagnosis of an opportunistic infection(s). However, a reduced CD4 count *alone* does not document the severity or functional consequences of HIV infection.

3. *Documentation of the manifestations of HIV infection.* The medical evidence must also include documentation of the manifestations of HIV infection. Documentation may be by laboratory evidence or other generally

acceptable methods consistent with the prevailing state of medical knowledge and clinical practice.

a. *Definitive documentation of the manifestations of HIV infection.* The definitive method of diagnosing opportunistic diseases or conditions that are manifestations of HIV infection is by culture, serologic test, or microscopic examination of biopsied tissue or other material (for example, bronchial washings). We will make every reasonable effort to obtain specific laboratory evidence of an opportunistic disease or other condition whenever this information is available. If a histologic or other test has been performed, the evidence should include a copy of the appropriate report. If we cannot obtain the report, the summary of hospitalization or a report from the treating source should include details of the findings and results of the diagnostic studies (including appropriate medically acceptable imaging studies) or microscopic examination of the appropriate tissues or body fluids.

b. *Other acceptable documentation of the manifestations of HIV infection.* We may also document manifestations of HIV infection without the definitive laboratory evidence described in 14.00F3a, provided that such documentation is consistent with the prevailing state of medical knowledge and clinical practice and is consistent with the other evidence in your case record. For example, many conditions are now commonly diagnosed based on some or all of the following: medical history, clinical manifestations, laboratory findings (including appropriate medically acceptable imaging), and treatment responses. In such cases, we will make every reasonable effort to obtain full details of the history, medical findings, and results of testing. The following are examples of how we may document manifestations of HIV infection with other appropriate evidence.

(i) Although a definitive diagnosis of PCP requires identifying the organism in bronchial washings, induced sputum, or lung biopsy, these tests are frequently bypassed if PCP can be diagnosed presumptively. Supportive evidence may include fever, dyspnea, hypoxia, CD4 count below 200, and no evidence of bacterial pneumonia. Also supportive are bilateral lung interstitial infiltrates on X-ray, a typical pattern on CAT scan, or a gallium scan positive for pulmonary uptake. Response to anti-PCP therapy usually requires 5–7 days, and such a response can be supportive of the diagnosis.

(ii) Documentation of *Cytomegalovirus* (CMV) disease (14.08D) may present special problems because definitive diagnosis (except for chorioretinitis, which may be diagnosed by an ophthalmologist or optometrist on funduscopic examination) requires identification of viral inclusion bodies or a positive culture from the affected organ and the absence of any other infectious agent likely to be causing the disease. A positive serology test does not establish a definitive diagnosis of CMV disease, but does offer supportive evidence of a presumptive diagnosis of CMV disease. Other clinical findings that support a presumptive diagnosis of CMV may include: fever, urinary culture positive for CMV, and CD4 count below 200. A clear response to anti-CMV therapy also supports a diagnosis.

(iii) A definitive diagnosis of toxoplasmosis of the brain is based on brain biopsy, but this procedure carries significant risk and is not commonly performed. This condition is usually diagnosed presumptively based on symptoms or signs of fever, headache, focal neurologic deficits, seizures, typical lesions on brain imaging, and a positive serology test.

(iv) Candidiasis of the esophagus (also known as *Candida* esophagitis) may be presumptively diagnosed based on symptoms of retrosternal pain on swallowing (odynophagia) and either oropharyngeal thrush (white patches or plaques) diagnosed on physical examination or by microscopic documentation of *Candida* fungal elements from a noncultured specimen scraped from the oral mucosa. Treatment with oral (systemic) antifungal agents usually produces improvement after 5 or more days of therapy, and such a response can be supportive of the diagnosis.

4. *HIV infection manifestations specific to women.*

a. *General.* Most women with severe immunosuppression secondary to HIV infection exhibit the typical opportunistic infections and other conditions, such as PCP, *Candida* esophagitis, wasting syndrome, cryptococcosis, and toxoplasmosis. However, HIV infection may have different manifestations in women than in men. Adjudicators must carefully scrutinize the medical evidence and be alert to the variety of medical conditions specific to, or common in, women with HIV infection that may affect their ability to function in the workplace.

b. *Additional considerations for evaluating HIV infection in women.* Many of these manifestations (for example, vulvovaginal candidiasis, pelvic inflammatory disease) occur in women with or without HIV infection, but can be more severe or resistant to treatment or occur more frequently in a woman whose immune system is suppressed. Therefore, when evaluating the claim of a woman with HIV infection, it is important to consider gynecologic and other problems specific to women, including any associated symptoms (for example, pelvic pain), in assessing the severity of the impairment and resulting functional limitations. We may evaluate manifestations of HIV infection in women under the specific criteria (for example, cervical cancer under 14.08E), under an applicable general category (for example, pelvic inflammatory disease under 14.08A4), or, in appropriate cases, under 14.08K.

5. *Involuntary weight loss.* For purposes of 14.08H, an involuntary weight loss of at least 10 percent of baseline is always considered "significant."

Loss of less than 10 percent may or may not be significant, depending on the individual's baseline weight and body habitus. For example, a 7-pound weight loss in a 100-pound woman who is 63 inches tall might be considered significant; but a 14-pound weight loss in a 200-pound woman who is the same height might not be significant. HIV infection that affects the digestive system and results in malnutrition can also be evaluated under 5.08.

G. *How do we consider the effects of treatment in evaluating your autoimmune disorder, immune deficiency disorder, or HIV infection?*
1. *General.* If your impairment does not otherwise meet the requirements of a listing, we will consider your medical treatment in terms of its effectiveness in improving the signs, symptoms, and laboratory abnormalities of your specific immune system disorder or its manifestations, and in terms of any side effects that limit your functioning. We will make every reasonable effort to obtain a specific description of the treatment you receive (including surgery) for your immune system disorder. We consider:

a. The effects of medications you take.

b. Adverse side effects (acute and chronic).

c. The intrusiveness and complexity of your treatment (for example, the dosing schedule, need for injections).

d. The effect of treatment on your mental functioning (for example, cognitive changes, mood disturbance).

e. Variability of your response to treatment (see 14.00G2).

f. The interactive and cumulative effects of your treatments. For example, many individuals with immune system disorders receive treatment both for their immune system disorders and for the manifestations of the disorders or co-occurring impairments, such as treatment for HIV infection and hepatitis C. The interactive and cumulative effects of these treatments may be greater than the effects of each treatment considered separately.

g. The duration of your treatment.

h. Any other aspects of treatment that may interfere with your ability to function.

2. *Variability of your response to treatment.* Your response to treatment and the adverse or beneficial consequences of your treatment may vary widely. The effects of your treatment may be temporary or long term. For example, some individuals may show an initial positive response to a drug or combination of drugs followed by a decrease in effectiveness. When we evaluate your response to treatment and how your treatment may affect you, we consider such factors as disease activity before treatment, requirements for changes in therapeutic regimens, the time required for therapeutic effectiveness of a particular drug or drugs, the limited number

of drug combinations that may be available for your impairment(s), and the time-limited efficacy of some drugs. For example, an individual with HIV infection or another immune deficiency disorder who develops pneumonia or tuberculosis may not respond to the same antibiotic regimen used in treating individuals without HIV infection or another immune deficiency disorder, or may not respond to an antibiotic that he or she responded to before. Therefore, we must consider the effects of your treatment on an individual basis, including the effects of your treatment on your ability to function.

3. *How we evaluate the effects of treatment for autoimmune disorders on your ability to function.* Some medications may have acute or long-term side effects. When we consider the effects of corticosteroids or other treatments for autoimmune disorders on your ability to function, we consider the factors in 14.00G1 and 14.00G2. Long-term corticosteroid treatment can cause ischemic necrosis of bone, posterior subcapsular cataract, weight gain, glucose intolerance, increased susceptibility to infection, and osteoporosis that may result in a loss of function. In addition, medications used in the treatment of autoimmune disorders may also have effects on mental functioning, including cognition (for example, memory), concentration, and mood.

4. *Refers to effects of treatment excluding HIV.*

5. *How we evaluate the effects of treatment for HIV infection on your ability to function.*

a. *General.* When we consider the effects of antiretroviral drugs (including the effects of highly active antiretroviral therapy (HAART)) and the effects of treatments for the manifestations of HIV infection on your ability to function, we consider the factors in 14.00G1 and 14.00G2. Side effects of antiretroviral drugs include, but are not limited to: bone marrow suppression, pancreatitis, gastrointestinal intolerance (nausea, vomiting, diarrhea), neuropathy, rash, hepatotoxicity, lipodystrophy (fat redistribution, such as "buffalo hump"), glucose intolerance, and lactic acidosis. In addition, medications used in the treatment of HIV infection may also have effects on mental functioning, including cognition (for example, memory), concentration, and mood, and may result in malaise, severe fatigue, joint and muscle pain, and insomnia. The symptoms of HIV infection and the side effects of medication may be indistinguishable from each other. We will consider all of your functional limitations, whether they result from your symptoms or signs of HIV infection or the side effects of your treatment.

b. *Structured treatment interruptions.* A structured treatment interruption (STI, also called a "drug holiday") is a treatment practice during which your treating source advises you to stop taking your medications temporarily. An STI in itself does not imply that your medical condition has improved, nor does it imply that you are noncompliant with your treatment because you are following your treating source's advice. Therefore, if you have stopped taking medication because your treating source prescribed or recommended an STI, we will not find that you are failing to follow treatment or draw inferences about the severity of your impairment on this fact alone. We will consider why your treating source has prescribed or recommended an STI and all the other information in your case record when we determine the severity of your impairment.

6. *When there is no record of ongoing treatment.* If you have not received ongoing treatment or have not had an ongoing relationship with the medical community despite the existence of a severe impairment(s), we will evaluate the medical severity and duration of your immune system disorder on the basis of the current objective medical evidence and other evidence in your case record, taking into consideration your medical history, symptoms, clinical and laboratory findings, and medical source opinions. If you have just begun treatment and we cannot determine whether you are disabled based on the evidence we have, we may need to wait to determine the effect of the treatment on your ability to function. The amount of time we need to wait will depend on the facts of your case. If you have not received treatment, you may not be able to show an impairment that meets the criteria of one of the immune system disorders listings, but your immune system disorder may medically equal a listing or be disabling based on a consideration of your residual functional capacity, age, education, and work experience.

H. *How do we consider your symptoms, including your pain, severe fatigue, and malaise?* Your symptoms, including pain, severe fatigue, and malaise, may be important factors in our determination whether your immune system disorder(s) meets or medically equals a listing or in our determination whether you are otherwise able to work. In order for us to consider your symptoms, you must have medical signs or laboratory findings showing the existence of a medically determinable impairment(s) that could reasonably be expected to produce the symptoms. If you have such an impairment(s), we will evaluate the intensity, persistence, and functional effects of your symptoms using the rules throughout 14.00 and in our other regulations. See §§404.1528, 404.1529, 416.928, and 416.929. Additionally, when we assess the credibility of your complaints about your symptoms and their functional effects, we will not draw any inferences from the fact that you do not receive treatment or that you are not following treatment without considering all of the relevant evidence in your case record, including any explanations you provide that may explain why you are not receiving or following treatment.

I. *How do we use the functional criteria in these listings?*

1. The following listings in this body system include standards for evaluating the functional limitations resulting from immune system disorders: 14.02B, for systemic lupus erythematosus; 14.03B, for systemic vasculitis; 14.04D, for systemic sclerosis (scleroderma); 14.05E, for polymyositis and dermatomyositis; 14.06B, for undifferentiated and mixed connective tissue disease; 14.07C, for immune deficiency disorders, excluding HIV infection; 14.08K, for HIV infection; 14.09D, for inflammatory arthritis; and 14.10B, for Sjögren's syndrome.

2. When we use one of the listings cited in 14.00I1, we will consider all relevant information in your case record to determine the full impact of your immune system disorder on your ability to function on a sustained basis. Important factors we will consider when we evaluate your functioning under these listings include, but are not limited to: your symptoms, the frequency and duration of manifestations of your immune system disorder, periods of exacerbation and remission, and the functional impact of your treatment, including the side effects of your medication.

3. As used in these listings, "repeated" means that the manifestations occur on an average of three times a year, or once every 4 months, each lasting 2 weeks or more; or the manifestations do not last for 2 weeks, but occur substantially more frequently than three times in a year or once every 4 months; or they occur less frequently than an average of three times a year or once every 4 months, but last substantially longer than 2 weeks. Your impairment will satisfy this criterion regardless of whether you have the same kind of manifestation repeatedly, all different manifestations, or any other combination of manifestations; for example, two of the same kind of manifestation and a different one. You must have the required number of manifestations with the frequency and duration required in this section. Also, the manifestations must occur within the period covered by your claim.

4. To satisfy the functional criterion in a listing, your immune system disorder must result in a "marked" level of limitation in one of three general areas of functioning: Activities of daily living, social functioning, or difficulties in completing tasks due to deficiencies in concentration, persistence, or pace. Functional limitation may result from the impact of the disease process itself on your mental functioning, physical functioning, or both your mental and physical functioning. This could result from persistent or intermittent symptoms, such as depression, severe fatigue, or pain, resulting in a limitation of your ability to do a task, to concentrate, to persevere at a task, or to perform the task at an acceptable rate of speed. You may also have limitations because of your treatment and its side effects (see 14.00G).

5. When "marked" is used as a standard for measuring the degree of functional limitation, it means more than moderate but less than extreme. We do not define "marked" by a specific number of different activities of daily living in which your functioning is impaired, different behaviors in which your social functioning is impaired, or tasks that you are able to complete, but by the nature and overall degree of interference with your functioning. You may have a marked limitation when several activities or functions are impaired, or even when only one is impaired. Also, you need not be totally precluded from performing an activity to have a marked limitation, as long as the degree of limitation seriously interferes with your ability to function independently, appropriately, and effectively. The term "marked" does not imply that you must be confined to bed, hospitalized, or in a nursing home.

6. *Activities of daily living* include, but are not limited to, such activities as doing household chores, grooming and hygiene, using a post office, taking public transportation, or paying bills. We will find that you have a "marked" limitation of activities of daily living if you have a serious limitation in your ability to maintain a household or take public transportation because of symptoms, such as pain, severe fatigue, anxiety, or difficulty concentrating, caused by your immune system disorder (including manifestations of the disorder) or its treatment, even if you are able to perform some self-care activities.

7. *Social functioning* includes the capacity to interact independently, appropriately, effectively, and on a sustained basis with others. It includes the ability to communicate effectively with others. We will find that you have a "marked" limitation in maintaining social functioning if you have a serious limitation in social interaction on a sustained basis because of symptoms, such as pain, severe fatigue, anxiety, or difficulty concentrating, or a pattern of exacerbation and remission, caused by your immune system disorder (including manifestations of the disorder) or its treatment, even if you are able to communicate with close friends or relatives.

8. *Completing tasks in a timely manner* involves the ability to sustain concentration, persistence, or pace to permit timely completion of tasks commonly found in work settings. We will find that you have a "marked" limitation in completing tasks if you have a serious limitation in your ability to sustain concentration or pace adequate to complete work-related tasks because of symptoms, such as pain, severe fatigue, anxiety, or difficulty concentrating, caused by your immune system disorder (including manifestations of the disorder) or its treatment, even if you are able to do some routine activities of daily living.

J. *How do we evaluate your immune system disorder when it does not meet one of these listings?*

1. These listings are only examples of immune system disorders that we consider severe enough to prevent you from doing any gainful activity. If your impairment(s) does not meet the criteria of any of these listings, we must also consider whether you have an impairment(s) that satisfies the criteria of a listing in another body system.

2. Individuals with immune system disorders, including HIV infection, may manifest signs or symptoms of a mental impairment or of another physical impairment. We may evaluate these impairments under any affected body system. For example, we will evaluate:

a. Musculoskeletal involvement, such as surgical reconstruction of a joint, under 1.00.

b. Ocular involvement, such as dry eye, under 2.00.

c. Respiratory impairments, such as pleuritis, under 3.00.

d. Cardiovascular impairments, such as cardiomyopathy, under 4.00.

e. Digestive impairments, such as hepatitis (including hepatitis C) or weight loss as a result of HIV infection that affects the digestive system, under 5.00.

f. Genitourinary impairments, such as nephropathy, under 6.00.

g. Hematologic abnormalities, such as anemia, granulocytopenia, and thrombocytopenia, under 7.00.

h. Skin impairments, such as persistent fungal and other infectious skin eruptions, and photosensitivity, under 8.00.

i. Neurologic impairments, such as neuropathy or seizures, under 11.00.

j. Mental disorders, such as depression, anxiety, or cognitive deficits, under 12.00.

k. Allergic disorders, such as asthma or atopic dermatitis, under 3.00 or 8.00 or under the criteria in another affected body system.

l. Syphilis or neurosyphilis under the criteria for the affected body system; for example, 2.00 Special senses and speech, 4.00 Cardiovascular system, or 11.00 Neurological.

3. If you have a severe medically determinable impairment(s) that does not meet a listing, we will determine whether your impairment(s) medically equals a listing. (See §§404.1526 and 416.926.) If it does not, you may or may not have the residual functional capacity to engage in substantial gainful activity. Therefore, we proceed to the fourth, and if necessary, the fifth steps of the sequential evaluation process in §§404.1520 and 416.920. We

use the rules in §§404.1594, 416.994, and 416.994a as appropriate, when we decide whether you continue to be disabled.

HIV Infection Listing

14.08 Human immunodeficiency virus (HIV) infection. With documentation as described in 14.00F and one of the following:

A. Bacterial infections:

1. Mycobacterial infection (for example, caused by *M. avium-intracellulare*, *M. kansasii*, or *M. tuberculosis*) at site other than the lungs, skin, or cervical or hilar lymph nodes, or pulmonary tuberculosis resistant to treatment; or
2. Nocardiosis; or
3. *Salmonella* bacteremia, recurrent non-typhoid; or
4. Multiple or recurrent bacterial infections, including pelvic inflammatory disease, requiring hospitalization or intravenous antibiotic treatment three or more times in a 12-month period.

OR

B. Fungal infections:

1. Aspergillosis; or
2. Candidiasis involving the esophagus, trachea, bronchi, or lungs, or at a site other than the skin, urinary tract, intestinal tract, or oral or vulvovaginal mucous membranes; or
3. Coccidioidomycosis, at a site other than the lungs or lymph nodes; or
4. Cryptococcosis, at a site other than the lungs (for example, cryptococcal meningitis); or
5. Histoplasmosis, at a site other than the lungs or lymph nodes; or
6. Mucormycosis; or
7. *Pneumocystis* pneumonia or extrapulmonary *Pneumocystis* infection.

OR

C. Protozoan or helminthic infections:

1. Cryptosporidiosis, isosporiasis, or microsporidiosis, with diarrhea lasting for 1 month or longer; or
2. Strongyloidiasis, extra-intestinal; or
3. Toxoplasmosis of an organ other than the liver, spleen, or lymph nodes.

OR

D. Viral infections:

1. *Cytomegalovirus* disease (documented as described in 14.00F3b(ii)) at a site other than the liver, spleen, or lymph nodes; or

2. Herpes simplex virus causing:

a. Mucocutaneous infection (for example, oral, genital, perianal) lasting for 1 month or longer; or

b. Infection at a site other than the skin or mucous membranes (for example, bronchitis, pneumonitis, esophagitis, or encephalitis); or

c. Disseminated infection; or

3. Herpes zoster:

a. Disseminated; or

b. With multidermatomal eruptions that are resistant to treatment; or

4. Progressive multifocal leukoencephalopathy.

OR

E. Malignant neoplasms:

1. Carcinoma of the cervix, invasive, FIGO stage II and beyond; or

2. Kaposi's sarcoma with:

a. Extensive oral lesions; or

b. Involvement of the gastrointestinal tract, lungs, or other visceral organs; or

3. Lymphoma (for example, primary lymphoma of the brain, Burkitt's lymphoma, immunoblastic sarcoma, other non-Hodgkin's lymphoma, Hodgkin's disease); or

4. Squamous cell carcinoma of the anal canal or anal margin.

OR

F. Conditions of the skin or mucous membranes (other than described in B2, D2, or D3, above), with extensive fungating or ulcerating lesions not responding to treatment (for example, dermatological conditions such as eczema or psoriasis, vulvovaginal or other mucosal *Candida*, condyloma caused by human *Papillomavirus*, genital ulcerative disease).

OR

G. HIV encephalopathy, characterized by cognitive or motor dysfunction that limits function and progresses.

OR

H. HIV wasting syndrome, characterized by involuntary weight loss of 10 percent or more of baseline (computed based on pounds, kilograms, or body mass index (BMI)) or other significant involuntary weight loss as described in 14.00F5, and in the absence of a concurrent illness that could explain the findings. With either:

1. Chronic diarrhea with two or more loose stools daily lasting for 1 month or longer; or

2. Chronic weakness and documented fever greater than 38°C (100.4°F) for the majority of 1 month or longer.

OR

I. Diarrhea, lasting for 1 month or longer, resistant to treatment, and requiring intravenous hydration, intravenous alimentation, or tube feeding.

OR

J. One or more of the following infections (other than described in A-I above). The infection(s) must either be resistant to treatment or require hospitalization or intravenous treatment three of more times in a 12-month period.

1. Sepsis; or
2. Meningitis; or
3. Pneumonia; or
4. Septic arthritis; or
5. Endocarditis; or
6. Sinusitis documented by appropriate medically acceptable imaging.

OR

K. Repeated (as defined in 14.00I3) manifestations of HIV infection, including those listed in 14.08A–J, but without the requisite findings for those listings (for example, carcinoma of the cervix not meeting the criteria in 14.08E, diarrhea not meeting the criteria in 14.08I), or other manifestations (for example, oral hairy leukoplakia, myositis, pancreatitis, hepatitis, peripheral neuropathy, glucose intolerance, muscle weakness, cognitive or other mental limitation) resulting in significant, documented symptoms or signs (for example, severe fatigue, fever, malaise, involuntary weight loss, pain, night sweats, nausea, vomiting, headaches, or insomnia) and one of the following at the marked level:

1. Limitation of activities of daily living.
2. Limitation in maintaining social functioning.
3. Limitation in completing tasks in a timely manner due to deficiencies in concentration, persistence, or pace.

PART B

The following sections in Part B are applicable to children under age 18 (where criteria in Part A do not give appropriate consideration to the particular disease process in childhood).

Section

100.00 Growth Impairment
101.00 Musculoskeletal System
102.00 Special Senses and Speech
103.00 Respiratory System
104.00 Cardiovascular System
105.00 Digestive System
106.00 Genitourinary Impairments

107.00 Hematological Disorders
108.00 Skin Disorders
109.00 Endocrine System
110.00 Impairments That Affect Multiple Body Systems
111.00 Neurological
112.00 Mental Disorders
113.00 Malignant Neoplastic Diseases
114.00 Immune System

HIV Infection Listing Introductory Text

114.00A. *What* disorders *do we evaluate under the* immune system *disorders listings?*

1. *We evaluate immune system disorders that cause dysfunction in one or more components of your immune system.*

a. The dysfunction may be due to problems in antibody production, impaired cell-mediated immunity, a combined type of antibody/cellular deficiency, impaired phagocytosis, or complement deficiency.

b. Immune system disorders may result in recurrent and unusual infections, or inflammation and dysfunction of the body's own tissues. Immune system disorders can cause a deficit in a single organ or body system that results in extreme (that is, very serious) loss of function. They can also cause lesser degrees of limitations in two or more organs or body systems, and when associated with symptoms or signs, such as severe fatigue, fever, malaise, diffuse musculoskeletal pain, or involuntary weight loss, can also result in extreme limitation. In children, immune system disorders or their treatment may also affect growth, development, and the performance of age-appropriate activities.

c. We organize the discussions of immune system disorders in three categories: Autoimmune disorders; Immune deficiency disorders, excluding human immunodeficiency virus (HIV) infection; and HIV infection.

2. *Autoimmune disorders (114.00D).* Autoimmune disorders are caused by dysfunctional immune responses directed against the body's own tissues, resulting in chronic, multisystem impairments that differ in clinical manifestations, course, and outcome. They are sometimes referred to as rheumatic diseases, connective tissue disorders, or collagen vascular disorders. Some of the features of autoimmune disorders in children differ from the features of the same disorders in adults. The impact of the disorders or their treatment on physical, psychological, and developmental growth of pre-pubertal children may be considerable, and often differs from that of post-pubertal adolescents or adults.

3. *Immune deficiency disorders, excluding HIV infection (114.00E).* Immune deficiency disorders are characterized by recurrent or unusual infections that respond poorly to treatment, and are often associated with complications affecting other parts of the body. Immune deficiency disorders are classified as either *primary* (congenital) or *acquired*. Children with immune deficiency disorders also have an increased risk of malignancies and of having autoimmune disorders.

4. *Human immunodeficiency virus (HIV) infection (114.00F).* HIV infection may be characterized by increased susceptibility to opportunistic infections, cancers, or other conditions, as described in 114.08.

B. *What information do we need to show that you have an immune system disorder?* Generally, we need your medical history, a report(s) of a physical examination, a report(s) of laboratory findings, and in some instances, appropriate medically acceptable imaging or tissue biopsy reports to show that you have an immune system disorder. Therefore, we will make every reasonable effort to obtain your medical history, medical findings, and results of laboratory tests. We explain the information we need in more detail in the sections below.

C. *Definitions*
1. *Appropriate medically acceptable imaging* includes, but is not limited to, angiography, x-ray imaging, computerized axial tomography (CAT scan) or magnetic resonance imaging (MRI), with or without contrast material, myelography, and radionuclear bone scans. "Appropriate" means that the technique used is the proper one to support the evaluation and diagnosis of the impairment.

2. *Constitutional symptoms or signs,* as used in these listings, means severe fatigue, fever, malaise, or involuntary weight loss. *Severe fatigue* means a frequent sense of exhaustion that results in significantly reduced physical activity or mental function. Malaise means frequent feelings of illness, bodily discomfort, or lack of well-being that result in significantly reduced physical activity or mental function.

3. *Disseminated* means that a condition is spread over a considerable area. The type and extent of the spread will depend on your specific disease.

4. *Dysfunction* means that one or more of the body regulatory mechanisms are impaired, causing either an excess or deficiency of immunocompetent cells or their products.

5. *Extra-articular* means "other than the joints"; for example, an organ(s) such as the heart, lungs, kidneys, or skin.

6. *Inability to ambulate effectively* has the same meaning as in 101.00B2b.

7. *Inability to perform fine and gross movements effectively* has the same meaning as in 101.00B2c.

8. *Major peripheral joints* has the same meaning as in 101.00F.

9. *Persistent* means that a sign(s) or symptom(s) has continued over time. The precise meaning will depend on the specific immune system disorder, the usual course of the disorder, and the other circumstances of your clinical course.

10. *Recurrent* means that a condition that previously responded adequately to an appropriate course of treatment returns after a period of remission or regression. The precise meaning, such as the extent of response or remission and the time periods involved, will depend on the specific disease or condition you have, the body system affected, the usual course of the disorder and its treatment, and the other facts of your particular case.

11. *Resistant to treatment* means that a condition did not respond adequately to an appropriate course of treatment. Whether a response is adequate or a course of treatment is appropriate will depend on the specific disease or condition you have, the body system affected, the usual course of the disorder and its treatment, and the other facts of your particular case.

12. *Severe* means medical severity as used by the medical community. The term does not have the same meaning as it does when we use it in connection with a finding at the second step of the sequential evaluation process in §416.924.

D. *Refers to autoimmune disorders excluding HIV.*

E. *Refers to immune deficiency disorders excluding HIV.*

F. *How do we document and evaluate human immunodeficiency virus (HIV) infection?* Any child with HIV infection, including one with a diagnosis of acquired immune deficiency syndrome (AIDS), may be found disabled under 114.08 if his or her impairment meets the criteria in that listing or is medically equivalent to the criteria in that listing.

1. *Documentation of HIV infection.* The medical evidence must include documentation of HIV infection. Documentation may be by laboratory evidence or by other generally acceptable methods consistent with the prevailing state of medical knowledge and clinical practice. When you have had laboratory testing for HIV infection, we will make every reasonable effort to obtain reports of the results of that testing. However, we will not purchase laboratory testing to establish whether you have HIV infection.

a. *Definitive documentation of HIV infection.* A definitive diagnosis of HIV infection is documented by one or more of the following laboratory tests:

(i) HIV antibody tests. HIV antibodies are usually first detected by an ELISA screening test performed on serum. Because the ELISA can yield false positive results, confirmation is required using a more definitive test, such as a Western blot or an immunofluorescence assay. Positive results on these tests are considered to be diagnostic of HIV infection in a child age 18 months or older. (See b. below for information about HIV antibody testing in children younger than 18 months of age.)

(ii) Positive "viral load" (VL) tests. These tests are normally used to quantitate the amount of the virus present but also document HIV infection. Such tests include the quantitative plasma HIV RNA, quantitative plasma HIV branched DNA, and reverse transcriptase-polymerase chain reaction (RT-PCR).

(iii) HIV DNA detection by polymerase chain reaction (PCR).

(iv) A specimen that contains HIV antigen (for example, serum specimen, lymphocyte culture, or cerebrospinal fluid) in a child age 1 month or older.

(v) A positive viral culture for HIV from peripheral blood mononuclear cells (PBMC).

(vi) An immunoglobulin A (IgA) serological assay that is specific for HIV.

(vii) Other tests that are highly specific for detection of HIV and that are consistent with the prevailing state of medical knowledge.

b. *Definitive documentation of HIV infection in children from birth to the attainment of 18 months.* For children from birth to the attainment of 18 months of age, and who have tested positive for HIV antibodies, HIV infection is documented by:

(i) One or more of the tests listed in F1a(ii)–F1a(vii).

(ii) For newborn and younger infants (birth to attainment of age 1), a CD4 (T4) count of 1500/mm^3 or less, or a CD4 count less than or equal to 20 percent of total lymphocytes.

(iii) For older infants and toddlers from 12 to 18 months of age, a CD4 (T4) count of 750/mm^3 or less, or a CD4 count less than or equal to 20 percent of total lymphocytes.

(iv) An abnormal CD4/CD8 ratio.

(v) A severely diminished immunoglobulin G (IgG) level (< 4 g/l or 400 mg/dl), or significantly greater than normal range for age.

c. *Other acceptable documentation of HIV infection.* We may also document HIV infection without the definitive laboratory evidence described in 114.00F1a, provided that such documentation is consistent with the prevailing state of medical knowledge and clinical practice and is consistent with the other evidence in your case record. If no definitive laboratory evidence is available, we may document HIV infection by the medical history, clinical and laboratory findings, and diagnosis(es) indicated in the medical evidence. For example, we will accept a diagnosis of HIV infection without definitive laboratory evidence of the HIV infection if you have an opportunistic disease that is predictive of a defect in cell-mediated immunity (for example, *Pneumocystis* pneumonia (PCP)), and there is no other known cause of diminished resistance to that disease (for example, long-term steroid treatment, lymphoma). In such cases, we will make every reasonable effort to obtain full details of the history, medical findings, and results of testing.

2. *CD4 tests.* Children who have HIV infection or other disorders of the immune system may have tests showing a reduction of either the absolute count or the percentage of their T-helper lymphocytes (CD4 cells). The extent of immune suppression correlates with the level or rate of decline of the CD4 count (relative to the age of the young child). By age 6, children have CD4 counts comparable to those levels found in adults. Generally, in these children when the CD4 count is below $200/mm^3$ (or below 14 percent of the total lymphocyte count) the susceptibility to opportunistic infection is greatly increased. Although a reduced CD4 count alone does not establish a definitive diagnosis of HIV infection, a CD4 count below 200 does offer supportive evidence when there are clinical findings, but not a definitive diagnosis of an opportunistic infection(s). However, a reduced CD4 count alone does not document the severity or functional consequences of HIV infection.

3. *Documentation of the manifestations of HIV infection.* The medical evidence must also include documentation of the manifestations of HIV infection. Documentation may be by laboratory evidence or other generally acceptable methods consistent with the prevailing state of medical knowledge and clinical practice.

a. *Definitive documentation of the manifestations of HIV infection.* The definitive method of diagnosing opportunistic diseases or conditions that are manifestations of HIV infection is by culture, serologic test, or microscopic examination of biopsied tissue or other material (for example, bronchial washings). We will make every reasonable effort to obtain specific laboratory evidence of an opportunistic disease or other condition whenever this information is available. If a histologic or other test has been performed, the evidence should include a copy of the appropriate report. If we cannot obtain the report, the summary of hospitalization or a report from the treating source should include details of the findings and results of the diagnostic studies (including appropriate medically acceptable imaging studies) or microscopic examination of the appropriate tissues or body fluids.

b. *Other acceptable documentation of the manifestations of HIV infection.* We may also document manifestations of HIV infection without the definitive laboratory evidence described in 114.00F3a, provided that such documentation is consistent with the prevailing state of medical knowledge and clinical practice and is consistent with the other evidence in your case record. For example, many conditions are now commonly diagnosed based on some or all of the following: Medical history, clinical manifestations, laboratory findings (including appropriate medically acceptable imaging), and treatment responses. In such cases, we will make every reasonable effort to obtain full details of the history, medical findings, and results of testing. The following are examples of how we may document manifestations of HIV infection with other appropriate evidence.

(i) Although a definitive diagnosis of PCP requires identifying the organism in bronchial washings, induced sputum, or lung biopsy, these tests are frequently bypassed if PCP can be diagnosed presumptively. Supportive evidence may include: Fever, dyspnea, hypoxia, CD4 count below 200 in children 6 years of age or older, and no evidence of bacterial pneumonia. Also supportive are bilateral lung interstitial infiltrates on X-ray, a typical pattern on CAT scan, or a gallium scan positive for pulmonary uptake. Response to anti-PCP therapy usually requires 5-7 days, and such a response can be supportive of the diagnosis.

(ii) Documentation of *Cytomegalovirus* (CMV) disease (114.08D) may present special problems because definitive diagnosis (except for chorioretinitis, which may be diagnosed by an ophthalmologist or optometrist on funduscopic examination) requires identification of viral inclusion bodies or a positive culture from the affected organ and the absence of any other infectious agent likely to be causing the disease. A positive serology test does not establish a definitive diagnosis of CMV disease, but does offer supportive evidence of a presumptive diagnosis of CMV disease. Other clinical findings that support a presumptive diagnosis of CMV may include: Fever, urinary culture positive for CMV, and CD4 count below 200 in children 6 years of age or older. A clear response to anti-CMV therapy also supports a diagnosis.

(iii) A definitive diagnosis of toxoplasmosis of the brain is based on brain biopsy, but this procedure carries significant risk and is not commonly performed. This condition is usually diagnosed presumptively based on symptoms or signs of fever, headache, focal neurologic deficits, seizures, typical lesions on brain imaging, and a positive serology test.

(iv) Candidiasis of the esophagus (also known as *Candida* esophagitis) may be presumptively diagnosed based on symptoms of retrosternal pain on swallowing (odynophagia) and either oropharyngeal thrush (white patches or plaques) diagnosed on physical examination or by microscopic documentation of *Candida* fungal elements from a noncultured specimen scraped from the oral mucosa. Treatment with oral (systemic) antifungal agents usually produces improvement after 5 or more days of therapy, and such a response can be supportive of the diagnosis.

4. *HIV infection manifestations specific to children.*

a. *General.* The clinical manifestation and course of disease in children who become infected with HIV perinatally or in the first 12 years of life may differ from that in adolescents (age 12 to attainment of age 18) and adults. Newborn and younger infants (birth to attainment of age 1) and older infants and toddlers (age 1 to attainment of age 3) may present with failure to thrive or PCP; preschool children (age 3 to attainment of age 6) and primary school children (age 6 to attainment of age 12) may present with recurrent infections, neurological problems, or developmental abnormalities. Adolescents may also exhibit neurological abnormalities, such as HIV encephalopathy, or have growth problems. HIV infection that affects the digestive system and results in malnutrition also may be evaluated under 105.08.

b. *Neurologic abnormalities.* The methods of identifying and evaluating neurologic abnormalities may vary depending on a child's age. For example, in an infant, impaired brain growth can be documented by a decrease in the growth rate of the head. In an older child, impaired brain growth may be documented by brain atrophy on a CAT scan or MRI. Neurologic abnormalities in infants and young children may present as serious developmental delays or in the loss of previously acquired developmental milestones. In school-age children and adolescents, this type of neurologic abnormality generally presents as the loss of previously acquired intellectual abilities. This may be evidenced in a child by a decrease in intelligence quotient (IQ) scores, by forgetting information previously learned, by inability to learn new information, or by a sudden onset of a new learning disability.

c. *Bacterial infections.* Children with HIV infection may contract any of a broad range of bacterial infections. Certain major infections caused by pyogenic bacteria (for example, some pneumonias) can be severely limiting, especially in pre-adolescent children. We evaluate these major bacterial infections under 114.08A4. Although 114.08A4 applies only to children under 13 years of age, children age 13 and older may have an impairment that medically equals this listing if the circumstances of the case warrant; for example, if there is delayed puberty. We will evaluate pelvic inflammatory disease in older girls under 114.08A5.

G. *How do we consider the effects of treatment in evaluating your autoimmune disorder, immune deficiency disorder, or HIV infection?*

1. *General.* If your impairment does not otherwise meet the requirements of a listing, we will consider your medical treatment in terms of its effectiveness in improving the signs, symptoms, and laboratory abnormalities of your specific immune system disorder or its manifestations, and in terms of any side effects that limit your functioning. We will make every reasonable effort to obtain a specific description of the treatment you receive (including surgery) for your immune system disorder. We consider:

a. The effects of medications you take.

b. Adverse side effects (acute and chronic).

c. The intrusiveness and complexity of your treatment (for example, the dosing schedule, need for injections).

d. The effect of treatment on your mental functioning (for example, cognitive changes, mood disturbance).

e. Variability of your response to treatment (see 114.00G2).

f. The interactive and cumulative effects of your treatments. For example, many children with immune system disorders receive treatment both for their immune system disorders and for the manifestations of the disorders or co-occurring impairments, such as treatment for HIV infection and hepatitis C. The interactive and cumulative effects of these treatments may be greater than the effects of each treatment considered separately.

g. The duration of your treatment.

h. Any other aspects of treatment that may interfere with your ability to function.

2. *Variability of your response to treatment.* Your response to treatment and the adverse or beneficial consequences of your treatment may vary widely. The effects of your treatment may be temporary or long term. For example, some children may show an initial positive response to a drug or combination of drugs followed by a decrease in effectiveness. When we evaluate your response to treatment and how your treatment may affect you, we consider such factors as disease activity before treatment, requirements for changes in therapeutic regimens, the time required for therapeutic effectiveness of a particular drug or drugs, the limited number of drug combinations that may be available for your impairment(s), and

the time-limited efficacy of some drugs. For example, a child with HIV infection or another immune deficiency disorder who develops otitis media may not respond to the same antibiotic regimen used in treating children without HIV infection or another immune deficiency disorder, or may not respond to an antibiotic that he or she responded to before. Therefore, we must consider the effects of your treatment on an individual basis, including the effects of your treatment on your ability to function.

3. *How we evaluate the effects of treatment for autoimmune disorders on your ability to function.* Some medications may have acute or long-term side effects. When we consider the effects of corticosteroids or other treatments for autoimmune disorders on your ability to function, we consider the factors in 114.00G1 and 114.00G2. Long-term corticosteroid treatment can cause ischemic necrosis of bone, posterior subcapsular cataract, impaired growth, weight gain, glucose intolerance, increased susceptibility to infection, and osteopenia that may result in a loss of function. In addition, medications used in the treatment of autoimmune disorders may also have effects on mental functioning, including cognition (for example, memory), concentration, and mood.

4. *How we evaluate the effects of treatment for immune deficiency disorders, excluding HIV infection, on your ability to function.* When we consider the effects of your treatment for your immune deficiency disorder on your ability to function, we consider the factors in 114.00G1 and 114.00G2. A frequent need for treatment such as intravenous immunoglobulin and gamma interferon therapy can be intrusive and interfere with your ability to function. We will also consider whether you have chronic side effects from these or other medications, including severe fatigue, fever, headaches, high blood pressure, joint swelling, muscle aches, nausea, shortness of breath, or limitations in mental function including cognition (for example, memory) concentration, and mood.

5. *How we evaluate the effects of treatment for HIV infection on your ability to function.*

a. *General.* When we consider the effects of antiretroviral drugs (including the effects of highly active antiretroviral therapy (HAART)) and the effects of treatments for the manifestations of HIV infection on your ability to function, we consider the factors in 114.00G1 and 114.00G2. Side effects of antiretroviral drugs include, but are not limited to: Bone marrow suppression, pancreatitis, gastrointestinal intolerance (nausea, vomiting, diarrhea), neuropathy, rash, hepatotoxicity, lipodystrophy (fat redistribution, such as "buffalo hump"), glucose intolerance, and lactic acidosis. In addition, medications used in the treatment of HIV infection may also have effects on mental functioning, including cognition (for example, memory), concentration, and mood, and may result in malaise, severe fatigue, joint and muscle pain, and insomnia. The symptoms of HIV infection and the side effects of medication may be indistinguishable from each other. We will consider all of your functional limitations, whether they result from your symptoms or signs of HIV infection or the side effects of your treatment.

b. *Structured treatment interruptions.* A structured treatment interruption (STI, also called a "drug holiday") is a treatment practice during which your treating source advises you to stop taking your medications temporarily. An STI in itself does not imply that your medical condition has improved; nor does it imply that you are noncompliant with your treatment because you are following your treating source's advice. Therefore, if you have stopped taking medication because your treating source prescribed or recommended an STI, we will not find that you are failing to follow treatment or draw inferences about the severity of your impairment on this fact alone. We will consider why your treating source has prescribed or recommended an STI and all the other information in your case record when we determine the severity of your impairment.

6. *When there is no record of ongoing treatment.* If you have not received ongoing treatment or have not had an ongoing relationship with the medical community despite the existence of a severe impairment(s), we will evaluate the medical severity and duration of your immune system disorder on the basis of the current objective medical evidence and other evidence in your case record, taking into consideration your medical history, symptoms, clinical and laboratory findings, and medical source opinions. If you have just begun treatment and we cannot determine whether you are disabled based on the evidence we have, we may need to wait to determine the effect of the treatment on your ability to develop and function in an age-appropriate manner. The amount of time we need to wait will depend on the facts of your case. If you have not received treatment, you may not be able to show an impairment that meets the criteria of one of the immune system disorders listings, but your immune system disorder may medically equal a listing or functionally equal the listings.

H. *How do we consider your symptoms, including your pain, severe fatigue, and malaise?* Your symptoms, including pain, severe fatigue, and malaise, may be important factors in our determination whether your immune system disorder(s) meets or medically equals a listing or in our determination whether you otherwise have marked and severe functional limitations. In order for us to consider your symptoms, you must have medical signs or laboratory findings showing the existence of a medically determinable impairment(s) that could reasonably be expected to produce the symptoms. If you have such an impairment(s), we will evaluate the intensity, persistence, and functional effects of your symptoms using the rules throughout 114.00 and in our other regulations. See §§416.928, and 416.929. Additionally, when we assess the credibility of your complaints about your symptoms and their functional effects, we will not draw any inferences from the fact that you do not receive treatment or that you are not following treatment without considering all of the relevant evidence in your case record, including any explanations you provide that may explain why you are not receiving or following treatment.

I. *How do we use the functional criteria in these listings?*

1. The following listings in this body system include standards for evaluating the functional limitations resulting from immune system disorders: 114.02B, for systemic lupus erythematosus; 114.03B, for systemic vasculitis; 114.04D, for systemic sclerosis (scleroderma); 114.05E, for polymyositis and dermatomyositis; 114.06B, for undifferentiated and mixed connective tissue disease; 114.07C, for immune deficiency disorders, excluding HIV infection; 114.08L, for HIV infection; 114.09D, for inflammatory arthritis; and 114.10B, for Sjögren's syndrome.

2. When we use one of the listings cited in 114.00I1, we will consider all relevant information in your case record to determine the full impact of your immune system disorder on your ability to function. Important factors we will consider when we evaluate your functioning under these listings include, but are not limited to: Your symptoms, the frequency and duration of manifestations of your immune system disorder, periods of exacerbation and remission, and the functional impact of your treatment, including the side effects of your medication.

3. To satisfy the functional criterion in a listing, your immune system disorder must result in an "extreme" limitation in one domain of functioning or a "marked" limitation in two domains of functioning depending on your age. (See 112.00C for additional discussion of these areas of functioning and §§416.924a and 416.926a for additional guidance on the evaluation of functioning in children.) Functional limitation may result from the impact of the disease process itself on your mental functioning, physical functioning, or both your mental and physical functioning. This could result from persistent or intermittent symptoms, such as depression, severe fatigue, or pain, resulting in a limitation of your ability to do a task, to concentrate, to persevere at a task, or to perform the task at an acceptable rate of speed. You may also have limitations because of your treatment and its side effects (see 114.00G).

J. *How do we evaluate your immune system disorder when it does not meet one of these listings?*

1. These listings are only examples of immune system disorders that we consider severe enough to result in marked and severe functional limitations. If your impairment(s) does not meet the criteria of any of these listings, we must also consider whether you have an impairment(s) that satisfies the criteria of a listing in another body system.

2. Individuals with immune system disorders, including HIV infection, may manifest signs or symptoms of a mental impairment or of another physical impairment. We may evaluate these impairments under any affected body system. For example, we will evaluate:

a. Growth impairment under 100.00.

b. Musculoskeletal involvement, such as surgical reconstruction of a joint, under 101.00.

c. Ocular involvement, such as dry eye, under 102.00.

d. Respiratory impairments, such as pleuritis, under 103.00.

e. Cardiovascular impairments, such as cardiomyopathy, under 104.00.

f. Digestive impairments, such as hepatitis (including hepatitis C) or weight loss as a result of HIV infection that affects the digestive system, under 105.00.

g. Genitourinary impairments, such as nephropathy, under 106.00.

h. Hematologic abnormalities, such as anemia, granulocytopenia, and thrombocytopenia, under 107.00.

i. Skin impairments, such as persistent fungal and other infectious skin eruptions, and photosensitivity, under 108.00.

j. Neurologic impairments, such as neuropathy or seizures, under 111.00.

k. Mental disorders, such as depression, anxiety, or cognitive deficits, under 112.00.

l. Allergic disorders, such as asthma or atopic dermatitis, under 103.00 or 108.00 or under the criteria in another affected body system.

m. Syphilis or neurosyphilis under the criteria for the affected body system, for example, 102.00 Special senses and speech, 104.00 Cardiovascular system, or 111.00 Neurological.

3. If you have a severe medically determinable impairment(s) that does not meet a listing, we will determine whether your impairment(s) medically equals a listing. (See §416.926.) If it does not, we will also consider whether you have an impairment(s) that functionally equals the listings. (See §416.926a.) We use the rules in §416.994a when we decide whether you continue to be disabled.

HIV Infection Listing

114.08 Human immunodeficiency virus (HIV) infection. With documentation as described in 114.00F and one of the following:

A. Bacterial infections:
1. Mycobacterial infection (for example, caused by *M. avium-intracellulare, M. kansasii*, or *M. tuberculosis*) at a site other than the lungs, skin, or cervical or hilar lymph nodes, or pulmonary tuberculosis resistant to treatment; or
2. Nocardiosis; or
3. *Salmonella bacteremia*, recurrent non-typhoid; or
4. In a child less than 13 years of age, multiple or recurrent pyogenic bacterial infections (sepsis, pneumonia, meningitis, bone or joint infection, or abscess of an internal organ or body cavity, but not otitis media or superficial skin or mucosal abscesses) occurring two or more times in 2 years (for children age 13 and older, see 114.00F4c); or
5. Multiple or recurrent bacterial infections, including pelvic inflammatory disease, requiring hospitalization or intravenous antibiotic treatment three or more times in 12-month period.

OR

B. Fungal infections:
1. Aspergillosis; or
2. Candidiasis involving the esophagus, trachea, bronchi, or lungs, or at a site other than the skin, urinary tract, intestinal tract, or oral or vulvovaginal mucous membranes; or
3. Coccidioidomycosis, at a site other than the lungs or lymph nodes; or
4. Cryptococcosis, at a site other than the lungs (for example, cryptococcal meningitis); or
5. Histoplasmosis, at a site other than the lungs or lymph nodes; or
6. Mucormycosis; or
7. *Pneumocystis* pneumonia or extrapulmonary *Pneumocystis* infection.

OR

C. Protozoan or helminthic infections:
1. Cryptosporidiosis, isosporiasis, or microsporidiosis, with diarrhea lasting for 1 month or longer; or
2. Strongyloidiasis, extra-intestinal; or
3. Toxoplasmosis of an organ other then the liver, spleen, or lymph nodes.

OR

D. Viral infections:
1. *Cytomegalovirus* disease (documented as described in 114.00F3b(ii)) at a site other than the liver, spleen, or lymph nodes; or

2. Herpes simplex virus causing:

a. Mucocutaneous infection (for example, oral, genital, perianal) lasting for 1 month or longer; or

b. Infection at a site other than the skin or mucous membranes (for example, bronchitis, pneumonitis, esophagitis, or encephalitis); or

c. Disseminated infection; or

3. Herpes zoster:

a. Disseminated; or

b. With multidermatomal eruptions that are resistant to treatment; or

4. Progressive multifocal leukoencephalopathy.

OR

E. Malignant neoplasms:

1. Carcinoma of the cervix, invasive, FIGO stage II and beyond; or

2. Kaposi's sarcoma with:

a. Extensive oral lesions; or

b. Involvement of the gastrointestinal tract, lungs, or other visceral organs; or

3. Lymphoma (for example, primary lymphoma of the brain, Burkitt's lymphoma, immunoblastic sarcoma, other non-Hodgkin's lymphoma, Hodgkin's disease); or

4. Squamous cell carcinoma of the anal canal or anal margin.

OR

F. Conditions of the skin or mucous membranes (other than described in B2, D2, or D3, above), with extensive fungating or ulcerating lesions not responding to treatment (for example, dermatological conditions such as eczema or psoriasis, vulvovaginal or other mucosal *Candida*, condyloma caused by human *Papillomavirus*, genital ulcerative disease).

OR

G. Neurological manifestations of HIV infection (for example, HIV encephalopathy, peripheral neuropathy) resulting in one of the following:

1. Loss of previously acquired, or marked delay in achieving, developmental milestones or intellectual ability (including the sudden onset of a new learning disability); or

2. Impaired brain growth (acquired microcephaly or brain atrophy—see 114.00F4b); or

3. Progressive motor dysfunction affecting gait and station or fine and gross motor skills.

OR

H. Growth disturbance, with:

1. An involuntary weight loss (or failure to gain weight at an appropriate rate for age) resulting in a fall of 15 percentiles from established growth curve (on standard growth charts) that persists for 2 months or longer, or

2. An involuntary weight loss (or failure to gain weight at an appropriate rate for age) resulting in a fall to below the third percentile from an established growth curve (on standard growth charts) that persists for 2 months or longer; or
3. Involuntary weight loss of 10 percent or more of baseline (computed based on pounds, kilograms, or body mass index (BMI)) that persists for 2 months or longer.

OR

I. Diarrhea, lasting for 1 month or longer, resistant to treatment and requiring intravenous hydration, intravenous alimentation, or tube feeding.

OR

J. Lymphoid interstitial pneumonia/pulmonary lymphoid hyperplasia (LIP/PLH complex), with respiratory symptoms that significantly interfere with age-appropriate activities, and that cannot be controlled by prescribed treatment.

OR

K. One or more of the following infections (other than described in A-J, above). The infection(s) must either be resistant to treatment or require hospitalization or intravenous treatment three or more times in a 12-month period.
1. Sepsis; or
2. Meningitis; or
3. Pneumonia; or
4. Septic arthritis; or
5. Endocarditis; or
6. Sinusitis documented by appropriate medically acceptable imaging.

OR

L. Any other manifestation(s) of HIV infection, including those listed in 114.08A-K, but without the requisite findings for those listings (for example, oral candidiasis not meeting the criteria in 114.08F, diarrhea not meeting the criteria in 114.08I), or other manifestation(s) (for example, oral hairy leukoplakia, hepatomegaly), resulting in one of the following:
1. For children from birth to attainment of age 1, at least one of the criteria in paragraphs A-E of 112.12; or
2. For children age 1 to attainment of age 3, at least one of the appropriate age-group criteria in paragraph B1 of 112.02; or
3. For children age 3 to attainment of age 18, at least two of the appropriate age-group criteria in paragraph B2 of 112.02.

Appendix B

Committee Charge

The Social Security Administration (SSA) charged the Institute of Medicine with completing a series of tasks and subtasks. This appendix serves as an index of the committee's responses to each question throughout the report.

1. *The Consensus Committee shall review, in a written report for the use of SSA, the most current medical literature to determine the latest standards of care, the latest technology for the understanding of disease processes, and the latest science demonstrating the impact of HIV infection on patients' health and functional capacity. As part of the review, the Consensus Committee shall perform the following subtasks:*

<u>Subtask 1A:</u> *The Consensus Committee shall survey published scientific literature, research, and studies to gather available information on the current medical and functional status (both mental and physical) of the cohort of very young children who (1) became HIV infected between 1988 and 1996 (primarily perinatal transmission), and (2) received serial antiviral monotherapy prior to the introduction of highly active antiretroviral therapy (HAART)(circa 1996–1997).*

The Consensus Committee shall survey published scientific literature, research, and studies to gather available information on the current medical and functional status (both mental and physical) of the cohort of very young children who (1) became HIV infected after 1996 and (2) have only received HAART therapy.

Specifically, the Consensus Committee shall compile a report based on the currently available information comparing the medical and functional status of both cohorts in order to determine if there is any medical or functional basis (either mental or physical) on which SSA would evaluate the impairments of each of these cohorts differently when adjudicating their disability claims at age 18 under the HIV Infection Listing (14.08) for adults.

Response: Information regarding HIV-infected children's medical and functional status can be found in Chapter 7. The incidence of perinatal infection has decreased greatly since the widespread use of antiretroviral therapy and aggressive testing; currently around 15,500 children live with HIV/AIDS as a result of increased survival (CDC, 2009). Prior to 1997, perinatal survival was low. In 1997, combination antiretroviral therapy became standard for treating children, leading to higher survival rates. As discussed in Chapter 7, children have benefited from advances in treatment in the same pattern as adults (McConnell et al., 2005). Combination antiretroviral therapy has resulted in reduced mortality, increased immune system functioning, and decreased complications from comorbidities and opportunistic diseases. Despite advances, challenges occur because options for therapy have been reduced as a result of multiple-resistance mutations. Little high-quality literature compares children of the above mentioned cohorts, and the committee found no literature indicating the cohorts should be treated differently when adjudicating claims.

Subtask 1B: The Consensus Committee shall survey published scientific literature, research, and studies to determine the following:

- *What published information (for example, medical and vocational literature) is available regarding the presence of chronic diarrhea in HIV-infected patients as an indicator of severity (both prognostically and functionally)?*
- *How is chronic diarrhea in HIV-infected patients defined?*
- *How is chronic diarrhea in HIV-infected patients documented?*
- *What are the medical treatments for chronic diarrhea in HIV-infected patients?*
- *How effective is treatment for diarrhea in HIV-infected patients?*
- *What is the association between chronic diarrhea in HIV-infected patients and HIV wasting syndrome?*

Response: The committee defined diarrhea as a change in an individual's stool pattern with ≥ 3 stools per day that are loose or watery for ≥ 3 weeks (see Chapter 5). In the literature, diarrhea is often defined by stool weight (greater than 200–300 grams/day), by stool frequency and character (greater than two to three loose or watery stools/day), or by stool viscosity (Dieterich et al., 1994; Doumbo et al., 1997; Fanning et al., 1991). A review of 46 studies of HIV-associated diarrhea showed most investigators defined diarrhea by duration and stool count (see Table B-1) (Tinmouth et al., 2007).

Relatively few studies address the problem of debilitating diarrhea associated with HIV and its treatment that reflect current experience. As a result, the committee found no literature regarding the presence of chronic diarrhea as an indicator of severity. Two reports deal with quality-of-life issues (Siddiqui et al., 2007; Tramarin et al., 2004), but both were conducted relatively early in the era of combination antiretroviral therapy when diarrhea complicating treatment was more common. For example, the Siddiqui et al. study (performed in New York City from 2001 to 2003) showed a significant difference in diarrhea rates due to protease inhibitor-based (PI-based) treatment at a time when the major agents used in that class (NFV, LPV/r) were associated with high rates of diarrhea. Nevertheless, the rate of diarrhea was still relatively high (17 percent) in patients receiving alternative agents.

The more recent experience with the PI class of antiretroviral agents is shown in Table B-2, which provides results of comparative trials using standard definitions for diarrhea. These data emphasize the differences between agents in this class and the relatively low rates with more recently introduced agents.

Occasional patients present with diarrhea reflecting late-stage HIV infection due to late HIV diagnosis or failed therapy. Possibly the most serious condition in terms of diarrhea is cryptosporidiosis with CD4 less than 50 cells/mm^3 because this may cause devastating diarrhea that can be controlled only with immune recovery. Other late-stage conditions may cause severe diarrhea, including microsporidiosis, dis-

TABLE B-1 Review of 46 Studies of Diarrhea Complicating HIV Infection

Characteristic	Number of Studies	Comment
Duration	33 (72%)	Ranged from 1–6 weeks 21/33 ≥ 4 weeks
Stools/day	29 (63%)	15/29 (52%) specified ≥ two stools/day and most used terms "loose" or "watery"
Stool weight	10 (22%)	7/10 used > 500 grams/day

SOURCE: Tinmouth et al., 2007.

TABLE B-2 Frequency of Diarrhea in Clinical Trials Using Protease Inhibitor-Based Therapy

	LPV/r		Comparator		
Study	N	%		N	%
KLEAN[a]	443	11	FPV/r	436	13
GEMINI[a]	168	14	SQV/r	163	7
M05-730[a]	331	15	LPV/r	333	17
ARTEMIS[b]	446	11	DRV/r	343	4
CASTLE[b]	437	12	ATV/r	441	2

NOTE: [a]KLEAN, GEMINI, and M05-730 represent 48-week data; [b]ARTEMIS and CASTLE represent 96-week data.
SOURCES: Eron et al., 2006; Gathe et al., 2009; Mills et al., 2009; Molina, 2008.

seminated *Mycobacterium avium*, and disseminated cytomegalovirus infection. The rates of these conditions are shown in Table B-3.

As discussed in Chapter 5, diarrhea in people infected with HIV can often be treated with antibiotics, but may require combination antiretroviral therapy. These therapies are generally quite effective; some nonspecific therapies such as loperamide also have been successful.

The literature is sparse about the current association between diarrhea and HIV-associated wasting syndrome. HIV-associated wasting has been defined as the following: unintentional weight loss of greater than 10 percent, body mass index (BMI) decreasing to less than 20, and a rapid weight loss of greater than 5 percent in 6 months (Mangili et al., 2006). In 466 participants with HIV in the Nutrition for Healthy Living Cohort, 18 percent lost greater than 10 percent of their weight, 8 percent had a BMI less than 20, and 21 percent lost greater than 5 percent in 6 months. Every 1 percent increase in weight loss correlated to an 11 percent increase risk of death. Weight loss was attributed to

TABLE B-3 AIDS-Defining Conditions That Often Present With Severe Diarrhea in the HOPS Cohort of 8,070 Participants

	Rate (per 1,000 patient years)	
Condition	Pre-HAART 1994–1997	HAART 2003–2007
Cryptosporidiosis	7.3	0.8
Mycobacterium avium	26.9	2.5
Cytomegalovirus	33.0	1.8

NOTE: HAART = highly active antiretroviral therapy.
SOURCE: Buchacz et al., 2010.

the following: (1) gastrointestinal dysfunction (malabsorption, AIDS enteropathy); (2) decreased dietary intake; (3) absence of HAART (leading to 0.9 kg reduction in body weight with each log increase in HIV viral load); (4) inflammatory cytokines, and (5) AIDS-defining conditions contribute, but "are not a major cause." It has been suggested that wasting should be defined by loss of body mass, with bioelectrical impedance measuring change in body cell mass (Wanke et al., 2004). Another study found weight loss and wasting to be important comorbidities in patients receiving combination antiretroviral therapy, although the cause of weight loss was not determined (Tang et al., 2002). A longitudinal study of 1,474 HIV-infected patients showed that total body weight correlated directly with physical functioning, as reported by patients; specific weight reduction that would be disabling was not described (Wilson et al., 2002).

<u>*Subtask 1C:*</u> *The Consensus Committee shall survey published scientific literature, research, and studies related to the opportunistic infections, cancers, or other conditions described in the criteria of immune system disorders listing 14.08 for adults with HIV infection to determine the following:*

- *How has the treatment of these related conditions changed recently?*
- *How effective are newer treatments for these conditions?*
- *How available are newer treatments?*
- *Are there indicators that these related conditions would prevent the ability to do any work for a continuous period of at least 12 months?*
- *Are there indicators that these related conditions would be expected to result in death?*

<u>Response:</u> The rates of opportunistic infections and cancers have decreased rapidly with widespread use of combination antiretroviral therapy. Chapter 2 described how opportunistic infections and cancers can continue to cause morbidity and mortality, but at much lower rates than at the beginning of the epidemic (Buchacz et al., 2010) (see Table C-1 in Appendix C). Some specific opportunistic infections, cancers, and other conditions can be expected to result in disability or death, as discussed in Chapters 4–6.[1] In cases where opportunistic

[1] Conditions discussed in Chapter 4 are HIV-associated dementia, multicentric Castleman's disease, Kaposi's sarcoma involving the pulmonary parenchyma, primary central nervous system lymphomas, primary effusion lymphoma, and progressive multifocal leukoencepha-

infections do occur, they would largely be captured by low CD4 count or limited functioning. Many opportunistic infections and cancers can now be prevented or treated with use of antiretroviral therapies. Some classes of antiretroviral therapies may induce development of cancers, but the literature in this area is inconclusive (Powles et al., 2009).

No specific indicators were identified in the literature showing opportunistic infections and cancers would prevent one's ability to work for a continuous period of at least 12 months or would result in death. The lack of indicators contributed to the development of the committee's recommendations.

<u>Subtask 1D:</u> *The Consensus Committee shall survey published scientific literature, research, and studies related to the opportunistic infections, cancers, or other conditions described in the criteria of immune system disorders listing 114.08 for children with HIV infection to determine the following:*

- *How has the treatment of these related conditions changed recently?*
- *How effective are newer treatments for these conditions?*
- *How available are newer treatments?*
- *Are there indicators that these related conditions would cause marked and severe functional limitations for a continuous period of at least 12 months?*
- *Are there indicators that these related conditions would be expected to result in death?*

<u>Response:</u> As discussed in Chapter 7, children have responded in similar patterns to combination antiretroviral therapy as adults (see response to Subtask 1C). The committee did not identify specific indicators of opportunistic infections, cancers, or other conditions that would lead to functional limitations or death in children.

<u>Subtask 1E:</u> *The Consensus Committee shall survey published scientific literature, research, and studies related to the coinfection of HIV infection and hepatitis to determine the following:*

---

lopathy. Conditions discussed in Chapter 5 are diarrhea, distal sensory polyneuropathy, HIV-associated neurocognitive disorders, HIV-associated wasting syndrome, Kaposi's sarcoma, lipoatrophy or lipohypertrophy, and osteoporosis. Conditions discussed in Chapter 6 are cardiovascular disease, chronic kidney disease, diabetes, hepatitis, and malignancies not mentioned elsewhere in the report.

- *Are there indicators that such a coinfection would prevent the ability to do any work for a continuous period of at least 12 months?*
- *Are there indicators that such a coinfection would result in death?*

Response: Infection with both HIV and hepatitis is a serious condition that can lead to chronic liver failure and potentially lead to death, but coinfection has not been found to be clinically distinct from hepatitis alone (see Chapter 6). No indicators were found suggesting coinfection as a primary reason why an individual would be prevented from working for at least 12 months or would result in death. This finding led to the committee's inclusion of hepatitis in Recommendation 5.

Subtask 1F: The Consensus Committee shall survey published scientific literature, research, and studies related to the coinfection of HIV infection and chronic pancreatitis to determine the following:

- *Are there indicators that such a coinfection would prevent the ability to do any work for a continuous period of at least 12 months?*
- *Are there indicators that such a coinfection would result in death?*

Response: As discussed in Chapter 2, chronic pancreatitis is not as common in patients with AIDS largely as a result of didanosine and stavudine being no longer widely used in the treatment of HIV/AIDS. Since the widespread use of combination antiretroviral therapies, the incidence of pancreatitis has been similar for both HIV-infected and non-HIV-infected populations (Gan et al., 2003). Chronic pancreatitis is usually the result of recurrent episodes of acute pancreatitis that results in permanent damage to the pancreas. The most common cause of chronic pancreatitis is alcohol use and, as such, this problem is not confined to patients with HIV/AIDS. Symptoms of chronic pancreatitis include abdominal pain and chronic diarrhea that leads to malabsorption. Patients can also develop diabetes. In patients with severe chronic pancreatitis, the diagnosis is easily made, but it is more difficult in early stages when endoscopic ultrasonography has been found to be quite sensitive. The differential diagnosis of chronic pancreatitis includes peptic ulcer disease, biliary tract disease and malignancy. Some HIV medications can increase the risk of developing pancreatitis, particularly the nucleoside reverse transcriptase inhibitor class of drugs and most notably didanosine and stavudine (Kahn et al., 1992; Moore et al., 2001; Smith et al., 2008). However, other drugs commonly used in patients with HIV/AIDS such as rifampin and trimethoprim/sulfamethoxazole can also cause pancreatitis. The committee found no current indicators that coinfection would prevent ability to work for a continuous period of 12 months or result in death.

2. *The Consensus Committee shall produce a written report for the use of SSA analyzing documents received in response to SSA's HIV Advance Notice of Proposed Rulemaking (ANPRM) request for public comment to determine which, if any, recommendations have the potential to become indicators of disability as defined by SSA (that is, to assess which, if any, comments or recommendations would be useful in developing listing criteria for determining disability).*

Response: The committee considered all comments responding to SSA's HIV ANPRM request. As discussed in Chapter 1, some of the responses were built on by the committee in the development of the report. For example, the committee recommended that HIV encephalopathy be broadened to include other neurocognitive conditions and added central nervous system lymphomas, both suggestions in response to the 2008 ANPRM. Other more specific responses (e.g., modifying "herpes zoster" to "herpes or varicella zoster") were not seen to be as relevant to the report, given the current state of medical practice and the committee's reconceptualization of the HIV Infection Listings.

3. *The Consensus Committee shall produce a written report for the use of SSA that compares and contrasts findings in the most current medical literature and ANPRM public comments with SSA's current HIV listings, as well as the key concepts included in the introduction of the HIV listings.*

Response: The current 14.08 Listing consists, for the most part, of opportunistic infections. Many of these infections are proposed to be excluded from being named specifically in a revised listing because they are not as common or disabling as they once were, such as bacterial and protozoan or helminthic infections (see Table B-4). The committee believes that claimants who are at significant risk of being disabled (i.e., those who were once at high risk for acquiring an opportunistic infection) would have at least one of the following:

- CD4 $\leq$ 50 cells/mm^3;
- Imminently fatal or severely disabling HIV-associated conditions;

TABLE B-4 Comparison of Current 14.08 Listing to Suggested Revisions

Current Listing		Suggested Revision	Explanation
14.08A	Bacterial infections	Remove from Listing	Bacterial infections themselves are no longer predictive of disability; claimants experiencing disability would qualify under low CD4 count or other categories of HIV-associated conditions
14.08B	Fungal infections	Remove from Listing	Fungal infections themselves are no longer predictive of disability; claimants experiencing disability would qualify under low CD4 count or other categories of HIV-associated conditions
14.08C	Protozoan or helminthic infections	Remove from Listing	Protozoan or helminthic infections themselves are no longer predictive of disability; claimants experiencing disability would qualify under low CD4 count or other categories of HIV-associated conditions
14.08D	Viral infections	Remove from Listing	Viral infections are no longer predictive of disability; claimants experiencing disability would qualify under low CD4 count or other categories of HIV-associated conditions
14.08E	Malignant neoplasms	Cross-reference to Malignant Neoplasms (13.00)	The current Malignant Neoplasms Listing is adequate to adjudicate claims of HIV-associated malignancies
14.08F	Conditions of the skin or mucous membranes with extensive fungating or ulcerating lesions not responding to treatment	Remove from Listing	These conditions are no longer predictive of disability; claimants experiencing disability would qualify under low CD4 count or other categories of HIV-associated conditions
14.08G	HIV encephalopathy	Revise to reflect current terminology	"HIV-associated neurocognitive disorders" is the current term used

continued

TABLE B-4 Continued

14.08H	HIV wasting syndrome	Retain as HIV-associated comorbidity currently without listings elsewhere	HIV-associated wasting syndrome can still be disabling if it impairs functioning
14.08I	Diarrhea	Retain as HIV-associated comorbidity currently without listings elsewhere	Diarrhea can still be disabling if it impairs functioning
14.08J	Other infections resistant to treatment or require hospitalization or intravenous treatment	Remove from Listing	These conditions are no longer predictive of disability; claimants experiencing disability would qualify under low CD4 count or other categories of HIV-associated conditions
14.08K	Other manifestations of HIV infection	Remove from Listing	These conditions are no longer predictive of disability; claimants experiencing disability would qualify under low CD4 count or other categories of HIV-associated conditions

- HIV-associated condition without a listing elsewhere in the Listing of Impairments; and/or
- HIV-associated condition with a listing elsewhere in the Listing of Impairments.

Some conditions in the current 14.08 Listing should be retained because they can still cause disability. These include HIV wasting syndrome (currently 14.08H) and diarrhea (currently 14.08I). Even when treated with combination antiretroviral therapy, these conditions continue to cause disability as discussed in Chapters 4–6. Additionally, the committee suggests updating the HIV encephalopathy sublisting (currently 14.08G) to "HIV-associated neurocognitive disorders." This suggestion reflects changes in the understanding of HIV's effect on the brain. The current 14.08K sublisting considers repeated occurrences of a number of manifestations, some of which the committee believes continue to present serious challenges for HIV patients, such as hepatitis and peripheral neuropathy.

With respect to Part B (sublisting 114.08), similar suggestions were made to that of Part A, with three differences. First, the committee concluded that neurological manifestations of HIV infection in children (currently 114.08G) still pose large challenges for children. Second, growth disturbance (currently 114.08H) continues to be a cause of severe disability in children. The committee suggests that both neurological manifestations and growth disturbance be retained as imminently fatal or severely disabling conditions. Finally, the committee decided lymphoid interstitial pneumonia/pulmonary lymphoid hyperplasia (LIP/PLH) complex (current 114.08J) should be removed from the Listing. As discussed in Chapter 7, LIP/PLH complex is an HIV-associated disease with no known etiology and was commonly observed in HIV-infected children before the availability of combination antiretroviral therapy. These suggestions are shown in Table B-5.

4. *The Consensus Committee shall recommend evidence-based guidance that, if incorporated into the HIV listings, would improve their utility for evaluating disability claims based on the HIV listings. The Committee will take into account considerations regarding the applicability of their recommendations in the SSA disability program. Examples of such considerations are: (1) consistency with standard medical practice; (2) cost and nationwide availability of any recommended tests; and (3) minimal risk and inconvenience to the claimant.*

Response: The committee's principles for developing its recommendations include feasibility and consistency with standard medical practice.

TABLE B-5 Comparison of Current 114.08 Listing to Suggested Revisions

Current Listing		Suggested Revision	Explanation
114.08A	Bacterial infections	Remove from Listing	Bacterial infections themselves are no longer predictive of disability; claimants experiencing disability would qualify under low CD4 count or other categories of HIV-associated conditions
114.08B	Fungal infections	Remove from Listing	Fungal infections themselves are no longer predictive of disability; claimants experiencing disability would qualify under low CD4 count or other categories of HIV-associated conditions
114.08C	Protozoan or helminthic infections	Remove from Listing	Protozoan or helminthic infections themselves are no longer predictive of disability; claimants experiencing disability would qualify under low CD4 count or other categories of HIV-associated conditions
114.08D	Viral infections	Remove from Listing	Viral infections themselves are no longer predictive of disability; claimants experiencing disability would qualify under low CD4 count or other categories of HIV-associated conditions
114.08E	Malignant neoplasms	Cross-reference to Malignant Neoplasms (113.00)	The current Malignant Neoplasms Listing is adequate to adjudicate claims of HIV-associated malignancies
114.08F	Conditions of the skin or mucous membranes with extensive fungating or ulcerating lesions not responding to treatment	Remove from Listing	These conditions are no longer predictive of disability; claimants experiencing disability would qualify under low CD4 count or other categories of HIV-associated conditions
114.08G	Neurological manifestations of HIV infection	Retain as severely disabling condition	Neurological manifestations of HIV infection continue to be disabling
114.08H	Growth disturbance	Retain as severely disabling condition	Growth disturbances continue to be disabling

114.08I	Diarrhea	Retain as HIV-associated comorbidity currently without listings elsewhere	Diarrhea can still be disabling if it impairs functioning
114.08J	Lymphoid interstitial pneumonia/pulmonary lymphoid hyperplasia complex (LIP/PLH)	Remove from Listing	LIP/PLH complex has been shown to be not disabling
114.08K	Other infections resistant to treatment or require hospitalization or intravenous treatment	Remove from Listing	These conditions are no longer predictive of disability; claimants experiencing disability would qualify under low CD4 count or other categories of HIV-associated conditions
114.08L	Other manifestations of HIV infection	Remove from Listing	These conditions are no longer predictive of disability; claimants experiencing disability would qualify under low CD4 count or other categories of HIV-associated conditions

The only test suggested in the recommendations is CD4 count, which is standard for HIV-infected patients and costs less than $50 per test, as discussed in Chapter 3. This will not inconvenience claimants or place them at risk, as CD4 is a standard part of care.

5. *The Consensus Committee shall produce a written report for the use of SSA indicating what evidence, laboratory findings, and signs and symptoms within the medical evidence of record may improve the sensitivity and specificity of the listing criteria to identify individuals who meet SSA's definition of disability.*

6. *The Consensus Committee will produce a written report for the use of SSA with all of its findings. The report may be made available to the interested public only after the Task Order has ended.*

REFERENCES

Buchacz, K., R. K. Baker, F. J. J. Palella, J. S. Chmiel, K. A. Lichtenstein, R. M. Novak, K. C. Wood, J. T. Brooks, and the HOPS Investigators. 2010. AIDS-defining opportunistic illnesses in US patients, 1994–2007: A cohort study. *AIDS* 24(10):1549–1559.

CDC (Centers for Disease Control and Prevention). 2009. *Cases of HIV Infection and AIDS in the United States and Dependent Areas, 2007, Table 1.* http://www.cdc.gov/hiv/topics/surveillance/resources/reports/2007report/pdf/table1.pdf (accessed May 7, 2010).

Dieterich, D. T., E. A. Lew, D. P. Kotler, M. A. Poles, and J. M. Orenstein. 1994. Treatment with albendazole for intestinal disease due to *Enterocytozoon bieneusi* in patients with AIDS. *Journal of Infectious Diseases* 169(1):178–183.

Doumbo, O., J. F. Rossignol, E. Pichard, H. A. Traore, M. Dembele, M. Diakite, F. Traore, and D. A. Diallo. 1997. Nitazoxanide in the treatment of cryptosporidial diarrhea and other intestinal parasitic infections associated with acquired immunodeficiency syndrome in tropical Africa. *American Journal of Tropical Medicine & Hygiene* 56(6):637–639.

Eron, Jr., J., P. Yeni, J. Gathe Jr., V. Estrada, E. DeJesus, S. Staszewski, P. Lackey, C. Katlama, B. Young, L. Yau, D. Sutherland-Phillips, P. Wannamaker, C. Vavro, L. Patel, J. Yeo, and M. Shaefer. 2006. The KLEAN study of fosamprenavir-ritonavir versus lopinavir-ritonavir, each in combination with abacavir-lamivudine, for initial treatment of HIV infection over 48 weeks: A randomised non-inferiority trial. *Lancet* 368(9534):476–482.

Fanning, M., M. Monte, L. R. Sutherland, M. Broadhead, G. F. Murphy, and A. G. Harris. 1991. Pilot study of sandostatin (octreotide) therapy of refractory HIV-associated diarrhea. *Digestive Diseases & Sciences* 36(4):476–480.

Gan, I., G. May, J. Raboud, J. Tilley, and R. Enns. 2003. Pancreatitis in HIV infection: Predictors of severity. *American Journal of Gastroenterology* 98(6):1278–1283.

Gathe, J., B. A. da Silva, D. E. Cohen, M. R. Loutfy, D. Podzamczer, R. Rubio, S. Gibbs, T. Marsh, C. Naylor, L. Fredrick, and B. Bernstein. 2009. A once-daily lopinavir/ritonavir-based regimen is noninferior to twice-daily dosing and results in similar safety and tolerability in antiretroviral-naïve subjects through 48 weeks. *Journal of Acquired Immune Deficiency Syndromes* 50(5):474–481.

Kahn, J., S. Lagakos, D. Richman, A. Cross, C. Pettinelli, S. Liou, M. Brown, P. Volberding, C. Crumpacker, G. Beall, H. Sacks, T. Merigan, M. Beltangady, L. Smaldone, R. Dolin, and the NIAID AIDS Clinical Trials Group. 1992. A controlled trial comparing continued zidovudine with didanosine in human immunodeficiency virus infection. The NIAID AIDS Clinical Trials Group. *New England Journal of Medicine* 327(9):581–587.

Mangili, A., D. H. Murman, A. M. Zampini, and C. A. Wanke. 2006. HIV/AIDS: Nutrition and HIV infection: Review of weight loss and wasting in the era of highly active antiretroviral therapy from the Nutrition for Healthy Living Cohort. *Clinical Infectious Diseases* 42(6):836–842.

McConnell, M., R. H. Byers, T. Frederick, V. Peters, K. Dominguez, T. Sukalac, A. Greenberg, H.-W. Hsu, T. Rakusan, I. Ortiz, S. K. Melville, and M. G. Fowler for the Pediatric Spectrum H. I. V. Disease Consortium. 2005. Trends in antiretroviral therapy use and survival rates for a large cohort of HIV-infected children and adolescents in the United States, 1989–2001. *Journal of Acquired Immune Deficiency Syndromes* 38(4):488–494.

Mills, A. M., M. Nelson, D. Jayaweera, K. Ruxrungtham, I. Cassetti, P.-M. Girard, C. Workman, I. Dierynck, V. Sekar, C. V. Abeele, and L. Lavreys. 2009. Once-daily darunavir/ritonavir vs. lopinavir/ritonavir in treatment-naive, HIV-1-infected patients: 96-week analysis. *AIDS* 23(13):1679–1688.

Molina, J. M. 2008. *Atazanavir/ritonavir vs lopinavir/ritonavir in antiretroviral-naïve HIV-1-infected patients: CASTLE 96 week efficacy and safety.* Poster Abstract H-1250b. Paper presented at 48th Interscience Conference on Antimicrobial Agents and Chemotherapy, Washington, DC, October 25–28.

Moore, R. D., J. C. Keruly, and R. E. Chaisson. 2001. Incidence of pancreatitis in HIV-infected patients receiving nucleoside reverse transcriptase inhibitor drugs. *AIDS* 15(5): 617–620.

Powles, T., D. Robinson, J. Stebbing, J. Shamash, M. Nelson, B. Gazzard, S. Mandelia, H. Moller, and M. Bower. 2009. Highly active antiretroviral therapy and the incidence of non-AIDS-defining cancers in people with HIV infection. *Journal of Clinical Oncology* 27(6):884–890.

Siddiqui, U., E. J. Bini, K. Chandarana, J. Leong, S. Ramsetty, D. Schiliro, and M. Poles. 2007. Prevalence and impact of diarrhea on health-related quality of life in HIV-infected patients in the era of highly active antiretroviral therapy. *Journal of Clinical Gastroenterology* 41(5):484–490.

Smith, C. J., C. H. Olsen, A. Mocroft, J. P. Viard, S. Staszewski, G. Panos, T. Staub, A. Blaxhult, N. Vetter, and J. D. Lundgren. 2008. The role of antiretroviral therapy in the incidence of pancreatitis in HIV-positive individuals in the EuroSIDA study. *AIDS* 22(1):47–56.

Tang, A. M., J. Forrester, D. Spiegelman, T. A. Knox, E. Tchetgen, and S. L. Gorbach. 2002. Weight loss and survival in HIV-positive patients in the era of highly active antiretroviral therapy. *Journal of Acquired Immune Deficiency Syndromes* 31(2):230–236.

Tinmouth, J., G. Tomlinson, G. Kandel, S. Walmsley, H. A. Steinhart, and R. Glazier. 2007. Evaluation of stool frequency and stool form as measures of HIV-related diarrhea. *HIV Clinical Trials* 8(6):421–428.

Tramarin, A., N. Parise, S. Campostrini, D. D. Yin, M. J. Postma, R. Lyu, R. Grisetti, A. Capetti, A. M. Cattelan, M. T. Di Toro, A. Mastroianni, E. Pignattari, V. Mondardini, G. Calleri, E. Raise, and F. Starace for the Palladio Study Group. 2004. Association between diarrhea and quality of life in HIV-infected patients receiving highly active antiretroviral therapy. *Quality of Life Research* 13(1):243–250.

Wanke, C., D. Kotler, and the HIV Wasting Collaborate Consensus Committee. 2004. Collaborative recommendations: The approach to diagnosis and treatment of HIV wasting. *Journal of Acquired Immune Deficiency Syndromes* 37:S284–S288.

Wilson, I. B., D. L. Jacobson, R. Roubenoff, D. Spiegelman, T. A. Knox, and S. L. Gorbach. 2002. Changes in lean body mass and total body weight are weakly associated with physical functioning in patients with HIV infection. *HIV Medicine* 3(4):263–270.

Appendix C

HIV Background Tables

This appendix includes information about HIV/AIDS to support discussion in Chapter 2. Table C-1 lists the AIDS-defining illnesses as determined by the Centers for Disease Control and Prevention, as well as a noninclusive list of contemporary, serious non-AIDS-defining illnesses. Table C-2 provides a nonexhaustive list of HIV/AIDS antiretroviral drugs and their potential side effects.

TABLE C-1 HIV/AIDS-Related Illnesses and Malignancies

AIDS-Defining Illnesses[a]	Serious Non-AIDS-Defining Illnesses[b]
• Cancers - Cervical (invasive) - Kaposi's sarcoma - Lymphoma (Burkitt's or equivalent, immunoblastic, or primary central nervous system) • Candidiasis of bronchi, trachea, lungs, oresophagus • Coccidioidomycosis, disseminated or extrapulmonary • Cryptococcosis, extrapulmonary • Cryptosporidiosis, chronic intestinal > 1 month • Cytomegalovirus disease (other than liver, spleen, or nodes) • Encephalopathy, HIV-related • Herpes simplex (chronic ulcers > 1 month, bronchitis, pneumonia, or esophagitis) • Histoplasmosis, extrapulmonary • Isosporiasis > 1 month • *Mycobacterium avium* complex or *Mycobacterium kansasii*, disseminated or extrapulmonary • *Mycobacterium tuberculosis*, any site (pulmonary or extrapulmonary) • *Pneumocystis jirovecii* pneumonia • Pneumonia (recurrent) • Progressive multifocal leukoencephalopathy • *Salmonella* septicemia (recurrent) • Toxoplasmosis of the brain • Wasting syndrome	• Avascular necrosis • Cardiovascular disease • Cholangiopathy • Diabetes • Gingivitis/periodontitis • Hepatic cirrhosis • HIV-associated nephropathy • Mental disorders - Anxiety - Bipolar disorder - Depression • Neutropenia • Non-AIDS malignancies - Cancer of the anus - Cancer of the larynx - Cancer of the mouth or pharynx - Cancer of the penis - Hodgkin's lymphoma - Liver cancer - Lung cancer - Sinonasal malignancies • Osteoporosis • Peripheral neuropathy • Sinusitis • Thromboembolic disease

[a]CDC AIDS-defining illnesses (CDC, 1994).

[b]See http://www.hopkins-hivguide.org/r.html?RequestingPage=http%3A%2F%2Fwww.hopkins-hivguide.org%2Fdiagnosis%2Findex.html&navigationId=8231&siteId=7151#8231.

TABLE C-2 Current HIV/AIDS Antiretroviral Drugs

Generic Name	Brand Name	Approval Date	Potential Side Effects
Multiclass Combination Products			
Efavirenz, emtricitabine, and tenofovir disoproxil fumarate	Atripla	July 12, 2006	• Hepatic steatosis +/– pancreatitis (severe mitochondrial toxicities) • Hepatotoxicity • Hyperlipidemia • Hyperpigmentation/skin discoloration • Lactic acidosis/Lipodystrophy • Nephrotoxicity • Osteopenia • Pancreatitis • Peripheral neuropathy
Nucleoside Reverse Transcriptase Inhibitors (NRTIs)			
Abacavir and lamivudine	Epzicom	August 2, 2004	• Hypersensitivity reaction
Abacavir, zidovudine, and lamivudine	Trizivir	November 14, 2000	• Cardiovascular effects • Hyperlipidemia • Hypersensitivity reaction • Lactic acidosis/hepatic steatosis +/– pancreatitis (severe mitochondrial toxicities) • Lipodystrophy • Stevens-Johnson syndrome • Toxic epidermal necrosis
Abacavir sulfate, ABC	Ziagen	December 17, 1998	• Hypersensitivity reaction • Lipoatrophy • Myocardial infarctions
Didanosine, dideoxyinosine, ddI	Videx	October 9, 1991	• Lactic acidosis • Pancreatitis • Peripheral neuropathy
Emtricitabine, FTC	Emtriva	July 2, 2003	• Lactic acidosis • Lipoatrophy
Enteric-coated didanosine, ddI EC	Videx EC	October 31, 2000	• Cardiovascular disease • Gastrointestinal intolerance • Hepatotoxicity • Hepatic steatosis +/– pancreatitis (severe mitochondrial toxicities) • Pancreatitis • Peripheral neuropathy • Stevens-Johnson syndrome • Toxic epidermal necrosis

continued

TABLE C-2 Continued

Generic Name	Brand Name	Approval Date	Potential Side Effects
Lamivudine and zidovudine	Combivir	September 27, 1997	• Hepatic steatosis +/– pancreatitis (severe mitochondrial toxicities) • Hepatotoxicity • Lactic acidosis • Lipodystrophy
Lamivudine, 3TC	Epivir	November 17, 1995	• Lipoatrophy
Stavudine, d4T	Zerit	June 24, 1994	• Insulin resistance • Lactic acidosis • Lipoatrophy • Lipohypertrophy • Neuromuscular weakness syndrome • Osteopenia • Peripheral neuropathy
Tenofovir disoproxil fumarate and emtricitabine	Truvada	August 2, 2004	• Hepatotoxicity • Hyperlipidemia • Hepatic steatosis +/– pancreatitis (severe mitochondrial toxicities) • Lipodystrophy • Nephrotoxicity • Osteopenia • Pancreatitis • Peripheral neuropathy
Tenofovir disoproxil fumarate, TDF	Viread	October 26, 2001	• Lipoatrophy • Nephrotoxicity • Osteopenia • Pancreatitis
Zalcitabine, dideoxycytidine, ddC (no longer marketed)	Hivid	June 19, 1992	• Unknown
Zidovudine, azidothymidine, AZT, ZDV	Retrovir	March 19, 1987	• Bone marrow suppression • Gastrointestinal intolerance • Hepatotoxicity • Hyperlipidemia • Insulin resistance/diabetes mellitus • Lactic acidosis/hepatic steatosis +/– pancreatitis (severe mitochondrial toxicities), lipodystrophy • Stevens-Johnson syndrome • Toxic epidermal necrosis

TABLE C-2 Continued

Generic Name	Brand Name	Approval Date	Potential Side Effects
Nonnucleoside Reverse Transcriptase Inhibitors (NNRTIs)			
Delavirdine, DLV	Rescriptor	April 4, 1997	• Stevens-Johnson Syndrome • Toxic epidermal necrosis
Efavirenz, EFV	Sustiva	September 17, 1998	• Birth defects (avoid in pregnant women) • Neuropsychiatric side effects • Short-term central nervous system toxicity
Etravirine	Intelence	January 18, 2008	• High blood pressure
Nevirapine, NVP	Viramune	June 27, 1996	• Hypersensitivity with hepatic failure
Protease Inhibitors (PIs)			
Amprenavir, APV	Agenerase	April 15, 1999	• Stevens-Johnson syndrome • Toxic epidermal necrosis
Atazanavir sulfate, ATV	Reyataz	June 20, 2003	• Jaundice • Kidney stones
Darunavir	Prezista	June 23, 2006	• Hepatotoxicity
Fosamprenavir calcium, FOS-APV	Lexiva	October 20, 2003	• Cholesteremia
Indinavir, IDV	Crixivan	March 13, 1996	• Kidney stones • Nephrotoxicity
Lopinavir and ritonavir, LPV/RTV	Kaletra	September 15, 2000	• Cardiovascular risk
Nelfinavir mesylate, NFV	Viracept	March 14, 1997	• Diarrhea
Ritonavir, RTV	Norvir	March 1, 1996	• Pancreatitis
Saquinavir (no longer marketed)	Fortovase	November 7, 1997	• N/A
Saquinavir mesylate, SQV	Invirase	December 6, 1995	• Many drug interactions
Tipranavir, TPV	Aptivus	June 22, 2005	• Cardiovascular risk

continued

TABLE C-2 Continued

Generic Name	Brand Name	Approval Date	Potential Side Effects
Fusion Inhibitors			
Enfuvirtide, T-20	Fuzeon	March 13, 2003	• Poorly tolerated (painful local subcutaneous reactions when injected)
Entry Inhibitors—CCR5 Coreceptor Antagonist			
Maraviroc	Selzentry	August 6, 2007	• Unknown
HIV Integrase Strand Transfer Inhibitors			
Raltegravir	Isentress	October 12, 2007	• Unknown

REFERENCE

CDC (Centers for Disease Control and Prevention). 1994. Revised classification system for HIV-infection in children less than 13 years of age. *Morbidity and Mortality Weekly Report* 43:1–10.

Appendix D

Literature Tables

METHODS

A review of published literature was conducted related to disability and HIV/AIDS to examine current evidence of related employment capability. Extensive search terms were used, yielding initial results of 9,295 studies published between January 1993 and October 2009. The studies were reviewed, analyzed, and categorized (see Box D-1). The most relevant studies were identified as Category 1, totaling 32 articles for more detailed review. The topics of these studies include return to work for people living with

BOX D-1
Definitions of Categories

- *Category 1:* Studies on clinical measures of treatment outcomes, diagnostic techniques, or health status indicators as they relate to employment capability (i.e., return to work, employability) for U.S.-based populations with HIV/AIDS.
- *Category 2:* Studies on one or more parameters of disability (e.g., comorbid conditions, quality of life, morbidity, mortality) as they affect functional capacity for populations with HIV/AIDS.
- *Category 3:* Studies on disability or employment factors, but which do not explicitly address, measure, or estimate medical treatment or functional capacity of populations with HIV/AIDS.
- *Category 4:* Studies not related to HIV disability and employment.

HIV/AIDS, the neuropsychological symptoms of HIV infection, and effect of combination antiretroviral therapy on vocational rehabilitation.

Search Strategy

The strategy of the literature review searched four databases: Medline, EMBase, Web of Science, and PsychINFO. Together these databases access information related to medicine, nursing, health care delivery, psychiatry, sociology, and psychology. Search strategies were developed for each database using text terms and Medical Subject Headings focused on eight subject areas, including HIV/AIDS, disability, employment, quality of life, functional capacity, treatment outcomes, severity of impairment, and comorbidities. Distinct terms were identified in each subject area to yield as many unique results as possible. Strategy parameters included limiting the search to human subjects, the English language, and studies published from 2004 to 2009. This time period was chosen to focus the studies on the most recent medical and scientific literature.

Preliminary Analysis and Results

A rigorous review of titles and abstracts determined which studies met the inclusion criteria. Each study was coded according to the category system. The preliminary results include 32 Category 1 articles, which focus on study populations with HIV/AIDS and employment capability. Table D-1 provides a detailed review of all Category 1 studies. An additional 331 articles were identified as Category 2 articles, which inform broader parameters potentially affecting functional capacity of populations with HIV/AIDS. These parameters include relative quality of life (with specific measurements for health-related quality of life), comorbid conditions, gender comparisons, and assessments of treatments for HIV/AIDS, or associated conditions that may lead to disability or impairment. The remaining 8,932 studies were categorized as either Category 3 or Category 4 studies. Category 3 studies informed background research during report writing. Category 4 studies did not meet the inclusion criteria and were not included in the study.

Table D-1 starts on
the following page.

TABLE D-1 Literature Review on Employment Capability and HIV

Study	Study Purpose	Study Type	Time Frame
Disability			
Anandan, N., B. Navaraj, B. Braveman, G. Kielhofner, and K. Forsyth. 2006. Impairments and perceived competence in persons living with HIV/AIDS. *Work* 27(3):255–266.	Determines occupational functioning required for various activities and describes impairments prevalent in HIV/AIDS population; examines impact of these impairments on individuals' perceived occupational competence	Observational	N/A
Cade, W. T., L. Peralta, and R. E. Keyser. 2004. Aerobic exercise dysfunction in human immunodeficiency virus: A potential link to physical disability. *Physical Therapy* 84(7):655–664.	Examines the biological factors possibly limiting the oxidative metabolic response to physical activity for people with HIV	Review	N/A
Levin, M., G. Kielhofner, B. Braveman, and L. Fogg. 2007. Narrative slope as a predictor of work and other occupational participation. *Scandinavian Journal of Occupational Therapy* 14(4):258–264.	Determines the utility of the narrative slope in predicting vocational outcomes of individuals with HIV/AIDS	Observational	9 months

Sample Size (Persons)	Method	Outcome Measures	Relevant Findings
35	• Convenience sample from the ongoing federally funded research project: Enabling Self-Determination (ESD) for Persons Living with HIV/AIDS	• Occupational Self-Assessment (OSA) • Sign and Symptom Checklist (SSC-HIV)	• Impairments most commonly identified by participants: - Fatigue - Fear/worries - Difficulty concentrating - Muscle aches - Depression • Primary areas of occupational functioning where individuals reported moderate to severe impairment: managing finances and physical activities
N/A	N/A	N/A	Physical functional disability measured by: • Fatigue • Diminished capacity to engage in peak aerobic exercise capacity • Inability to engage in instrumental activities of daily living
65	• SSC-HIV • Occupational Performance History Interview (OPHI-II) includes: - Occupational identity scale - Occupational competence scale - Occupational behavior settings scale • Model of Human Occupation	Narrative slope measure of employment status or other productive activity at 3- and 6-month follow-up	• Positive narrative slope predictive of employment or engagement in other productive activity • Relationships were statistically significant at 3- and 6-month follow-up; 9-month follow-up not statistically significant

continued

TABLE D-1 Continued

Study	Study Purpose	Study Type	Time Frame
Employment			
Arns, P., D. Martin, and R. Chernoff. 2004. Psychosocial needs of HIV-positive individuals seeking workforce re-entry. *AIDS Care* 16(3):377–386.	Examines a population entering a vocational rehabilitation program designed for individuals with HIV, examining the population's indicated objective and subjective needs to gain employment	Observational	January 1997–December 1999
Braveman, B., G. Kielhofner, G. Albrecht, and C. Helfrich. 2006. Occupational identity, occupational competence and occupational settings (environment): Influences on return to work in men living with HIV/AIDS. *Work* 27(3):267–276.	Examines and describes the efforts of 12 men living with AIDS to reestablish a role in the workforce following the completion of a vocational rehabilitation program	Observational	12 months
Braveman, B., M. Levin, G. Kielhofner, and M. Finlayson. 2006. HIV/AIDS and return to work: A literature review one-decade post-introduction of combination therapy (HAART). *Work* 27(3):295–303.	Reviews literature on employment and combination antiretroviral therapy	Review	1995–2005
Burns, S. M., L. R. Young, and S. Maniss. 2006. Predictors of employment and disability among people living with HIV/AIDS. *Rehabilitation Psychology* 51(2):127–134.	Explores the relationship between employment and disability as well as selected demographic, biological, and functionality variables for people living with HIV/AIDS	Observational	N/A
Conover, C. J., P. Arno, M. Weaver, A. Ang, and S. L. Ettner. 2006. Income and employment of people living with combined HIV/AIDS, chronic mental illness, and substance abuse disorders. *Journal of Mental Health Policy and Economics* 9(2):71–86.	Examines the labor market outcomes of individuals diagnosed with HIV, mental disorders, and substance abuse disorders	Observational	2000–2002

Sample Size (Persons)	Method	Outcome Measures	Relevant Findings
235	• Questionnaires of individuals recruited from local health care agencies, HIV mental health programs, HIV case management programs	• Employment status • Education • Finances • Housing • Access to health care • Health status	• Employed participants exhibited a marked decline in vocational functioning relative to pre-HIV status, with related and accompanying financial declines
12	• OPHI-II • Completion of Employment Options Program	• Employment history before and after onset of disability • Narratives • Narrative slope analysis	• Resumption of roles and engagement in new activities resulted in increased confidence in occupational identity, competence, and setting
N/A	N/A	N/A	• Employment is a possibility for HIV-infected people, but many face multiple challenges, including: • Side effects of treatment • Ongoing social stigma • Psychological burden associated with the disease
152	• Questionnaire	• Age • Clinical markers • Race • Time since diagnosis	• Significant predictors of employment: - Minority race - Higher CD4 count - Higher mental health or physical health functioning
1,138	• Interviews	• HIV transmission risk activities • Medication adherence • Employment • Source of income	• Less than 15 percent of sample employed, including both full- or part-time • High education levels and better physical health were indicators for employment • More than 33 percent reported not working due to a permanent disability

continued

TABLE D-1 Continued

Study	Study Purpose	Study Type	Time Frame
Conyers, L. M. 2004. The impact of vocational services and employment on people with HIV/AIDS. *Work* 23(3):205–214.	Explores the perceptions of 25 individuals with HIV/AIDS who engage in vocational services in attempt to return to work	Observational	N/A
Conyers, L. M. 2008. HIV/AIDS and employment research: A need for an integrative approach. *The Counseling Psychologist* 36(1):108–117.	Reviews three articles on HIV/AIDS and employment that recommend future directions for theory integration, HIV health outcomes, and interdisciplinary approaches	Review	N/A
Escovitz, K., and K. Donegan. 2005. Providing effective employment supports for persons living with HIV: The KEEP project. *Journal of Vocational Rehabilitation* 22(2):105–114.	The Kirk Employment Empowerment Project (KEEP), a 3-year demonstration project, identified effective employment service strategies for individuals with HIV/AIDS	Observational	36 months
Goldman, D. P., and Y. Bao. 2004. Effective HIV treatment and the employment of HIV(+) adults. *Health Services Research* 39:1691–1712.	Examines whether combination antiretroviral therapy helps HIV-infected patients return to work, remain employed, or maintain hours of work	Observational	24 months

Sample Size (Persons)	Method	Outcome Measures	Relevant Findings
25	• Focus groups	• Impact of vocational rehabilitation • Programmatic qualities of vocational services • Impact of employment	• Vocational rehabilitation services led to the following: - Improved confidence - Higher motivation - Increased skills - Increased self-respect - Diversion from HIV - Improved health • Vocational services engender the following among participants: - Individualized approach to HIV management - Peer support
N/A	N/A	N/A	• Integrating multiple disciplines—such as psychology, vocational rehabilitation, and community development—in addition to approaches to clinical care are important for helping individuals with HIV/AIDS return to work
148	• Focus groups • Interviews at 6-month intervals	• Employment status • Motivation to work • Quality of life	• Most participants experienced the following barriers to employment: - Psychiatric disability - Substance abuse - Domestic violence - Low education levels - Incarceration history - Unstable housing
2,864	• Interviews • Multistage sampling frame	• Return to work within 6 months of treatment • Remaining employed within 6 months of treatment • Hours at work	• Beginning treatment at less advanced stages of infection leads to greatest gain in employment status • Employed patients are more likely to remain employed because of therapy

continued

TABLE D-1 Continued

Study	Study Purpose	Study Type	Time Frame
Gorman, A. A., J. M. Foley, M. L. Ettenhofer, C. H. Hinkin, and W. G. van Gorp. 2009. Functional consequences of HIV-associated neuropsychological impairment. *Neuropsychology Review* 19(2):186–203.	Reviews the implications of HIV-associated neuropsychological disorders (HAND)	Review	N/A
Hergenrather, K. C., S. D. Rhodes, and G. Clark. 2005. The employment perspectives study: Identifying factors influencing the job-seeking behavior of persons living with HIV/AIDS. *AIDS Education & Prevention* 17(2):131–142.	Explores factors influencing the job-seeking behaviors of individuals living with HIV/AIDS, using the planned behavior theory	Observational	N/A
Maguire, C. P., C. J. McNally, P. J. Britton, J. L. Werth Jr., and N. J. Borges. 2008. Challenges of work: Voices of persons with HIV disease. *The Counseling Psychologist* 36(1):42–89.	Provides in-depth descriptions of vocational experiences of individuals with HIV	Observational	N/A
Martin, D. J., P. G. Arns, R. A. Chernoff, and M. Steckart. 2004. Working with HIV/AIDS: Who attempts workforce reentry following disability? *Journal of Applied Rehabilitation Counseling* 35(3):28–38.	Compares factors influencing individuals with HIV/AIDS who attempt workforce reentry; at entry to the program, participants were unemployed and disabled	Observational	1997–2001, 24-month periods
Martin, D. J., R. A. Chernoff, and M. Buitron. 2005. Tailoring a vocational rehabilitation program to the needs of people with HIV/AIDS: The Harbor–UCLA experience. *Journal of Vocational Rehabilitation* 22(2):95–103.	Reviews three vocational rehabilitation programs to better understand the workforce-reentry process for individuals living with HIV/AIDS	Review	N/A

Sample Size (Persons)	Method	Outcome Measures	Relevant Findings
N/A	N/A	N/A	• Patients with HAND have limited or challenged ability to engage and persist in employment, driving, medication adherence, mood, fatigue, and interpersonal functioning
54	• Focus groups • Planned behavior model	• Responses elicited from individuals on interest in and potential barriers to employment	• Work perceived as having value • Participants expressed need for assistance to address barriers to employment such as education/training or social stigma
93	• Focus groups • Grounded theory approach	• Responses elicited from individuals on interest in and potential barriers to employment	• Primary areas of concern for participants: - Employment - Community - Health
235	• Questionnaire • Short Form 36 (SF-36): Evaluates individuals on eight domains of functioning	• Income and source • Employment status • CD4 count • Viral load • History of opportunistic infections	• Individuals who attempted return to work showed more improved health status (i.e., higher CD4 counts, fewer opportunistic infections, higher SF-36 scores for physical functioning, among other measures)
N/A	N/A	N/A	• Continuing need for workforce reentry programs exists • Population affected by HIV shifts; programs should reflect this change • Full-time employment may not be an appropriate goal for individuals with HIV/AIDS

continued

TABLE D-1 Continued

Study	Study Purpose	Study Type	Time Frame
Martin, D. J., M. J. Steckart, and P. G. Arns. 2006. Returning to work with HIV/AIDS: A qualitative study. *Work* 27(3):209–219.	Studies the workforce-reentry process for individuals with HIV/AIDS	Observational	24 months
Rabkin, J. G., M. McElhiney, S. J. Ferrando, W. van Gorp, and S. Hsing Lin. 2004. Predictors of employment of men with HIV/AIDS: A longitudinal study. *Psychosomatic Medicine* 66(1):72–78.	Identifies patterns and predictors of work status and number of hours employed in a group of men with HIV/AIDS	Observational	30 months
Razzano, L. A., and M. M. Hamilton. 2005. Health-related barriers to employment among people with HIV/AIDS. *Journal of Vocational Rehabilitation* 22(3):179–188.	Evaluates two issues identified in previous research on HIV/AIDS and employment: health perceptions and sources of insurance and health benefits	Observational	N/A
Razzano, L. A., M. M. Hamilton, and J. K. Perloff. 2006. Work status, benefits, and financial resources among people with HIV/AIDS. *Work* 27(3):235–245.	Focuses on the factors related to employment status, sources of health benefits, and entitlements among people with HIV/AIDS; results demonstrate differences in work status, benefits, and financial support received based on gender	Observational	6 months

Sample Size (Persons)	Method	Outcome Measures	Relevant Findings
104	• Questionnaire	• Income • Health indexes - CD4 count - Viral load • Work in the past month	• Employment barriers include: - Poor physical health - Poor mental health - Education deficiencies - Lack of motivation - Social barriers - Cognitive deficits - Substance abuse - Incarceration history
141	• Beck Depression Inventory • Axis I diagnosis of lifetime and current depressive disorders	• Medical measures (CD4 count, viral load, physical limitations) • Hours employed: (full or part time, unemployed) • Financial measures (SSI, SSDI) • Neuropsych-ological measures (seven tests—not listed)	• 20 percent of men were continuously employed full time • 9 percent of men were continuously employed part time • 40 percent of men were continuously unemployed • Barriers to work included: - Structure of disability benefits - Depressive disorder - Physical limitations - Cognitive impairment
63	• Beck Depression Inventory • Medical Outcome Survey-HIV Health Survey (MOS-HIV)	• Functional status • Well-being - Pain - Mental health - Energy/fatigue - Health distress - Quality of life • Changes in health status (i.e., CD4 count, viral load)	• Patients faced health-related barriers to employment, including personal concerns of health and functional status • Depression affected the ability to consider or continue work • Physical impairments remained despite higher CD4 counts
98	• Medication Adherence Program Study (MAPS protocol)	• Employment status • Health benefit sources • Medication adherence • Alcohol or drug use • Physical and mental health indicators • Employment status • Financial status	• More men than women reported working at 6-month follow-up • Men receive higher Social Security Disability Insurance benefit based on higher average lifetime earnings • Employment and gender affect amount of benefits and financial resources for individuals living with HIV/AIDS

continued

TABLE D-1 Continued

Study	Study Purpose	Study Type	Time Frame
Timmons, J. C., and S. L. Fesko. 2004. The impact, meaning, and challenges of work: Perspectives of individuals with HIV/ AIDS. *Health & Social Work* 29(2):137–144.	Reveals the value and significance of employment for individuals with HIV/ AIDS, concerns related to Social Security benefits	Observational	N/A
van Gorp, W. G., J. G. Rabkin, S. J. Ferrando, J. Mintz, E. Ryan, T. Borkowski, and M. McElhiney. 2007. Neuropsychiatric predictors of return to work in HIV/AIDS. *Journal of the International Neuropsychological Society* 13(1):80–89.	Followed individuals with HIV/AIDS who initiated return to work processes to identify existing supports or barriers to employment	Observational	24 months

Sample Size (Persons)	Method	Outcome Measures	Relevant Findings
29	• Focus groups	• Employment status • Perceptions and intentions of participants	• The loss of Social Security benefits was a notable concern for participants who considered returning to work
118	• Neuropsychological tests: - Wechsler Adult Intelligence Scale III - Wide Range Achievement Test-3 - Trail Making Test I and II - California Verbal Learning Test - Faces I and III - Stroop Color Interference Test - California Computerized Assessment Package - Wisconsin Card Sorting Test • Structured Clinical Interview for DSM (SCID) • Beck Depression Inventory • Endicott Quality of Life Enjoyment and Satisfaction Questionnaire • Wortman Social Support Scale	• Financial status • Health status • Neuropsych-ological measures • Psychiatric/ psychosocial measures • Employment status assessed at each 6-month follow-up	• Predictors of employments: - Younger age - Reporting higher quality of life - Performing significantly better on timed motor measure with dominant hand - Evidence of better learning and recall on recognition and learning memory measures

continued

TABLE D-1 Continued

Study	Study Purpose	Study Type	Time Frame
Functional Capacity			
Bernell, S. L., and J. A. Shinogle. 2005. The relationship between HAART use and employment for HIV-positive individuals: An empirical analysis and policy outlook. *Health Policy* 71(2):255–264.	Analyzes the determinants of combination antiretroviral therapy use and employment status for individuals who are infected with HIV	Observational	1996, 2 months
Berry, J. D., and B. Hunt. 2005. HIV/AIDS 101: A primer for vocational rehabilitation counselors. *Journal of Vocational Rehabilitation* 22(2):75–83.	Provides an overview of medical and psychosocial, information on HIV/AIDS related to vocational rehabilitation	Review	N/A
Conyers, L., and P. Datti. 2008. The unmet vocational rehabilitation needs of women with HIV/AIDS. *Work* 31(3):277–290.	Discusses unique needs of women with HIV/ AIDS and their needs for vocational rehabilitation services	Observational	N/A

Sample Size (Persons)	Method	Outcome Measures	Relevant Findings
2,864	• HIV Cost and Services Utilization Study: A test of independence between individuals on therapy and those not, and unemployed and employed individuals	• Employment status • Combination antiretroviral therapy • Covariates: - Comorbidities - Injection drug use - Mental health status	• Fully or partially employed individuals were more likely to be on therapy (26 versus 22 percent) • Individuals on therapy were less likely to have difficulties with activities of daily living (7 versus 26 percent)
N/A	N/A	N/A	• Vocational rehabilitation may include: - Training for employers to reduce stigma or discrimination of the individual with HIV/AIDS - Address employment gaps for individuals with HIV/AIDS - Improve job seeking and interviewing skills
122	• National Working Positive Coalition Employment Needs Survey (NWPC-ENS)	• Economic and health characteristics and how they differ by employment status • Patterns of employment and use of employment services of NWPC-ENS • Incentives to work and effect of loss of employment	• 59 percent of study respondents were employed at time of survey (compared to 68 percent at time of diagnosis) • Maintaining or increasing income was cited as the most important incentive for employment • 70 percent of employed individuals self-reported they were mostly to very healthy, compared to 49 percent of unemployed participants

continued

TABLE D-1 Continued

Study	Study Purpose	Study Type	Time Frame
Kielhofner, G., B. Braveman, M. Finlayson, A. Paul-Ward, L. Goldbaum, and K. Goldstein. 2004. Outcomes of a vocational program for persons with AIDS. *American Journal of Occupational Therapy* 58(1):64–72.	Describes the development, implementation, and outcomes of a program of vocational services for individuals with HIV/AIDS	Observational	N/A
O'Brien, K. K., A. M. Bayoumi, C. Strike, N. L. Young, and A. M. Davis. 2008. Exploring disability from the perspective of adults living with HIV/AIDS: Development of a conceptual framework. *Health & Quality of Life Outcomes* 6(76).	Develops a conceptual framework of disability from the perspective of adults living with HIV/AIDS	Observational	N/A
Paul-Ward, A., B. Braveman, G. Kielhofner, and M. Levin. 2005. Developing employment services for individuals with HIV/AIDS: Participatory action strategies at work. *Journal of Vocational Rehabilitation* 22(2):85–93.	Details the development of employment and independent living services of a 3-year federally funded demonstration project: Enabling Self-Determination (ESD) for Persons Living with AIDS	Observational	12 months

Sample Size (Persons)	Method	Outcome Measures	Relevant Findings
129	• OPHI-II • Narrative slope	• Other physical diagnoses besides HIV or AIDS • Mental health history • Substance abuse history • Incarceration history • OPHI-II scale scores • Narrative slope	• Significant outcomes included return to work, school, or volunteer or intern activities: - 60 participants successfully completed the program - 30 participants did not successfully complete the program because they did not return to work or seek education or volunteer opportunities • An additional 39 individuals dropped out of the program prior to its completion: reasons included becoming sick, deciding vocational goals were not realistic, relapse into substance abuse, or difficulty maintaining a routine to come to the program; 39 individuals did not complete the program
38	• Focus groups • Grounded theory techniques	• Health-related challenges • Physical, social, and psychological areas of life affected • Overall impact on health	• Participants' concepts of disability emerged as multidimensional and episodic • Disability spanned physical, mental, and psychological domains • Inability to access needed services (e.g., housing, medications) reduced the individual's ability to participate in society
14	• Survey • Focus groups	• OPHI-II • MOS-HIV • HIV impairment checklist • The Worker Role (structured interview)	Intensive, personalized, coordinated independent living services positively affect the lives of individuals living with HIV/AIDS: • Two clients obtained part-time jobs • One client returned to school • One client enrolled in a full-time technical training program • One client transitioned to independent living

continued

TABLE D-1 Continued

Study	Study Purpose	Study Type	Time Frame
Quality of Life			
Martin, D. J., P. B. Arns, P. J. Batterham, A. A. Afifi, and M. J. Steckart. 2006. Workforce reentry for people with HIV/AIDS: Intervention effects and predictors of success. *Work* 27(3):221–233.	Predicts the likelihood of return to work of individuals living with HIV/AIDS participating in a specialized program	Observational	24 months
Ryu, E., S. G. West, and K. H. Sousa. 2009. Mediation and moderation: Testing relationships between symptom status, functional health, and quality of life in HIV patients. *Multivariate Behavioral Research* 44(2):213–232.	Examines the relationships among symptoms, functional capacity, and quality of life for individuals living with HIV/AIDS	Observational	1992–1994
Severity of Impairment			
Vetter, C. J., and J. P. Donnelly. 2006. Living long-term with HIV/AIDS: Exploring impact in psychosocial and vocational domains. *Work* 27(3):277–286.	Reviews literature addressing medical, psychological, and psychosocial challenges related to living with HIV/AIDS	Review	N/A

Sample Size (Persons)	Method	Outcome Measures	Relevant Findings
235	• Questionnaire	• Income and income source • Current employment status • Health status: - CD4 count - Viral load - History of opportunistic infections - SF-36	• Participants receiving Social Security Disability Income benefits were less likely to return to work • Participants with higher income levels prior to study were less likely to return to work than those with low income levels • Those with higher health status were more likely to return to work
956	• Questionnaire	• Symptoms • Functional health • Health-related quality of life	• Symptom status has an indirect relationship to quality of life • Relationship partially mediated by functional health: having more symptoms increases disability (i.e., decreases functional health) and lowers quality of life
N/A	N/A	N/A	• In 5 of 10 reviewed studies, respondents cited loss of medical benefits through Social Security as a barrier to seeking or resuming employment • Social stigma cited as a barrier to employment • Receiving support services after attaining employment were cited as important in one study

Appendix E

Committee Member and Staff Biographies

COMMITTEE BIOGRAPHIES

Paul Volberding, M.D. (Chair), serves as professor and vice chair of the Department of Medicine at the University of California–San Francisco (UCSF) and chief of the Medical Service at the San Francisco Veterans Affairs Medical Center. He is the Principal Investigator and codirector of the UCSF-Gladstone Institute of Virology and Immunology Center for AIDS Research. He chairs the Scientific Advisory Board of the Infectious Disease Institute of Makerere University in Kampala, Uganda. For 20 years, Dr. Volberding's professional activities centered on San Francisco General Hospital, where he established a model program of AIDS patient care, research, and professional education. He became the chief of the Medical Service at the San Francisco VA Medical Center in 2001. His research career began with investigations of HIV-related malignancies, especially Kaposi's sarcoma. His primary research focus, however, shifted to clinical trials of antiretroviral drugs. He has been instrumental in testing many compounds, including early studies in asymptomatic infection that led to the concept of HIV disease, not simply AIDS as the target of treatment. Dr. Volberding has written many research and review articles. He is coeditor in chief of the *Journal of Acquired Immune Deficiency Syndrome*, and a founder of HIV InSite, a comprehensive source of HIV information. He served as coeditor of the major textbook *Global HIV/AIDS Medicine*. He is the founder and chair of the Board of the International AIDS Society—USA. He has served as president of the HIV Medical Association of the Infectious Diseases Society of America (IDSA) and of the International AIDS Society. He was elected a member of the Institute of Medicine (IOM) in 1999. He has served on several IOM committees, including the first review of the AIDS epidemic, Confronting AIDS, in 1986, and No Time to Lose, an assessment of HIV prevention programs at the Centers for Disease Control and Prevention (CDC) in 2001. He received his undergraduate and medical degrees at the University of Chicago and the University of Minnesota, respectively, and finished training at the University of Utah and UCSF, where he studied for 2 years as a Research Fellow in the virology laboratory of Dr. Jay Levy, later a codiscoverer of HIV.

John G. Bartlett, M.D., is a professor of medicine in the Division of Infectious Diseases at The Johns Hopkins University School of Medicine. Prior to this role, he served as chief of the Infectious Diseases Division at the school for 26 years, stepping down in 2006. In addition, Dr. Bartlett has served as a faculty member at the University of California–Los Angeles (UCLA) and Tufts University School of Medicine. He was associate chief of staff for research at the Boston VA Hospital. Dr. Bartlett is a member of the IOM, master of the American College of Physicians, past president of the IDSA, and recipient of the Kass Award from the IDSA. In 2005, Dr. Bartlett was awarded the Alexander Fleming Award by the IDSA and the Finland Award from the National Foundation for Infectious Diseases. Dr. Bartlett received his undergraduate degree at Dartmouth College and his M.D. at Upstate Medical Center, Syracuse, New York. He trained in internal medicine at the Peter Bent Brigham Hospital in Boston and the University of Alabama–Birmingham, and he completed his fellowship training in infectious diseases at UCLA.

Carlos del Rio, M.D., is professor and chair of the Hubert Department of Global Health at the Rollins School of Public Health and professor of medicine in the Division of Infectious Diseases at the Emory University School of Medicine. He is also codirector for Clinical Science and International Research of the Emory Center for AIDS Research. He has held numerous leadership roles, including executive director of the National AIDS Council of Mexico, the federal agency of the Mexican government responsible for AIDS policy in that country; program director and principal investigator of the Emory AIDS International Training and Research Program; member of the CDC/Health Resources and Services Administration Advisory Committee on HIV/Sexually Transmitted Disease Prevention and Treatment; and member of the Board of the International AIDS Society USA and the HIV Medical Association of the IDSA. Dr. del Rio is associate editor of *AIDS Clinical Care* and *AIDS Research and Human Retroviruses* and a member of the editorial board of the *Journal of AIDS*; *Women, Children* *and HIV*; and *Global Public Health*. He has coauthored 5 books, 30 book chapters, and more than 150 scientific papers.

Patricia M. Flynn, M.D., is the Arthur Ashe chair in pediatric AIDS research and director of clinical research in the infectious disease department at St. Jude Children's Research Hospital. Dr. Flynn's research interests include infections in immunocompromised hosts, HIV/AIDS, and epidemiology. She has been an investigator on several AIDS clinical trials. She has authored numerous publications and abstracts. Dr. Flynn received her undergraduate degree at Rhodes College; her master's in epidemiology from the University of Tennessee, and her medical degree from Louisiana State University Medical Center.

Larry M. Gant, L.M.S.W., Ph.D., is a professor of social work at the University of Michigan. Dr. Gant's research has focused on studying health-related physiological and psychosocial outcomes of structural, social, and individual factors leading to health disparities in urban communities nationally and globally. An HIV/AIDS outreach worker, case management consultant, and clinical consultant during the first two decades of the HIV/AIDS epidemic, Dr. Gant's research has focused on the creation, implementation, and evaluation of urban, community-based health prevention initiatives in the areas of substance abuse prevention, sexually transmitted diseases, and HIV/AIDS among African-American heterosexual populations. His current work involves comparative analysis of HIV behavioral outreach interventions in mainland and interior China, Sub-Saharan Africa, and the United States. Dr. Gant has contributed to numerous scholarly publications and is principal investigator or coinvestigator in several National Institutes of Health (NIH), CDC, and Substance Abuse and Mental Health Services Administration grants, including R01s from the National Institute on Drug Abuse (NIDA) to conduct clinical trials of an HIV prevention program with urban drug-dependent men, and the National Institute on Mental Health (NIMH) for a citywide demographic analysis and prospective study of ecologic stressors, posttraumatic stress disorder, and drug use in urban areas. Dr. Gant earned his bachelor's from the University of Notre Dame and his master's and doctorate in psychology and social work from the University of Michigan.

Igor Grant, M.D., is a distinguished professor of psychiatry and director of HIV neurobehavioral research programs at the University of California–San Diego. Dr. Grant's academic interests focus on the effects of various diseases on brain and behavior, with an emphasis on translational studies in HIV, and drugs of abuse. Dr. Grant has contributed to approximately 500 scholarly publications and is principal investigator of several NIH studies, including a NIDA P50 (Translational Methamphetamine AIDS Research Center, or TMARC) and the NIMH-funded HIV Neurobehavioral Research Center, California NeuroAIDS Tissue Network, and Central Nervous System HIV Antiretroviral Therapy Effects Research (CHARTER). Dr. Grant is a neuropsychiatrist who graduated from the University of British Columbia School of Medicine. He received specialty training in Psychiatry at the University of Pennsylvania, and additional training in Neurology at the Institute of Neurology (Queen Square), London, United Kingdom.

H. Clifford Lane, M.D., is the clinical director of the National Institute of Allergy and Infectious Diseases at the NIH. His areas of interest include the study of the pathogenesis and treatment of HIV infection. He has received the Commendation Medal, Meritorious Service Medal, Outstanding Service Medal, and Distinguished Service Medal from the U.S. Public Health Service; the NIH Director's Award; and the Chevalier du' Mali from the President of Mali. He is also a member of the IOM and several other professional societies. Dr. Lane received his B.S. in chemistry and his M.D. from the University of Michigan. He is board-certified in internal medicine, infectious diseases, and diagnostic and clinical laboratory immunology.

Celia Maxwell, M.D., is assistant vice president for Health Sciences and director of the Women's Health Institute at Howard University. She has been appointed to several national boards and committees, including serving as a member of the Healthcare Reform Task Force chaired by then-First Lady, Hillary Rodham Clinton, and the Office of the AIDS Advisory Council at the NIH. She was selected for the nationally renowned Robert Wood Johnson Health Policy Fellowship and served as a health legislative assistant for Senator Tom Harkin (D-IA). Dr. Maxwell obtained her B.S. in nursing from Hunter College and her M.D. from Columbia University College of Physicians and Surgeons. She completed her residency training in internal medicine at Howard University Hospital and completed her fellowship in infectious diseases/tropical medicine at the NIH and Howard University.

Heidi Nass, J.D., is director of Treatment Education and Community Advocacy at the University of Wisconsin Hospital's HIV/AIDS Comprehensive Care Program. Ms. Nass has published dozens of articles, pamphlets, and newsletters. She is the founder of southern Wisconsin's only AIDS legal services program, and served as managing editor of *Wisconsin Women's Law Journal*. Ms. Nass consults with the UNAIDS on issues related to women and clinical HIV research and serves on a panel that is reviewing guidelines for biomedical HIV prevention trials. She has also been a community representative in the NIH Adult AIDS Clinical Trials Group. She is widely recognized as a national leader in HIV/AIDS activism.

Ira Shoulson, M.D., is the Louis C. Lasagna Professor of Experimental Therapeutics and professor of Neurology, Pharmacology, and Medicine at the University of Rochester School of Medicine and Dentistry. He founded the Parkinson Study Group in 1985 and the Huntington Study Group in 1994. He is considered a pioneer in research methods that have led to new treatments for Huntington's disease, Parkinson's disease, and other neurodegenerative diseases. Dr. Shoulson has authored more than 270 scientific reports and is associate editor of *Archives of Neurology*. In addition, he is a former member of the National Institute of Neurological Disorders and Stroke Council, and past president of the American Society for Experimental NeuroTherapeutics. Dr. Shoulson is an elected member of the IOM. He earned his bachelor's from the University of Pennsylvania and his M.D. from the University of Rochester School of Medicine and Dentistry.

Ann Williams, Ed.D., R.N.C., FAAN, is currently professor of Nursing at UCLA, where she is also associate dean for Research. A certified family nurse practitioner, Dr. Williams has worked for more than two decades caring for persons living with HIV/AIDS. She designed and conducted some of the earliest studies of AIDS among drug users. Her work tested interventions to decrease HIV transmission, improve gynecologic care of women living with HIV, and increase patient adherence to antiretroviral medication. She led the Connecticut AIDS Education and Training Center for two decades. Her current research examines the prevalence and incidence of combination antiretroviral therapy resistance and seeks to evaluate an intervention to improve medication adherence among drug users in south central China. Dr. Williams, an accomplished author and researcher, has been honored many times for her work. Dr. Williams earned a degree in history from Roosevelt University, an M.S. in nursing from Yale School of Nursing, and a doctorate in adult education from Columbia University. She completed her postdoctoral studies in HIV/AIDS research at UCSF.

STAFF BIOGRAPHIES

Samantha M. Chao, M.P.H., is a program officer at the IOM, where she has primarily worked on issues such as health care quality, continuing education, and integrative medicine. She directed the Forum on the Science of Health Care Quality Improvement and Implementation, which brought together leaders in the field to discuss methods to improve the quality and value of health care through the strengthening of research. She previously staffed the Pathways to Quality Health Care Series, which reviewed performance measures to analyze health care delivery, evaluated Medicare's Quality Improvement Organization Program, and assessed pay for performance and its potential role in Medicare. Prior to joining the IOM, she completed an M.P.H. in health policy with a concentration in management at the University of Michigan School of Public Health. As part of her studies, she interned with the American Heart Association.

Frederick (Rick) Erdtmann, M.D., M.P.H., spent 30 years as a commissioned officer in the U.S. Army Medical Department. He had a variety of assignments, including Chief of the Preventive Medicine Services at Fitzsimons Army Medical Center, Frankfurt Army Medical Center in Germany, and Madigan Army Medical Center. He also served as division surgeon for the Second Infantry Division and as chief of the Preventive Medicine Consultant's Division in the Surgeon General's Office. Dr. Erdtmann served as Commander of Evans Army Community Hospital from 1995 to 1997. He was the deputy chief of staff for Clinical Operations within the Department of Defense's TRICARE Region 1, prior to assuming Hospital Command at Walter Reed Army Medical Center in 1998. Following that he was assigned to the Office of the Surgeon General as the deputy assistant surgeon general for Force Development. Following military retirement in 2001, Dr. Erdtmann joined the IOM. He currently serves as director of the Medical Follow-up Agency and of the Board on the Health of Select Populations (formerly the Board on Military and Veterans Health). Dr. Erdtmann is a graduate of Bucknell University, where he received a B.S. in biology. He earned an M.P.H. from the University of California–Berkeley. He attended Temple University School of Medicine, where he earned his M.D. He is board certified in preventive medicine.

Susan R. McCutchen, M.A., is a senior program associate for the IOM Board on the Health of Select Populations. She has been on staff at The National Academies for nearly 30 years and has worked in several institutional divisions and with many different boards, committees, and panels within those units. The studies in which she has participated have addressed a broad range of subjects and focused on a variety of issues related to science and technology for international development, technology transfer, aeronautics and the U.S. space program, natural disaster mitigation, U.S. education policy and science curriculums, needle exchange for the prevention of HIV transmission, the scientific merit of the polygraph, human factors/engineering, research ethics, disability compensation programs, health hazard evaluation, and medical and public health preparedness for catastrophic events, including nuclear detonations. She has assisted in the production of more than 50 publications and was an editor for *A 21st Century System for Evaluating Veterans for Disability Benefits* and *Assessing Medical Preparedness to Respond to a Terrorist Nuclear Event: Workshop Report*. Ms. McCutchen has a B.A. in French, with minors in Italian and

Spanish, from Ohio's Miami University, and an M.A. in French, with a minor in English, from Kent State University.

Joi D. Washington, B.S., is a senior program assistant for the IOM Board on the Health of Select Populations. Prior to joining the IOM in 2008, Ms. Washington held the position of registrar at the National Minority AIDS Council, for which she oversaw the registration process for two large national conferences. Ms. Washington received her B.S. in public and community health from the University of Maryland–College Park. She is currently pursuing a dual master's degree in health care administration and business administration from the University of Maryland–University College.

Erin E. Wilhelm, M.P.H., is a research associate with the IOM Board on the Health of Select Populations, serving both the Committee on Social Security HIV Disability Criteria and the Committee on Social Security Cardiovascular Disability Criteria. She is a health policy researcher and writer with experience in global health, nutrition, flood disasters and their impact on mental health, and disability issues. Prior to joining the IOM and The National Academies in 2009, Ms. Wilhelm served as a guest researcher at Fogarty International Center of the NIH, where she contributed to a literature review and portfolio analysis for the Trans-NIH Working Group on Climate Change and Health. Among other roles, she has served as a publications editor for the Corporate Executive Board, a best practice research firm in Washington, DC, and a staff writer for the *St. Petersburg Times* in Florida. Ms. Wilhelm holds an M.P.H. in global health from The George Washington University and a dual Bachelor of Arts in broadcast journalism and political science from the University of South Florida.

Index